Racing to Justice

RACING TO JUSTICE

TRANSFORMING OUR CONCEPTIONS OF SELF AND
OTHER TO BUILD AN INCLUSIVE SOCIETY

john a. powell
Foreword by David R. Roediger

INDIANA UNIVERSITY PRESS

Bloomington & Indianapolis

This book is a publication of

INDIANA UNIVERSITY PRESS
601 North Morton Street
Bloomington, Indiana 47404-3797 USA

iupress.indiana.edu

Telephone orders 800-842-6796
Fax orders 812-855-7931

♾ The paper used in this publication
meets the minimum requirements of
the American National Standard for
Information Sciences – Permanence
of Paper for Printed Library
Materials, ANSI Z39.48–1992.

*Manufactured in the
United States of America*

*Library of Congress
Cataloging-in-Publication Data*

Powell, John A. (John Anthony)
  Racing to justice : transforming our conceptions of self and other to build an inclusive society / John A. Powell; foreword
by David R. Roediger.
    p. cm.
  Includes bibliographical references and
index.
  ISBN 978-0-253-00629-5 (cloth : alk.
paper) – ISBN 978-0-253-00735-3
(eb) 1. Racism – United States. 2.
Equality – United States. 3. Social
justice – United States. 4. United
States – Social policy. I. Title.
  E184.A1P6637 2012
  305.800973 – dc23

                                2012018655

    2 3 4 5   17 16 15 14 13

To my children, Saneta and Fon DeVuono-powell
and Travis and Caitlin Vorland, to everyone else's children,
and to Ray, my recently deceased brother.

Through our scientific and technological genius, we have made of this world a neighborhood and yet we have not had the ethical commitment to make of it a brotherhood. But somehow, and in some way, we have got to do this. We must all learn to live together as brothers or we will all perish together as fools. We are tied together in the single garment of destiny, caught in an inescapable network of mutuality. And whatever affects one directly affects all indirectly. For some strange reason I can never be what I ought to be until you are what you ought to be. And you can never be what you ought to be until I am what I ought to be. This is the way God's universe is made; this is the way it is structured.

DR. MARTIN LUTHER KING JR.,
"Remaining Awake through a Great Revolution"

CONTENTS

FOREWORD

DAVID R. ROEDIGER

said, "Nobody is only one thing"

In the late 1990s, partly because john powell and I were consulting at
Macalester College on their curriculum on racial justice, I attended a
keynote lecture on that campus by the late literary critic and theorist
Edward Said. His health already failing, Said spoke with even more than
usual grandeur and in passages with a particularly spare eloquence. "Nobody," he said at one point, "is only one thing." This insight, so simple but
so hard won, is a central subject of the book you hold. Pushing not only
toward an analysis of the "intersectional" matrices in which race, class,
gender, sexuality, and more collide and collude, powell shows that even
a single category compounds the others in ways defying claims to purity.
Indeed powell's challenging concluding sections recall the insistence of
his and my former University of Minnesota colleague, the sociologist
Rose Brewer, that not only "intersectionality" but also "simultaneity"
characterize the ways in which we are more than one thing.

Thinking about Said's words over the years, I have often been
tempted to add addenda, two of which particularly apply to powell's
work. The first would hold that while we are never one thing, we often
and tragically try to suppose that we are. Thus multiplicity and its denial,
even repression, are both facts of modern life. In making whiteness central to his analysis, powell names what is in his country and much of the
overdeveloped world the most powerful false universal, one implying an
ersatz unity not only among whites of different classes but also within
individual white psyches. Thus for powell the "problematic and isolated
white self" constitutes a "backbone of resistance" to a changed world.

To thus indict whiteness is about as far as imaginable from "playing the race card." Indeed, as a particularly brilliant chapter below suggests, powell struggles to make us see race as a "verb" always being made structurally, not as a noun capable of being invoked to separate enlightened and unenlightened. In 1998, when he and I designed a questionnaire on whiteness for a special issue of the journal *Hungry Mind Review* on that theme, powell included the searching question, "When are you white?" – one meant to be answered by people of color as well as those categorized as white. Indeed, he got the African American mixed-race writer Walter Mosley to tackle that question in a response in the special issue. "When are you white?" Mosley offered, "is a Black person's question."

Said's aphorism secondly suggests a way to explain his, and powell's, extraordinary insight. To be consciously and militantly many things – in Said's case to be immersed in music, literature, history, theory, nationalist politics, and a dissent from nationalist politics based on aspirations toward humanism – enables (if it can never ensure) a critical positioning interested in the here-and-now of social change and the largest questions of life and meaning.

I cannot imagine that john powell, or anyone, would fail to be humbled by comparisons with Edward Said. But the soaring intellectual curiosity, the willingness to challenge even himself, and the ability to do the work of learning about everything from neuroscience to urban sprawl, so present in powell, does matter in accounting for the very unusual, indeed marvelous, shape of *Racing to Justice*.

My own friendship with powell has seldom failed to produce surprises regarding his breathtaking range of interests. Like the polymath historian C. L. R. James, john's passion for beauty and ideas sometimes took the form of a literal generosity. That is, he (and James) would get so excited about a work that it was given to friends, so that it could be discussed and enthused over together. My first Cassandra Wilson CD came to me that way. It was at john's insistence that I came to see *Genghis Blues*, a stirring film on U.S. blues and throat singing in central Asia. Nor was the street one-way. Constant requests from john for references to historical work on all manner of subjects have been a regular part of our relationship, as have follow-up conversations. I long regarded such habits on john's part as atypical of people whose day job is to teach about contracts or torts, but through him I came to know a broad set of almost equally inquisitive legal scholars.

My most vivid memory of powell's commitment to being adventuresome comes from the "Making and Unmaking of Whiteness" conference at Berkeley in 1997. This first major conference on critical whiteness studies drew over a thousand participants, attracting interest far beyond academia. Press attention ran high, in part because major media outlets misunderstood the event and ran pieces implying that disgruntled whites were finally claiming a place denied them in the rainbow of multiculturalism. The atmosphere was electric, and almost all speakers, myself included, responded as professors do, by clinging even more closely to the reading of a written text. In contrast, powell pushed his prepared remarks aside, saying it seemed more urgent to discuss dreams and why his law students reported (as he discusses in the pages below) often dreaming that they were another species, sometimes of another gender, and almost never of another race.

One further necessarily embarrassing comparison deserves to be made – indeed the most humbling one possible for a writer in these areas of inquiry. In its structure, *Racing to Justice* calls to mind the great James Baldwin collection *The Price of the Ticket* (1986). That massive volume shows how much of Baldwin's work, published in many venues over many years, was unified around a profound appreciation of the costs of being white – a price exacted across the color line. In particular, the price of whiteness for working class Europeans adapting to the U.S. racial system is relentlessly reckoned by Baldwin. This ability to convincingly connect whiteness and misery, including misery for whites, is shared by powell and by very few writers, notably the novelist Toni Morrison, the theologian Thandeka, the historian George Rawick, and the political scientist Michael Rogin.

But as big as their topics are, both Baldwin's *Price of the Ticket* and powell's *Racing to Justice* use their last sections to raise the stakes yet again. Baldwin closes with "Here Be Dragons," a work powell uses in his book as inspiration. In that essay the focus is far less on race than on sexuality, gender, and the ways in which boundaries are conjured up. In closing powell likewise expands the frame, making a book on race more fully a book on the need to make categories, the need to unmake them, and need to exercise care and courage in the process of that unmaking.

ACKNOWLEDGMENTS

The idea of collecting some of my essays came originally from colleagues in social justice work who asked me to make more of my writing available to those who do not routinely read law journals. Another friend suggested a collection centered around my writings on identity, the self, community, and social justice, as well as the impact that race has on all of them. The results are in your hands. I am grateful to these friends and to the following organizations and publications, in which earlier versions or parts of these essays appeared: *Social Policy* ("Moving beyond the Isolated Self"); the *Denver University Law Review* ("Post-Racialism or Targeted Universalism?"); the *University of San Francisco Law Review* ("The Color-Blind Multiracial Dilemma," in "Symposium: In Honor of Professor Trina Grillo; and "Whites Will Be Whites"); *Law and Inequality* ("The Racing of American Society," in "Symposium: Our Private Obsession, Our Public Sin"); *Washington University Law Review* ("Dreaming of a Self beyond Whiteness and Isolation"); *University of Minnesota Law Review* ("The Multiple Self"); and the *University of St. Thomas Law Journal* ("Lessons from Suffering"). I extend my thanks to all of these organizations for the important work that they do, with special thanks to Sandy Levitsky and the *Minnesota Law Review* for publishing the tribute in memory of Trina Grillo, who is a continuing source of inspiration to me.

These essays have been edited for this volume under the leadership of my friend and colleague, Rebecca High, whose research and insights have enriched the collection in numerous ways. Earlier versions of the essays benefited from the work of excellent researchers: Mark Girouard,

Gavin Kearney, Jessica Larson, Bonniee Mookherjee, Mellody Parchia, Eric Stiens, and Colleen Walbran.

David Roediger and Anna Meigs read earlier drafts of "The Racing of American Society" and provided insightful comments and criticism; Dr. Donna Waters contributed valuable suggestions for "The Multiple Self"; and Terri Karis shared comments and suggestions for "Lessons from Suffering." Derek Black reviewed "White Innocence and the Courts" with care and generosity. Richard Delgado made valuable suggestions in the early stages of the project, as did Chester Hartman, whose support has been much appreciated.

At Indiana University Press, my editor Robert Sloan provided great support and assistance in addition to soliciting the thoughtful and very helpful suggestions of two anonymous readers. Sarah Wyatt Swanson, Angela Burton, Susanna Sturgis, and others at the press improved the work with skill and energy, and Mandy Clarke helped get the book into circulation.

A number of colleagues at the Kirwan Institute for the Study of Race and Ethnicity helped create this book. Kathy Baird's energy and commitment made an enormous difference. Philip Kim's and Mary Griffith's suggestions helped shape the collection, as did Gretchen Hirsh's many editorial and organizational ideas. Stephen Menendian's extensive research and writing have benefited this collection and my work over the years. I especially want to thank Andrew Grant-Thomas for his insights and leadership on many of the issues discussed here.

Finally I would like to thank my father, Marshall Powell, Jr.; my mother, Florcie Mae Powell; my adopted father, Bill Sutherland; my spiritual brother, Farokh Merat; and my spiritual friend and social justice fellow traveler, Marguerite Spencer. I would also like to express my empathy to all those who suffer and my gratitude to all those who work to end suffering.

Moving beyond the Isolated Self

Justice involves claiming a shared, mutual humanity. It is about inter-relationships. Until now, every major attempt to achieve racial justice in this country has come up short, and each time, we have seen race and racial hierarchy reinscribed in different ways. Slavery gave way to Jim Crow. The explicit discrimination of Jim Crow laws was replaced with tacit segregation through spatial arrangements, like white suburbs that wall themselves off from the larger regions of which they are a part. Today many of the older suburbs have become diverse, yet racial hierarchy shows no sign of going away but instead continues to mutate. Institutional supports for the racial caste system, such as anti-miscegenation laws, have been dismantled, but with no corresponding increase in the fluidity of the racialized self.

Indeed, although we may try to ignore or explain them as choice, racialized disparities persist across all areas of life opportunity, and segregation divides us not only in our neighborhoods, schools, and businesses but also in non-competitive spheres like spirituality or music. Without an examination of the construction and presence of whiteness, and specifically the role of whiteness in the formation of the modern separate self, inequitable arrangements based on fear and exclusion will endure. Even laws and policies considered fair, equal, and universal will continue to falter or fail as long as they rest on a foundation of racialized injury and injustice.

The problematic and isolated white self forms the backbone of resistance to a truly robust, inclusive America and energizes much of the conservative movement. This self is all too easily controlled by fears – in part because it was born of fear – whether of declining property values, the "predatory" black man, the other's "culture of poverty," or any of a range of similar racialized images. Beyond these distortions, however, lies a more fundamental fear: self-annihilation. For in the context of this society's unwillingness to come to terms with its racial organization, to ask people to give up whiteness is to ask them to give up their sense of self. We cannot expect people to expose themselves to ontological death or worse. Instead, we must provide space – institutional space, political space, social space, and conceptual space – for the emergence of new relationships and a new way of being that exists beyond isolation and separation.

The Western self, especially the American self, is particularly isolated and separate. This conception of the self has a history, a large part of which is its construction in conjunction with ideals that assert a radical individualism: rationality, objectivity, private property, market capitalism, and race. This notion of the self is at the core of the American dream of liberty and opportunity for all, of pure meritocracy, but also of exclusion and domination. Certainly we can see this idea of the self active in the conservative movement today. The visceral fear of terrorists, the tightening of national borders, racial profiling, and tough rhetoric on crime would all make Hobbes proud – the authoritarian state protecting us, each one from the other. The liberal worldview, however, is based on the same isolated and autonomous self, especially in its dogmatic adherence to secularism, rationality, and a strict separation of church and state.

Jeremy Rifkin has asserted that the American Dream is in decline and that we should look to Europe for an alternate vision. Even today, with crises rippling through its Union, such an inquiry can provide a starting point in questioning our views of self and community. Rifkin writes that "[f]or Europeans, freedom is found not in autonomy but in embeddedness. To be free is to have access to many interdependent relationships. The more communities one has access to, the more options one has for living a full and meaningful life. It is *inclusivity* that brings security – belonging, not belongings."[1] We might take exception to looking toward Europe, but the sense of America's decline is largely shared. There is a need for an alternative vision, a beloved community where being connected to the other is seen as the foundation of a healthy self, not its destruction, and where the racial other is seen not as the infinite other, but rather as the other that is always and already a part of us.

Even aspirations like these are not enough, however; visions must be reflected in social structures and institutions, or they remain merely dreams deferred. Rifkin points to the increasingly interconnected infrastructure of Europe as an indication that this dream is starting to be realized. News reports reflect daunting problems, indeed dangers, in this process – not least of all the economic crises that spread now at the speed of light and the ever-present struggle with inequality. In spite of the challenges, however, the recognition of shared vulnerability and shared yearnings reflects an accurate assessment of the issues of a globalized society, as well as the steps needed to make it a just and democratic society. To take these steps, we must also move beyond prevailing notions of the self, in all its egoistic separateness.

This project cannot be thought of as strictly political or even philosophical; this "moving beyond" implicates spirituality. The liberation from the separate egoist self is one of the grand goals of most religious traditions, whether through union with God or through realization of our inherent interconnectedness. In every major religious tradition, the ideal is unity, and separation is recognized as the path that leads to suffering. Many Americans, even when they do not explicitly articulate this need, are interested in moving beyond a vision of public life and politics as fundamentally separate from spirituality. They understand that our interests extend beyond purely material concerns. But the progressive movement in this country, perhaps because of its determination to preserve an inclusive secularism in public life, has often failed to speak to the hunger for meaning in human life.

When progressives fail to support this realm of understanding, important values, spirituality, and even the radical promise of liberation from selfishness and the separate self are abandoned to fundamentalists, to imperialists. Cornel West reminds us of the tradition of interweaving social activism and prophetic Christianity in this country – of Daniel Berrigan, Dr. Martin Luther King Jr., William Sloane Coffin Jr., and Dorothy Day. Social theorist Roberto Unger rejects any spirituality that is not intertwined with the secular. Unger believes that our religious existential project can only be worked out through engagement with others. We must remake the world, heal separation, and create structures and institutions that support relationships and love – the same inclusivity and contextuality that Rifkin sees as underlying the "European Dream."

When we look at racial justice, which certainly needs to be brought more to the forefront of a progressive social agenda, we often fail to recognize that we are looking at it through the eyes of the modern separate self already infected with surplus anxiety and fear. Yet this problematic self came into being at the same time that modern white racial consciousness came into being. It is, indeed, a racialized separate self, or more pointedly, a white self. Here I am not talking about phenotypical characteristics necessarily, but instead about a sense of how a person exists in and interacts with the world – something that may be called identity. There are certainly people who look white, for example, who are moving toward a more contextual self; but the white social category was inscribed in the separate Hobbesian self and defined by its ability to exclude and distance itself from the other, especially the black other. This self commands a rejection of relationship and responsibility for one another that is both disheartening, in the truest sense, and disabling.

These essays on race, identity, and social policy, drawn from my writing and reflection on social justice work, are offered with the hope that they might help in efforts to claim our mutual, shared humanity; to heal ourselves; and to secure our future. For I believe that the struggle for racial and social justice provides an unparalleled lens through which to visualize – and achieve – more honest, just, and positive interrelationships in all aspects of our lives together. The volume is organized into four parts: the first describes the roles and effects of race and racialization; the second takes on whiteness as an all too often invisible barrier to social justice; the third addresses the effects of racialization on us as individuals and suggests ways of increasing integration of our selves; and the fourth calls for a greater integration of our spiritual and social needs, directed toward peace and justice.

In the first chapter, I review aspects of our racial legacies, mostly from a policy standpoint, in the context of suggestions that with the election of an African American president, the United States is at last "post-racial." Post-racialism is analyzed in tandem with color blindness with respect to the weakness of past "universal," or race-blind, programs, policies, and institutions. The Interstate Highway Act and the Federal

Housing Administration, for example, drove the creation of current spatial patterns, including the now-familiar white suburbs surrounding urban poverty. Government programs that instead target currently marginalized communities as beneficiaries could help deconstruct the results of this racialization and increase overall productivity and societal cohesiveness through access to opportunity.

The insistence, however, of our courts on a blindness to race that ignores both history and differences in how people are situated instead predictably supports policies that perpetuate current patterns and suppress the potential of significant parts of the population. Political factors also make purportedly universal programs less accessible to non-white groups, as do poverty-based solutions that decline to address racial effects. Targeting universal programs, by incorporating race-sensitive aspects, can correct many failures of past policies and accelerate progress toward racial equality.

The second chapter begins an analysis of the current racial landscape of the United States. I take up in more depth what we mean by race, looking mainly at two currents of thought and activism that purport to solve our race problems without addressing racism. The first is color blindness, introduced in the previous chapter, in which conservatives make the claim that race, lacking biological reality, has no meaning. The second has to do with conflicts over the identity and categorization of the growing population of families with diverse racial ancestry. Multiracial individuals have been a part of racial categorizing for almost as long as our racial hierarchy has existed. So too have colorism and pigmentocracy, both in the United States and abroad. The histories of both multiracial designations and pigmentocracy indicate that neither multiplying racial categories, nor declaring people multiracial, nor blindness to color is likely to undo racial hierarchy. Instead, because the very nature of racism makes it a problem that is not solvable at the individual level – a problem that must be solved at a systemic level – keeping the focus on racial hierarchy rather than race is key. Examining some of the turning points in the development of and struggle against that hierarchy can help light the path forward.

A review of the development of racial categories continues in the third chapter, including another look at hypodescent, an artifact of slavery that both reflects and perpetuates the idea of whiteness as "pure" and keeps it at the top of the unofficial racial hierarchy. The top-down process of racialization first labeled non-whites, then denied them the benefits of the society, even after the end of legal slavery. Denial of this hierarchy only helps maintain the structures that support it: "not seeing race" too often means preserving white gains. And lopsided white gains egregiously worsen the deepening inequality that threatens our economy. Indeed, although we hear more about the undeserving poor than we hear about the undeserving rich, our racial hierarchy is unsustainable – economically, politically, environmentally, and from any semblance of a humanitarian point of view. Dismantling that hierarchy requires, among other things, a close examination of whiteness.

The fourth chapter challenges whiteness by delineating white privilege in an era of amorphous but powerful de facto segregation. Within white-defined structural and institutional arrangements, whiteness is generally not viewed as privilege; rather, privilege is defined as normality and those without this white normality as defective. White Americans need not seek white privilege; they simply exist within it. Non-whites in turn are asked to qualify as normal and deserving (not as unprivileged or underprivileged and thus undeserving). White privilege is deeply ingrained thereby, even automatic, throughout our society. The voices and perspectives of those for whom privilege does not attach automatically through group membership can therefore provide a critical context in which to assess privilege.

I suggest that white privilege may be overstated in terms of the privilege it brings, while understated in its cost. I also suggest that white privilege is changing and in decline. After reviewing some of the challenges of struggles against group-based exclusions and hierarchies – whether based on race, gender, class, or some other characteristic – I advocate a transformative model, in which we reserve judgment on group characteristics while altering institutions and removing structural barriers to participation.

The fifth chapter specifically addresses the role of our laws and judicial system. The Supreme Court's most persistent and effective evasions with regard to race include the establishment of a requirement that plaintiffs prove an explicit intent to discriminate; insistence on viewing social justice issues apart from history or context; and invocation of the dangers of a slippery slope (toward justice). Under these standards, our courts continue to claim an objective application of law to fact, in spite of the increasingly clear role of unconscious bias – which affects decisions on many levels, from which evidence to include to how credible a witness or defendant is. New legal strategies can help, but with the courts generally in color-blind mode, more than good lawyering will be required. More and better organization will have to be brought to efforts to prevent racial injustice at the level of the school, the workplace, the bank, and the neighborhood, as well as in the criminal justice system. In these efforts, affirmative goals and targets, as well as affirmative duties, can increase the rate of progress while providing transparency and a sense of fairness.

Dramatic new ways of seeing the internal workings of our brains can only help as we seek understand the depth of our internalization of racial boundaries and the way these boundaries have controlled not only the distribution of rights and opportunity in our society but also how we experience our selves and our world. The sixth chapter describes how these boundaries are drawn, and where the dividing lines lie within our communities and our minds and hearts. Here I review some of the history and effects of boundary-drawing and make suggestions for opening up internal and external spaces. Within our current racial arrangements, any alternative (non-white) self-conception amounts to a kind of social death for whites. One obvious approach to this problem is to reduce racialized disparities in health, education, and housing, such that race ceases to be such a strong determinant of access to opportunity. Altering structural barriers that impede progress for non-whites would result in a wide array of benefits: freeing minds, increasing social and geographical diversity and space, reducing poverty and alienation, and healing communities. But another undertaking is crucial as well: the reconceptualization of selfhood that could occur in this new social space.

In chapter 7, I review some former and current understandings of the self as well as some of the challenges to the Enlightenment model of an autonomous, rational individual. The latter is especially important because while that notion of the self may have been born in Europe and the Enlightenment project, it reached full expression in the United States, which was less constrained by existing pre-Enlightenment structures and institutions. The obsession with the independent, disconnected, free self in the young (and not so young) America has been part of American exceptionalism. But this "free" child was born not of one parent but of two. Enlightenment ideals shaped many of the philosophical and political aspirations of the new America, but it was slavery in our midst that formed the motivation, fear, and obsession around freedom and independence. Orlando Patterson has argued that freedom in the West had its earlier roots in the fear of slavery in Greece, but Eric Foner and David Roediger remind us that new America created both an extreme form of slavery and an extreme – one could even say a twisted, unhealthy – view of freedom. To help evaluate the current state of our assumptions and aspirations in this realm, this chapter reviews some of the understandings of the self emerging from postmodern, feminist, and intersectional perspectives, as well as two alternatives to Western individualistic understandings of the self, the psychoanalytic and the Buddhist.

To complete the needed transformation to a society based on liberty and its complement equality, pain created and maintained through institutional arrangements must be alleviated. In the final chapter, I emphasize the importance of work to ameliorate suffering. As we engage in such work, we recognize the connections between social and spiritual suffering and gain insight into the words and actions of some of our greatest spiritual leaders, who explain that social justice work is more a source than a result of spiritual pursuits. Highly attuned seekers and leaders have the ability to see across categories and to recognize the importance of bringing love into even the most potentially mathematical equations. They also, importantly – and here I think especially of Dr. King – place themselves in service to more than caring for those in pain. They also place themselves in service to the public face of love: justice. And they call upon each and all of us to do the same.

From our current context, this will not be an immediate transformation. We may be too socialized in systems of separation to even conceive of viable beginning steps. This is one reason that other possibilities buried in the past or in our myths become so important. We may see these vague shadows in spiritual traditions and practices that embrace our common and collective humanity. We may see signposts in other countries and cultures. We may find hope in the understanding of mutuality that appears in some families and beloved communities. Ultimately, if we are to avoid failure in the most critical work of this century, the deepest reaches of our beings must be brought to bear in honestly reevaluating the most basic structures of our society. This book is about race, but not in the narrow sense in which we usually talk about it. Race has been a defining part of the DNA of this country, but it is also ever-changing and evolving. If we look more deeply at race, not just as bodies, but as structures and practices as well, then race can be used as a heuristic that can help us understand and claim our humanity.

This effort is no small project. Is it even doable? Can we stop focusing simply on transactional moves we see as winnable and start working for the transformation of the institutions that perpetuate suffering? Can we speak to people's deepest needs – to feel a sense of connection, to feel love? Can we realize that working for the elimination of social suffering is an integral part of any spiritual project? Can we have a discussion about values that is grounded in hope and acknowledgment of our connected being? I believe that we can, and I believe that we must, if we are to heal the self and have a future at all.

Racing to Justice

Race and Racialization

ONE

Post-Racialism or Targeted Universalism?

We hear it said nowadays that there is no "race problem," but only a "class problem." . . . From a practical angle there is a point in this reasoning. But from a theoretical angle it contains escapism in new form. . . . And it tends to conceal the whole system of special deprivations visited upon the Negro only because he is not white.

Gunnar Myrdal, An American Dilemma

Executive and legislative branches, which for generations now have considered these types of policies and procedures, should be permitted to employ them with candor and with confidence that a constitutional violation does not occur whenever a decisionmaker considers the impact a given approach might have on students of different races.

Justice Anthony M. Kennedy, Parents Involved in Community Schools v. Seattle

The United States made history on November 4, 2008, by electing Barack Obama as its first African American president, generating a sense of pride and a collective celebration that was shared worldwide. The installation of a black president who was supported by a significant minority of white voters was an occasion imbued with great political, social, historical, and cultural meaning. That meaning has been interpreted and expressed in many different ways, and Americans will continue to attempt to determine its contours and synthesize its various strands far into the future. As we engage in this process, different segments of society will continue to identify and promote different meanings, any of which may have important ramifications. Perhaps no aspect of the election compares, however, with the milestone that it represents with respect to the history of race. Questions about how we are to understand racial conditions in society and what the proper role of public policy and law should be in addressing – or avoiding – racial issues will gain greater salience as we seek ways of building upon the understandings the election has fostered. These questions about where we are on the issue of race are not just factual or descriptive; they are deeply political as well, having implications for how and when we respond to social problems and how we define the scope of our collective obligations.

RACE, RACISM, AND RACIALIZATION

In exploring these questions, I will add the term "racialization" to the more common terms "race" and "racism," which are understood in a way that is too limited and specific to fully address these important issues. By racialization, I refer to the set of practices, cultural norms, and institutional arrangements that both reflect and help to create and maintain race-based outcomes in society. Because racialization is a set of historical and cultural processes, it does not have one particular meaning. Instead, it describes conditions and norms that are constantly evolving and interacting with the sociopolitical environment, varying from location to location as well as throughout different periods in history.[1] These processes are not uniformly present or static. They respond to what we collectively do and think and are therefore highly contested.[2] As a society, however, we are not inclined to consider the nuances of race and racism. Rather, we tend to see them as a limited set of discrete practices that remain constant over time, in spite of social changes.

Even as we use "racialization" to connote the fluid nature of the phenomena we are describing and the broader context in which racial outcomes are manifested and understood, the use of this term will not automatically break us of our reflexive thinking and mental habits around race and racism. In this country, the cultural understanding of racism is most closely associated with Jim Crow. In this context, it is imagined as conscious discriminatory activity, directed at a particular victim, by racist individuals.[3] Issues of race and racism, therefore, have come to be understood as explicit acts by individuals or explicit laws or policies implemented by institutions such as school boards or municipal governments.[4] This overly individualistic definition of race and racism fits well with our country's individualistic approach to many life issues. Consequently, issues of race are likely to be seen primarily as deliberate psychosocial events, instigated by individual bad actors or by institutions managed or directed by them. This view was made law in the 1976 case *Washington v. Davis*, which sets out the Supreme Court's discriminatory purpose doctrine, requiring that a plaintiff prove intent in racial discrimination claims.[5] From the point of view of the Court in this case, the Jim Crow system – a highly institutionalized and extensive regime of racial oppression that was only partly legal – is reduced to the behavior of bigots, whose policies can be purged or reversed in an election cycle or by excising the offending de jure rules. In this individualistic frame of analysis, if one does not engage in conscious acts of racism, or, better still, does not consciously see race, then there can be no racism or racialization.

This requirement of proof of intentional discrimination became the legal standard at the same time that our society more consciously embraced a public position of racial egalitarianism. Virtually all sectors of society now renounce racism. To call someone racist impugns not only the legality of that person's actions but also his or her morality. Indeed, to call someone racist today is seen as incendiary and a form of character assassination. The good American refuses to engage in conscious racially motivated behavior and refuses to see race or call it out. He is race-blind, purportedly embracing the dream of Dr. Martin Luther King, Jr., that our children "will one day live in a nation where they will not be judged by the color of their skin but by the content of their character."[6] Unfortunately, this line is too often used to suggest that were Dr. King alive today, he would oppose policies such as affirmative action or race-conscious voluntary integration. This allows the good American to claim that as long as others share this blindness, race does not matter.

RACE BLINDNESS AND POST-RACIALISM

The conservative form of race blindness has been extremely callous at times. Consider the Supreme Court's 2007 opinion in *Parents Involved in Community Schools v. Seattle School District No. 1*. The case actually involved two school districts: Seattle, in which racial segregation had not been legally mandated, and metropolitan Louisville, in which court-imposed desegregation had been terminated when the district was deemed "unitary" – meaning that it no longer operated a racially segregated, dual school system. Both districts had created student assignment plans that took race into account in order to maintain diversity, equality of opportunity, and broad support for public schools. Writing for a plurality of the Court, Chief Justice Roberts adopted language from the struggle to remove racial barriers to education, but uncoupled it from both history and current patterns of racialization:

> Before *Brown*, schoolchildren were told where they could and could not go to school based on the color of their skin. The school districts in these cases have not carried the heavy burden of demonstrating that we should allow this once again – even for very different reasons. . . . The way to stop discrimination on the basis of race is to stop discriminating on the basis of race.[7]

The chief justice seems to be arguing that when school districts devise student assignment plans that foster diversity and integration, it is as injurious a practice as intentional race-based exclusion. From this perspective, racial hierarchy is legally irrelevant to the constitutional principle of Equal Protection. Other conservatives assert that "moving beyond race" is not just an aspiration or a description of where we ought to be, but is also the best means to get us there. They are all but indifferent to segregation and other forms of racial stratification unless the intent to create or foster them can be located in the conscious minds of specific perpetrators. This position not only ignores the policies, structures, and conditions of racial marginalization; it also ignores the extent to which our behavior and motivation are unconscious.

Though Chief Justice Roberts asserts that color blindness is the appropriate mechanism for addressing racial hierarchy, a race-blind stance not only does not address racialized conditions, such as failing minority-majority schools; it also fails to avoid the divisiveness that many conservatives say they are attempting to mitigate through this form of denial. In fact, this use of color blindness bars engagement on the issue of race. It also precludes intervention. It offers a narrative that supports the racial status quo, even blaming marginalized groups for their status and conditions.[8] Fortunately, eloquent voices are raised in dissent, as in Justice Stevens's reminder that "the history books do not tell stories of white children struggling to attend black schools. In this and other ways, the Chief Justice rewrites the history of one of this Court's most important decisions."[9]

Color-blind conservatives focus only on the purity of the conscious mind with respect to awareness of race, which allows them to remain purposefully unconcerned with racial realities or the complicity of the unconscious mind. The evil they seek to guard against is the psychological state of those in power – the noticing of race – not the condition of various racial groups or current and historical patterns in the distribution of opportunity.[10] Indeed, if conservatives do take notice of them, they are likely to explain existing racial arrangements as caused by a non-white "culture of poverty," a term often used to excuse the lack of effort to improve conditions in low-income communities of color by implying that the problems are caused by blameworthy and immutable group behavior. Justice Thomas, for example, expresses indifference to racial arrangements, practices, and conditions, telling us that real harm ensues when we see race, whether our intentions are benevolent or malign.[11] In *Parents Involved*, Thomas and the plurality assert that only harms caused by intentionally discriminatory state action can be remedied using race, with a very limited set of exceptions.[12]

This is not the position of many of the liberals who supported President Obama. The word "post-racialism" has been adopted to describe their race blindness. Like their conservative counterparts, many liberals believe that racialization is primarily a psychological event and that good Americans are beyond race.[13] "Race doesn't matter!" – much.[14] These liberals focus, as do conservatives, primarily on the conscious mind, the least important area for understanding our motivation and actions. Growing evidence reveals that even if the conscious mind does not notice race, the unconscious is likely to notice and to act on this awareness unconsciously. Unlike color-blind conservatives, post-racial liberals are willing, under some conditions, to be race-sensitive, but they agree that a frontal attack on racial conditions is divisive.

Naturally, in the wake of President Obama's victory, the question of where we are with regard to race has surfaced again and again. The president has specifically rejected the claim that we are in a post-racial world, citing continuing racial disparities:

> When I hear commentators interpreting my speech to mean that we have arrived
> at a "postracial politics" or that we already live in a color-blind society, I have to
> offer a word of caution. To say that we are one people is not to suggest that race
> no longer matters – that the fight for equality has been won, or that the problems
> that minorities face in this country today are largely self-inflicted. . . . [A]s much
> as I insist that things have gotten better, I am mindful of this truth as well: Better
> isn't good enough.[15]

Yet there is and likely will continue to be stubborn insistence that we are
in a post-racial world, evidenced most poignantly by President Obama's
own success.[16]

For both color-blind conservatives and liberal post-racialists, we
are all but beyond race. In their view, a few old-style racists may remain,
especially in the South, but those individuals, like many civil rights ac-
tivists, are still stuck in old paradigms, locked in a struggle that is anti-
quated, outmoded, and distracting. The alternative to this tired old battle
is post-racialism. Adolph Reed asserts that we should stop using race and
deal with the real issue of class.[17] Some post-racialists also use changing demographics to support the claim that we are beyond race.[18] From
these perspectives, the question of where we are with regard to race then
becomes binary. We are either in a divisive space from the past where
we continue to assert the dominance of conscious racism, or we are in a
post-racial world where race really does not matter to most Americans.

To post-racialists, white support of President Obama is proof positive that we are in, or rapidly approaching, a new, post-racial era. They
argue that young people do not even see race, and that only persons
over forty are still likely to think in racial terms. All we must do is wait
patiently, and post-racialism will grow as the older generations pass on.
Post-racialists further assume that there is a direct connection between
improved conscious racial attitudes, by which they mean race blindness, and the end of racial inequality.[19] While there is a certain intuitive
logic to this assumption, it is often incorrect. During the counterculture
movement of the 1960s, for example, many young Americans rejected
materialism, but the assumption that materialism would therefore decline as the young became the leaders of the country did not pan out.
Likewise, we should not assume that the hopes we have now will lead
naturally to racial nirvana. Post-racialists claim to remain blind to growing evidence of the racialized work of structures on one hand and the

powerful role of racial anxiety and unconscious bias on the other. They insist on a simple notion of race and racism: either you are a racist, or you are not. A more realistic picture would accommodate the reality that one can have and act on racial anxiety and bias in one situation and have and act on racial openness and fairness in the next. We now know that one can have inconsistent racial positions at both conscious and unconscious levels. So as it turns out, it is the post-racial position that is stuck in the past, ignoring mounting evidence from neuroscience.[20]

FALSE NEUTRALITY

One way of expressing color blindness is to be neutral on the issue of race. Proponents of this position apparently are most interested in neutrality in the design of policies and programs. They pay less attention to the administration or implementation of what they design and, more importantly, often ignore the effects of the policies and procedures they create. Although a policy that is neutral in design is not necessarily neutral in effect, the courts and the public seem all but obsessed with the design and, even more narrowly, with the *intent* of the design, rather than the results.[21] Fairness is not advanced by treating those who are situated differently as if they were the same, however. For example, it would make little sense to provide the same protections against hurricanes to midwestern communities as to coastal communities or to provide the same level of investment against diseases such as malaria to communities in which the risks of an outbreak are dramatically different. If the institutions managing and distributing resources in such contexts are merely neutral, the effects of their work may not be, given that the intended beneficiaries are differently situated. This kind of blindness, moreover, is wasteful as well as inadequate. Equality of effort can produce very different overall outcomes, depending not only on the beneficiaries' individual needs, but also on their environments. These policy views – and the goal of neutrality of *results* in targeted spending – would spark little debate in most contexts. Applying them with respect to racial disadvantage, however, is often controversial. It need not be.

Aristotle, who gave us much of our understanding of equality, asserted that it is just to treat those who are situated similarly the same, but it would be unjust to treat those who are situated differently the same.[22] Once stated, this seems obvious; yet we have difficulty acknowledging that we are differently situated. Even when we are more attuned to the fact that differences matter, we are inclined to focus on a single factor, which causes us to misunderstand the situation. The debate over neutrality in relation to those differently situated has a particular history in jurisprudence. Legal scholar Herbert Wechsler argued that *Brown* was not rightly decided because it was not based on the neutrality principle.[23] According to Wechsler, even if segregation harmed blacks, legal neutrality required also considering the harm of integration and association for whites. This argument was rejected by other legal scholars such as Charles Black, who asserted that the Fourteenth Amendment and other Civil War Amendments were not meant to be neutral, but instead embodied certain constitutional values.[24] As the case *Parents Involved* indicates, however, the Supreme Court has been moving toward the neutrality principle, effectively overturning *Brown* and changing the meaning of the Civil War Amendments.

With these considerations in mind, what are we to do with our existing racialized conditions and arrangements, from schools to housing to the criminal justice system? Will these problems really fix themselves automatically with the passage of time? Many conservatives say that the proper response – the only possible response – is to do nothing.[25] They argue that color blindness prohibits us from doing anything that would either be sensitive to race or require the use of racial classifications. Other conservatives argue that we must convince racially marginalized groups to adopt the proper cultural values so that they may benefit from the new race-blind landscape: The opportunity is there; if African Americans and Latinos fail to take advantage of this new arrangement, it is their own fault. For conservatives, state intervention is thus a moral and legal mistake.

FALSE UNIVERSALISM

Post-racialists are more likely to support state intervention, but they are reluctant to support ideas that cannot be framed in a universal manner, and an explicit consideration of race is largely off the table.[26] This course of action has the apparent advantage of helping those who have been historically excluded without mentioning a topic seen as "divisive." This approach, which I will call false universalism, presents a number of problems. One set of concerns is conceptual, another is empirical, and a third is problematic from a legal or policy perspective.

Conceptual Concerns

Universal programs begin with a conception of the universal that is based on background assumptions that are non-universal. Virtually all universal approaches are in fact particular.[27] Robert Lieberman notes that the analysis must focus on the targeting as well as on the administration and funding of a program.[28] For example, although it is often described as the quintessential universal policy, the Social Security Act was universal only insofar as the universe was composed of white, male, able-bodied workers. In its early years, the program excluded the elderly because they did not have a history of paying contributions into the system.[29] Exclusions of agricultural and domestic work, adopted to appease southern resistance to the act, caused 65 percent of African American workers to be denied protection as well.[30] Under the cultural norms and discriminatory patterns of the era, men were the primary wage earners, and women typically worked in the home. Indeed, unpaid household labor and child-rearing responsibilities are not counted toward Social Security earnings even today. Those who take time off or select careers with more flexible working hours in order to care for children or other family members will therefore earn less, on average, than those who do not and will have lower Social Security benefits upon retirement. This continues to disproportionately affect women, but even if it didn't, does it make sense? We all have families, and we all have, or are, dependents during some stages of our lives. Assessing programs in terms of how they interact with other systems, rather than in isolation, reveals that even Social Security is not universal. Our aim therefore should be for universal goals and outcomes, not just universal processes or strategies.

Targeted policies and programs (poorhouses in the nineteenth century, mother's pensions in 1910, the War on Poverty in the 1960s), however, are likely to be viewed through the prism of zero-sum politics. At a time of perceived scarcity and contracting government budgets, targeted policies may be viewed as favoring specific constituencies rather than promoting the common good. If the target group is historically disfavored or considered "undeserving," targeted policies risk being labeled "preferences" for "special interests." To avoid alienating voters in these circumstances, policies are often packaged for broad appeal.[31] President Obama has expressed a preference for universal programs to address racialized disparities, but he also acknowledges the need for targeted programs. In particular, he asserts that a targeted focus will be needed for both "underclass" blacks and undocumented immigrants.[32] The approach I advocate here is much in agreement but is different in scope. Programs should be universal in goals, but unless they are targeted in approach, the goals of fairness and inclusion will falter – not just for the most marginalized blacks and the undocumented, but also for many other racialized and non-racialized groups, such as people living in rural areas, people with disabilities, and the elderly. Accepting this is in part simple responsiveness to empirical information. Where untargeted universal approaches fall short, we should be willing to adjust. We can learn to communicate about these needs in ways that avoid most of the racial divisiveness.

We can also work to expose the conceptual problem: Why is it divisive to focus on race-specific programs or talk about race? Many liberals are concerned that no targeted program will work because it cannot garner the necessary support.[33] Another stock explanation for avoiding race-conscious programs is that race does not matter. The energy invested in the need for race not to matter to whites, however, in and of itself indicates that race does indeed matter. Some express concern that racially targeted programs may cause whites who see themselves as playing by the rules to resent having things given to undeserving non-whites who do not play by the rules. These whites may see themselves as resenting only those they perceive as rule breakers. This attitude may hold more promise for racial fairness, but it also turns out to be wanting, as white opposition to affirmative action can also be viewed as based mostly on the fear of losing white privileges and on the sense that something is being "taken" unfairly.[34] But consider issues such as fair housing, school integration, or reform of the criminal justice system. Why should these efforts be controversial or divisive? George Lipsitz points out that the challenge arising in these contexts is not so much to a material zero-sum policy, but is instead an urge to protect what he calls a "possessive investment in whiteness."[35] The need to keep the racial "other" out of schools and neighborhoods and under the control of the criminal justice system makes sense only if race does matter. What the overused resentment argument conceals is how concern for possible white anger is employed to block action to ameliorate existing, egregious racial injustice and protect white prerogative and privilege instead.[36] But why would whites vote for Obama and still insist that schools, neighborhoods, and other opportunities continue to be racialized? Are they racist or not?

Empirical Concerns

In addition to the conceptual problems, problems with outcomes plague approaches based on false universalism. These problems, which I think of as empirical, are not with design or administration as much as with results. What are we trying to achieve in our universal efforts? There is no single answer to this question. Some are trying to achieve race blindness, others to guarantee racial justice or fairness.[37] While the two goals could work in tandem, in practice they are often in conflict.[38] Dona and Charles Hamilton have examined many efforts to use universal programs, and they conclude that to the extent that we are concerned with racial justice, virtually all of them fail.[39] Ira Katznelson looked at some of the most popular universal programs coming out of the New Deal and World War II and concluded that by and large these programs benefited whites disproportionately.[40] Even programs that did benefit non-whites often exacerbated disparities between whites and non-whites. We have to recognize that in some situations, universalism simply will not work to address the needs of marginalized racial and ethnic groups. Indeed it is possible, even likely, that universal programs will continue to worsen existing inequalities.

Some universal programs were *intended* to benefit whites more than non-whites, but let us consider programs in which this was not the case. Hailed as one of this country's greatest accomplishments, the Interstate Highway Act of 1956 – at the time the largest public works project in

American history – used federal dollars to subsidize the creation of the suburbs. The act gave impetus to waves of migrating middle- and upper-class families to abandon central cities for the suburbs. At the same time, many downtown regions were surrounded or demolished by massive highway construction, and the revenue generated by these projects did not return to the communities that lost their churches, schools, and homes. As Kevin Douglas Kuswa has noted, "[h]ighways made subur-ban housing available on one end while destroying urban housing on the other."[41] The ensuing arrangement of racially isolated urban and suburban communities, hastened by the white flight that followed 1954's *Brown v. Board of Education* decision, is a pattern we live with even today.

Consider as well the Veterans Administration (va) programs, which helped millions of Americans attend college, acquire homes, and start businesses. With the introduction of the GI Bill, interest rates and thirty-year mortgage loans made Americans, for the first time, more likely to purchase a home than to rent. The resulting building boom, from 1945 to 1954, created more than thirteen million new homes in the United States.[42] va mortgages paid for five million new homes.[43] The educa-tional benefits of the va were equally impressive. Millions of Americans acquired college degrees. By 1950, the federal government had spent more on schooling for veterans than on the Marshall Plan.[44] These edu-cational programs were race- and gender-neutral in design, yet in prac-tice they increased disparities between blacks and whites and between white men and white women.[45] In fact, no other single instrument did as much to widen the racial gap in postwar America. The bill provided for local and state administration with congressional oversight, but this oversight was controlled by southern congressmen. As a result, blacks were excluded, rejected, and discouraged from partaking in the benefits of a generous federal program.[46] Explicit racial barriers to non-whites trying to join the military resulted in disproportionate numbers of white servicemen, but impediments from non-military institutions also lim-ited the number of blacks who could join. For example, given the limited access to education that most blacks had at the time, reading and writing requirements were much harder to meet.[47] Even black men who served did not receive benefits on par with those of their white counterparts. As Amartya Sen notes, they were not able to benefit from the educational program to the same extent as whites, partly because the colleges they were allowed to attend were highly segregated, uneven in quality, and often underfunded.[48] Thus, although it might have seemed fair, awarding federal college grants to all soldiers on a racially neutral basis had the effect of worsening inequality in educational outcomes, as whites received a greater advantage for the same tax dollar spent.

Another disparity that worsened under the GI Bill was challenged in an important Supreme Court case. In 1979, in *Personnel Administrator of Massachusetts v. Feeney*, female plaintiffs proved that 98 percent of the benefits of some portions of this federal program went to men.[49] The Court found no discrimination, however, because there was no proof of any explicit, conscious desire to exclude women.[50] The fact that the program was for veterans, and that women were not as likely to be veterans, was deemed coincidental and not legally or morally significant. Although the disparities were not as stark as between men and women, white men thus benefited disproportionately relative to both non-white men and women. Thus a "universal" program helped create a middle class insensitive to the conditions of women and non-white men. It was indeed what Ira Katznelson calls an affirmative action program for white men.[51]

Problems with outcomes also result from resistance to recognition of differences in individual and group circumstances. One major assumption today is that if universal programs focus on an area, such as poverty, where a marginalized group is overrepresented, the benefit will disproportionately benefit the marginalized group. This would allow race-blind universal policies to do race-sensitive work. This approach is favored not only by policy makers but also by the Supreme Court, which has limited race-conscious remedial efforts.[52] While the idea is intuitively appealing, efforts to use income as a soft proxy for race often simply do not deliver.[53]

As Gunnar Myrdal noted in 1944, poor blacks and poor whites are not similarly situated.[54] African Americans suffer from cumulative causation, or mutually reinforcing restraints.[55] What false universalism fails to address is that groups of people are differently situated in relation to institutional and policy dynamics. If one looks at only one or two constraints, one is likely to inaccurately assume that groups in very different circumstances are in fact similar. But let us assume for simplicity's sake that there are ten constraints reducing opportunity for group A, and that two of those constraints also are reducing opportunity for group B. Suppose that the presence of any of the constraints is sufficient to deny opportunity. Let us also assume that group A is overrepresented on constraints 1 and 2, which are also the constraints holding back group B. A universal policy that removed constraints 1 and 2 would vastly increase the opportunity movement of group B. It would not, however, change the conditions of group A, because the eight remaining constraints continue to reduce opportunity for that group. Yet the failure of group A to translate the policy into opportunity might be seen as a failure by group A, rather than as a policy failure. This flaw in false universalism is not overcome by anti-discrimination policies. One could even argue that the disfavored group is not being discriminated against in a traditional sense. But in order for progress to occur, that group's situation must be seen as a whole, including prior discrimination in education, housing, and health care, and the ways those earlier factors contribute to the problem at hand.[56] Some may object to considering social situations. Which conditions should count or be considered for policy concerns? There are a couple of responses to this. One is that we are discussing group, not just individual, differences. But more importantly, it is critical in a democracy that we be attentive to how opportunity is distributed, and to and for whom. While we cannot determine the outcome of such a discussion, it would be beneficial to have it. It would also be useful for policymakers to deliberately consider how groups of people are situated, and the relevance of these situations, when designing and adopting policies.

The failure to do so limited progress in the wake of the *Southern Burlington County* N.A.A.C.P. *v. Mount Laurel Township* cases, in which the plaintiffs challenged land-use regulations that operated to exclude low- and moderate-income persons from housing in Mount Laurel, New Jersey.[57] Although the plaintiffs were predominantly African American and Latino, the action was reframed as a case about class rather than race. The reasoning was that because African Americans and Latinos were in greater need of affordable housing than were whites, a victory achieved in the universal frame of socioeconomic status would provide the needed relief. In a landmark ruling, the New Jersey Supreme Court struck down exclusionary zoning and ordered municipalities to take affirmative steps to provide their "fair share" of low-income housing.[58] The state legislature followed with the New Jersey Fair Housing Act, which it viewed as its constitutional obligation in light of the court's ruling.[59] The program proved successful in producing affordable housing, but it – along with initiatives elsewhere that were designed to reduce economic segregation – increased the racial isolation of blacks, who were also further segregated from opportunity. As had happened in the VA programs and the New Deal, the program increased the material and social distance between low-income whites and non-whites by failing to take into account important differences in how groups are situated in relation to institutional interactions and processes.

To fully understand the importance of situatedness, one must look at how the interaction of institutions creates and distributes opportunity benefits and burdens. The political philosopher Iris Young observed that the more complex society becomes, the more our relationships and opportunities will be mediated through institutional arrangements.[60] This statement is true for all groups in society. At a rudimentary level, Young's insight is not particularly surprising. Most of our modes of commerce, from the purchase of groceries to banking, have been depersonalized. Instead of buying produce from a farmer or taking out a loan from the local banker, we may mediate these exchanges through supermarkets or websites. At a deeper level, we know that the neighborhood we live in may be more important than the house we live in.[61] We know that where we live will largely determine which schools our children attend and how safe we feel, as well as our access to jobs, other people, and both material and social wealth. A middle-income person living in a poor neighborhood is situated differently from a low- or middle-income person in a middle-income neighborhood. Moreover, the importance of institutional arrangements and the interactions within these structures for the distribution of opportunity in our society is only increasing.

Universal programs often operate on the unstated assumption that the particular conditions of the more favored group exist for all groups – that they are universal. Thus, as noted earlier, the Social Security Act, a program considered quintessentially universal, began with a conception of a recipient who was a working, white male. The development of such a policy or program, with an ostensibly universal norm that in fact favors or disfavors a particular group, is likely to be an unconscious and unintentional process but harmful nonetheless.

Legal Concerns

When Hurricane Katrina struck New Orleans, confusion reigned. As photos and news reports emerged, so did disbelief and questions: Were we not already in a largely color-blind society, where if race mattered at all, it mattered very little? Why, then, were so many blacks stranded? I received several calls from media outlets asking me if I thought President Bush was racist. It is not that we do not know that there still is persistent racial inequality in our society, but we have a story line that allows us to justify and explain this fact when it rudely intrudes into our otherwise public stance that race does not matter. We tell the stories about the culture of poverty and the lack of personal and collective responsibility in racially marginalized communities. We talk about segregation from opportunity as a choice, and about people just wanting to live with their own. We become armchair sociologists, uninterested in and unconcerned with the facts and even less aware of our institutional arrangements and the work they do.

What made Hurricane Katrina particularly difficult to explain was that these stories of institutional racialization were less available. We never asked why blacks in New Orleans were so segregated and so poor. We never asked how they came to be in harm's way. We never asked why the disinvestment in their communities and lives had been extended to such shameful levels. We never asked ourselves why a universal evacuation plan required cars when so many blacks had no vehicles. We assumed we knew. And if we thought some unjustified racial play was at work, we looked for the conscious racist. Thus even in the wake of a disaster so dramatic that many ordinarily complacent or resistant whites vividly witnessed the tragic and ongoing effects of race in America, the structural and institutional underpinnings of racialization held firm.[62]

So the final problem for the post-racial position is a legal and policy limitation. Once a race-blind position is adopted, it becomes difficult to justify race-sensitive or race-specific policies or laws. Proponents of color-blindness who oppose considering race have an easier path. If race is irrelevant, what is the justification, legal or otherwise, for using it? The conservative position, while concerned about the socially explosive consequences of using race, is not concerned with racial conditions. But again, the assertion that the use of race is explosive belies the claim that it does not matter.[63] The conservative position, however, not only rejects the use of race; it is also very skeptical of race-sensitive policies. Of course, race and racialization will matter more in some situations than in others, but simplistic notions about these concepts can make those situations difficult to distinguish. We need help not only in seeing that race matters, but also in seeing when and how it matters. Race blindness cannot help us do that work.

Consider the issue of voluntary integration measures implemented by democratically elected school boards struggling to overcome legacies of educational and residential segregation.[64] As we saw in the Supreme Court case on voluntary school desegregation, *Parents Involved*, a plurality of justices made the case for color blindness, arguing that no matter how well intentioned, the Constitution forbids the use of racial classifications.[65] According to this same group, *Brown* was about classification, not racial conditions or subordination.[66] Fortunately, this position is not the law at this point, because Justice Kennedy, in the tie-breaking vote, rejected the claim that the Constitution is color-blind.[67]

Consider as well the post-racial argument raised in a challenge to section 5 of the Voting Rights Act of 1965 (VRA).[68] The VRA prohibits voting practices or procedures that discriminate on the basis of race, color, or membership in one of the language minority groups. Section 5 requires that certain state and local governments, mostly in the South, obtain permission, or "pre-clearance," from the Justice Department or a federal court before making changes that could affect participation in voting.[69] A Texas municipal utility district, using the election of the nation's first African American president as proof, challenged this provision, arguing that, in reauthorizing the act in 2006, Congress had not taken sufficient account of more than four decades of progress toward racial equality. As the district put it: "The country has its first African-American president, who received a larger percentage of the white vote than each of the previous two Democratic presidential nominees."[70] But does this historic event really mean that the central justification for the Voting Rights Act has now dissipated?

The Supreme Court decided the case on narrow statutory grounds, but the 8–1 opinion was written by Chief Justice Roberts, who currently challenges any governmental use of racial classifications and who, as a young lawyer in the Reagan administration, opposed efforts to expand the VRA.[71] In the Court's opinion, the chief justice noted that "[i]n part due to the success of that legislation, we are now a very different Nation. Whether conditions continue to justify such legislation is a difficult constitutional question we do not answer today."[72]

Even if post-racial liberals can succeed in maintaining the VRA or addressing racial isolation in schools or neighborhoods, such efforts are likely to be seen as inconsistent with the fundamental position that race does not matter. We could take a more nuanced position that race matters under some circumstance and not others. And, of course, this is true, but it conflicts with the attraction to simplistic answers and with our eagerness to be done with race.

Today the country faces a housing and credit crisis that disproportionately affects African Americans and Latinos.[73] With little residential or commercial lending from mainstream banking institutions, isolated communities of color were indeed easy prey for high-cost credit institutions that faced little competition.[74] These communities have been undercapitalized since World War II, when affirmative action was white and redlining was in full bloom, but they remain largely invisible other than when they are criticized for taking out loans they could not afford.[75]

Things have changed since World War II. We could not have had a black president a decade ago, let alone in the 1940s. Conscious racial attitudes have improved greatly. Whites may be more willing to support targeted universal programs, which perhaps represents a meaningful shift in attitudes. Still, it would be wise for us to remember the euphoria after the *Brown* decision, when many Americans thought racialization and racism would be dead within ten years. Today many pundits assert that racialization is or soon will be a thing of the past. Thomas Friedman has stated that the Civil War is finally over and the North has won.[76] Others tell us that the country is going through a major realignment that will put an end to Richard Nixon's (and the Republican Party's) Southern Strategy of racializing politics to win white votes.[77] The writers making these assertions have failed to consider, however, that only a few years ago most Americans had not even heard of the Southern Strategy, and that conservatives have been claiming for decades that we are beyond race.

RACIALIZATION AND BIAS

The process of racialization has changed and is changing. The number of old-style explicit racists is declining. Even though we talk about white and non-white attitudes, a range of attitudes and conditions is reflected in each racialized group. What may be more interesting is that most of us carry conflicting racial attitudes within ourselves.[78] President Obama accurately noted that "None of us – black, white, Latino, or Asian – is immune to the stereotypes that our culture continues to feed us, especially stereotypes about [blacks]."[79] It is a serious mistake therefore to define racialization narrowly and then dismiss it. There are more possibilities than just the Jim Crow racial practices challenged in the 1950s and 1960s, the color-blind position, or post-racialism. We are in a space in which our old ways of thinking about race do not serve us well and can easily lead us to misunderstand the opportunities and challenges before us.

Two emerging areas of racialization are most salient today. The first is in the processes and practices of inter-institutional arrangements that continue to distribute racialized outcomes in part because of differences in how groups are situated. The second is ambivalence that unconsciously affects our racial meanings and practices. The first is called "structural racialization"[80] and the second "implicit bias." To start with the latter, research suggests that most of us have implicit biases that can affect our behaviors and understandings.[81] Because we have conscious control over – or, indeed, access to – only a small part of the processes going on in our brains, many of our thoughts and feelings, even during waking hours, occur without our express command or permission. This recognition helps explain inconsistencies between our conscious attitudes and our behavior. Although most of us are completely unaware of their influence on our subconscious, these biases affect how we perceive, interpret, and understand one another. Because of these implicit biases, identical actions or opinions of two people of different social groups may be interpreted quite differently, depending upon the groups to which they, and a given viewer, belong.[82] Because these attitudes – unrecognized on the conscious level but powerful at the unconscious level – influence choices and decisions, individual and institutional discrimination can and does occur even in the absence of blatant prejudice, ill will, or animus. This bias has been measured and documented in the Harvard Implicit Association Tests.[83]

These biases are formed as social and physical structures lead us to create mental associations that become embedded in our unconscious and affect how we process the world. When we hear several unrelated words repeatedly grouped together, the mental associations between those words grow stronger, and our brains "arrange" the words accordingly. For example, in our society, many people associate African American men with crime – a cognitive association. Currently, African American men in the United States are several times more likely to go to prison than white men, a structural "verification" of that association.[84] When such associations form in both mental and structural contexts, they reinforce one another, creating a vicious cycle. If history, context, and facts are then removed from the analysis, as they are in the color-blind worldview, it can become unclear which came first, the cognitive or the social construct. Structures support policies, and the policies further reinforce stereotypes. The more often African American men are charged with crimes, the more the mental association is reinforced, which in turn primes the thinking of law enforcement and court officials.

To add to the frustrating nature of this problem, studies have shown that when an individual's behavior disproves or conflicts with an ingrained assumption or stereotype, the mind – rather than discarding more deeply embedded thought patterns – perceives that individual as a mere outlier or anomaly.[85] Because these mental associations operate below the level of conscious control, the stereotypes are not easily willed away. The tendency is instead toward framing information to match strongly held concepts and refusing to believe facts that tend to disprove them.

The existence of implicit bias does not mean that we are all secretly racist. It does suggest that we are complex and conflicted and that this conflict can be organized to make either our biases or our egalitarian aspirations more salient. A particularly egregious example of the former – the Southern Strategy – mobilized racial resentment, and the tactic worked well from 1968 until the election of Barack Obama. We can challenge these nefarious efforts, but we cannot do so by being race-blind, as President Obama reminds us:

> If an internalization of antidiscrimination norms over the past three decades – not to mention basic decency – prevents most Whites from consciously acting on [negative racial] stereotypes in their daily interactions with persons of other races, it's unrealistic to believe that these stereotypes don't have some cumulative impact on the often snap decisions of who's hired and who's promoted, on who's arrested and who's prosecuted, on how you feel about the customer who just walked into your store or about the demographics of your children's school.[86]

Research on implicit bias can help us understand more about these forces that continue to feed the racial hierarchy. It can also help make the case that the requirement to prove "intent" in racial discrimination is, at best, out of touch. Charles Lawrence has proposed an alternative test that would take unconscious racism into account.[87]

Beyond individual thought patterns are the structural factors that influence how race affects human interactions. Harmful practices, cultural norms, and institutional arrangements, if left unchallenged, create and maintain racialized outcomes. To address this structural racialization effectively, we must understand the work that our institutions and policies are, in fact, doing – not just what we hope they will do. To understand the current state of institutions, we must take seriously the ways in which groups are situated. I have already argued that a universal approach is unlikely to be effective. Others insist that targeted racial efforts are likely to fail in part because of the continuing racial resentment that such efforts may create or preserve. For a sincere policy maker, these arguments suggest a difficult choice: either avoid race and leave existing racial practices and arrangements largely undisturbed, or deal with race and excite racial resentment that will undermine the policies and the electability of the politician. Fortunately there are powerful and effective alternatives to these two choices.

TARGETED UNIVERSALISM

One alternative is to learn a great deal about how to talk about race in ways that are not divisive. The second is to make sure our institutions do the work we want them to do. The latter is accomplished by adopting strategies that are both targeted and universal. A targeted universal strategy is inclusive of the needs of both dominant and marginalized groups, but pays particular attention to the situation of the marginalized group. For example, if the goal is to open up housing opportunity for low-income whites and non-whites, one would look at the different constraints for each group. Targeted universalism rejects a blanket approach that is likely to be indifferent to the reality that different groups are situated differently relative to the institutions and resources of society. It also rejects the claim of formal equality that would, as a way of denying difference, treat all people the same. Any proposal would be evaluated by the outcome as well as the intent. While the effort would be universal for the poor, it would be especially sensitive to the most marginalized groups.

Because institutions interact and affect one another's impacts, it will be necessary to be mindful of synergistic effects as well. This is an approach that I have advocated under the rubric of opportunity communities or opportunity structures. Synergy was a key issue in *Parents Involved*, where a majority of the Court acknowledged the interactions of institutions and softened the requirement that there be proof of conscious racially motivated wrongdoing before race-sensitive policy interventions could be allowed.[88]

In complex real-world settings, policies often have unintended consequences and can generate resistance that thwarts the best intentions. It is critical, therefore, that targeted universal policies set clear goals and use mechanisms to closely monitor and correct for negative feedback loops and other impediments to the achievement of those goals. A targeted universal approach also recognizes that problems faced by particular segments of American society are problems that could spill over into the lives of everyone, just as the Lower Ninth Ward was not the only part of New Orleans to suffer in the wake of Katrina. In this sense, marginalized populations in American society are like the canary in the coal mine, to borrow a metaphor developed by Lani Guinier and Gerald Torres.[89] Likewise, although low-income communities of color were its prime targets, the subprime crisis did not end in poor, urban communities but spread far beyond, with staggering effects on even the global economy.

In times of economic crisis, however, there is increased danger that commitments to racial fairness will be jettisoned in favor of expedience or ostensibly universal concerns. This is a mistake. As President Obama has written, "[N]owhere is it ordained that history moves in a straight line, and during difficult economic times it is possible that the imperatives of racial equality get shunted aside."[90] The experience of the New Deal taught us that even universal policies, if not well designed, can worsen rather than ameliorate racial conditions. Yet a number of current proposals for infrastructure spending look to divert much of the funding to existing road projects.[91] This broad and regressive use of infrastructure stimulus funds may produce jobs in the short term, but the strategy is simply a replication of existing models of public investment that have produced inequitable and unsustainable growth. What is truly needed are strategic investments that produce economic development on a broad scale while transforming communities and cities.

The manifold crises we face have produced a rare opportunity to change our institutional and regulatory arrangements. The post–New Deal and post–World War II arrangements laid the groundwork for the generations that followed them, and the policies we promulgate are likely to do the same. The window of opportunity will remain open for only so long, however. In this moment, we can work toward building a more equitable future, or we can repeat the mistakes of the past. If we fail at promoting equity, we will be trying to correct our missteps for years – if not generations – to come.

In *The Audacity of Hope,* President Obama discusses targeting within universalism, specifically mentioning health care: "We should support programs to eliminate existing health disparities between minorities and whites . . . but a plan for universal health-care coverage would do more to eliminate health disparities between whites and minorities than any race-specific programs we might design."[92] This statement, which might at first sound the same as other "universal" approaches, sounds different in light of the health disparities initiative of the Department of Health and Human Services (HHS). It is true that a universal approach will help increase access to insurance for the far higher percentages (as compared with whites) of African American, Latino, and American Indian workers who have no access to employer-provided health insurance.[93] But the disparities initiative goes further. Secretary of Health & Human Services Kathleen Sebelius has announced that "It is time to refocus, reinforce, and repeat the message that health disparities exist and that health equity benefits everyone."[94] The Health Disparities Initiative will use research and outreach to address areas of greatest need, whether they are related to environmental factors, quality of provider-patient interaction, systemic social and economic disadvantage, or lack of medical knowledge and/or health education in vulnerable communities.[95]

In using a two-step process – establishing "universal," then targeted programs aimed at eliminating disparities – President Obama may be breaking ground that could result in greater public understanding and recognition of the significant benefits of this approach.[96] Even so, although it is hard to argue with the truly universal benefits of broad access to essentials such as health care or education, even targeted universal programs can cause racial resentment. Such resentment does not simply represent racist attitudes; it also represents ambivalence and confusion. A more sophisticated understanding of implicit bias as well as of our common yearnings for fairness and connectedness can help us learn how to communicate in ways that greatly increase our potential to build a society we can all be proud to call home.

The fact that some such communication is even possible suggests that we have made progress, though it should not be overstated. Ambivalence on matters of race is deeply rooted in the history of the United States. Thomas Jefferson hated slavery and worried about what it was doing to the country and the psyches of whites.[97] He also had a long-term, intimate relationship with a woman he held in slavery, and thus contributed simultaneously to the ideals of democracy and freedom and to the ideology of racial inferiority and subordination.[98] Lincoln supported the end of slavery but for many years did not believe that the races could ever live together. More generally, our very concept of freedom is bound up with the concept of slavery.[99]

In analyzing how Barack Obama's ascent to the presidency has changed and will change the process of racialization, we should congratulate ourselves. We must also be deliberate and thoughtful about how to make the most of this important opportunity. The popular media and culture like the idea of post-racialism and color blindness so much that Ian Haney López has cautioned that we may be entering a new era of color-blind racial dominance.[100] Others have warned that we may be moving from a white/non-white society to a black/non-black one, where educated and professional blacks would be embraced as non-black, while those considered black would be marginalized to an even greater extent.[101] To be effective in this context, the struggle for racial justice and fairness will need to focus on both structural racism and bias.

We must develop a more sophisticated understanding of the human mind, building on the new research on neurolinguistics and implicit bias. Perceptions of unfairness and resentment are present in many spheres of life, but our racial history and ongoing racial segregation can make these biases even more difficult to access or reform, even through active cross-cultural experiences and engagement. Moreover, mental associations formed at unconscious levels may operate even in individuals whose self-concept is organized around racial fairness, and these biases are difficult to change at the level of individual consciousness.

As important as it is to address the negative thought processes that can keep us trapped in our nation's tragic racial history, however, it is critically important to focus on institutional arrangements and policy interactions and how they work with respect to differently situated groups. Where we are and where we are going in terms of racial justice is fluid and in flux. We are changing both as a matter of demographics and, more importantly, as a matter of our history and practices. Where this journey and process will lead us is not predetermined, but certainly it must be to a place beyond our present failure to alleviate needless suffering and to build sustaining community.

As we develop as a pluralistic nation, we must also acknowledge that the racial binary is not a useful way to think about our journey. The language of race and racism does not adequately express all that needs to be conveyed in our discussion. We need a new way to talk about race and racialization and a meaningful way to analyze racialization. Our communication must be tailored to garner support for policies that are broad enough to encompass universal concerns but also sensitive to particular needs and situations. Recognition of the harms to the whole caused by inequality and exclusion must be expanded and deepened. Rare moments of insight, as in the wake of Katrina, or the cascading effects of the financial fraud centered on the housing markets must be more than momentary upheavals, forgotten in the next news cycle. Such sensitivities must gain ground and guide social policy, to the ultimate betterment of all of our lives.

We cannot allow even so important a milestone as the election of an African American to the highest office in the land to blind us to the important work that needs to be done. We are not there yet, wherever "there" is. Although not in the same way it did forty years ago, race still matters. Perhaps most importantly, what we do – and what our institutions do – matters. If we do not change our institutions to reflect our expressed attitudes and ideals, those ideals will increasingly lose their rightful centrality, and Americans of all races will be the poorer for it.

TWO

The Color-Blind Multiracial Dilemma

RACIAL CATEGORIES RECONSIDERED

> We're teaching our kids all of it, all their history. My 5-year-old asks, "People who looked like you, why did they treat them so bad?" It's hard to explain to a biracial child in 2011. In a perfect world, race wouldn't matter, but that day's a while off.
>
> *Sonia Cherail Peeples, quoted in Susan Saulny, "Black and White and Married in the Deep South"*

> Racism is like an eclipse. But unlike a solar eclipse that may blind us, it is more like a lunar eclipse that may cause us to trip in the dark.
>
> *John O. Calmore, "Exploring Michael Omi's 'Messy' Real World of Race"*

What are you? What race are you? For some, the answer takes less than half a second; others may need a paragraph to respond; and some may have their own question: Why do you ask? For despite our obsession with race, which sometimes takes the form of an aversion to discussing it, our national discourse on the subject is disturbingly confused, highly charged, and often unproductive. The concept of race is hotly contested and deconstructed in literature, law, and politics, yet our language seems wooden and rehearsed, and the way that we talk about it in conflict with our stated ideals. All the while, we constantly make assumptions about one another based on literal or figurative racial check boxes, not only as a society, but also as individuals. The racial categories we use are therefore well worth examining, both because of their societal role and because of the intense interest they evoke among thoughtful people.

A number of theories about race and its meaning in the United States currently compete for primacy. Here I will examine two of them: The first, the color-blind position, calls for an end to racial categories. The second, the multiracial position, calls for the proliferation of racial categories, with particular attention to expanding multiracial categories. Both positions make similar mistakes, and, more importantly, neither position seriously challenges racism. For this reason, I will also discuss some political implications of the multiracial project as well as the importance, under any categorical scheme, of emphasizing an anti-racist agenda.

THE COLOR-BLIND POSITION

With strong roots in the political liberalism of the 1960s, especially since Dr. King's electrifying calls for racial equality and justice for all, the color-blind position continues to receive support from traditional liberals and from those who believe that identity politics dangerously fracture our society.[1] In recent decades, however, neoconservatives have adopted the color-blind philosophy and recast it in ways that are often at odds with its original meaning and with liberal social goals.[2] This use of color-blind and race-neutral discourse has greatly expanded the right's control over the center and even over parts of the liberal political spectrum.[3]

The raceless proposal is partly rooted in the view that race is a social construct and not a biological fact. Its proponents argue that since we have learned that race is an illusion, we should drop racial categories altogether: minor differences in appearance are irrelevant, and only those who are either racist or badly misinformed would insist that we continue to use these pernicious categories. These ideals are popular behind the walls of academia, but they have found a more public voice in law and politics as well.

Much of the conservative rhetoric about color blindness rests on the recognition that racial categories are rooted in discredited biology and gene theory.[4] The sooner we remove references to race from law and politics, the reasoning goes, the better. Indeed, in this camp's view, we will only solve the race problem by eliminating all racial categories. Certainly the disappearance of racial discrimination is an important goal, but a ban on the recognition of race is not its equivalent, even if it were enforceable, or even possible to achieve. Yet, the Supreme Court has already used

color-blind reasoning to attack the validity of programs such as affirmative action, the redrawing of voting districts, and school desegregation,
all of which were specifically designed to achieve greater equality.[5] Only
fifty-odd years after declaring educational apartheid unconstitutional in
Brown v. Board of Education, for example, the Supreme Court in *Parents
Involved* cautioned two school districts, Seattle and metropolitan Louisville, about considering race when crafting assignment plans meant to
reduce racial isolation and increase public support districtwide.[6]

Conceptual Position

The new right's position is both conceptual and pragmatic. The conceptual part is the claim that because race does not have a substantial
scientific basis, it is only a problematic illusion. The claim that race is an
illusion draws on the work of late modernists and postmodernists – particularly that of Omi and Winant – that asserts that race is socially constructed. The conclusion that race is not real, however, does not comport
with the deeper implications of their insights. Omi and Winant, for example, do not support the position that the collection of data on race
can or should be dropped. Omi, citing *The Journal of Blacks in Higher
Education*, notes that while race may not be a scientific reality, it is a social
fact.[7] The color-blind argument is based on the seriously flawed assumption that whatever is not grounded in objective scientific data is not real.[8]

Constructionists, however, see all reality, including all concepts, as
socially constructed. So although the insight that race is socially constructed is based in part on postmodernist teaching, making the assertion out of context distorts these understandings.[9] Limiting the scope of
the inquiry to race leaves unchallenged both existing racial hierarchies
and the spectrum of socially constructed forces that sustain them. The
insight is not that the socially constructed world is an illusion; rather, it is
that that world is not pre-given.[10] The claim that the socially constructed
world is an illusion suggests that there is a more real world behind the
illusion. But late modernists and postmodernists disagree with the idea
that the real world is separate from us and from our perceptions of it.

In other words, it is not simply that the real world is unavailable to
us and that we misunderstand what is real, but instead that our percep-

tions and categories both represent and participate in the constitution of the world that we know.[11] Postmodernism asserts that the self, like race, is socially constructed; but few would claim that the self is merely an illusion, or that the concept of the self should be discarded.[12] The recognition of the social construction of the self may point to an illusion or error, but it does not follow that the self does not exist. Rather, the assertion is that the unconstituted and disembodied self that forms the basis of much of liberal thinking does not exist.[13] Similarly, those who would abandon race because a biological or genetic foundation for it proves inadequate fail to engage other ways of understanding or taking seriously the significance of race.[14]

An example of this type of limited understanding comes from my experience as a young college student. In our first year, my friends and I often flexed and stretched our intellectual muscles with discussions of the existence or nonexistence of God. As the year drew to a close, we moved toward greater consensus and a conviction that God did not exist or was dead. As we collectively announced our conclusion, one of the students pointed out a significant error in our examination. She noted that, at best, what we had achieved were strong arguments against the existence of the Judeo-Christian representation of God. Our interrogation had been so limited that it was silent on other possibilities.

Denying the reality of race because of its lack of biological support mirrors the limitations of our collegiate theological discussions. Even the position that race is socially constructed instead of biologically based underestimates the force of the postmodernist claim that everything is socially constructed – race and the self, but also biology and science.[15] This does not mean that all claims are either arbitrary or illusory. It means that the way we think of reality, as being presented to us by our senses, rather than interactive with our senses and language, is illusionary.

There is another conceptual error that is as seductive as it is wrong: the assertion that in a liberal society, we should not trade in categories, but should instead see each person solely as an individual. This position holds that race as a classification and category is part of a larger problem – classification and categorization generally, which necessarily bias and distort our perceptions of reality. There are volumes of work rejecting the false goal of interacting with and perceiving reality directly, as it simply is not possible to see reality without categories. This recognition comes not only from postmodernist thought and linguistics but also from neuropsychology and neuroscience. The meaning and content of categories can be contested, certainly, but to insist upon living without them is to re-inscribe a foundational error that has implications for all areas of life, not just race. Unfortunately, our Supreme Court presently appears to be wedded to this error.

Pragmatic Position

A second color-blind position is pragmatic and political. This position errs in assuming that the major race problem in our society is race itself, rather than racism. These proponents of a raceless, color-blind society argue that the categories of race are both irrelevant and politically and racially divisive.[16] In the larger political sphere, there is ongoing discussion of dropping race from the census altogether. Newt Gingrich, for example, has advocated that the census move beyond merely including a multiracial category to replacing all census categories with just one: American.[17] Others, as noted above, have appropriated the language of Dr. King and the civil rights movement to give force to the call for color blindness. This occurred in California during the struggle over Proposition 209 – the California ballot initiative that amended the state's constitution to prohibit public institutions from considering race, sex, or ethnicity. Invoking a raceless, color-blind society as a means to dismantle anti-racist programs, however, is less an error than a strategy to maintain white supremacy and racial hierarchy.[18]

Whether it is intentional or in error, moreover, powerful evidence suggests that the color-blind, race-aversive language adopted by the new right has the effect of shoring up racial hierarchy, masking both the subordination of the racial minority and white privilege.[19] Indeed, in many respects, the focus on racelessness not only masks racism but also actively supports what Patricia Williams calls racism in drag.[20] The racial project of the new right can be viewed as maintaining the racial order without specific reference to race – allowing the speaker to send coded messages in apparently race-neutral terms such as welfare, crime victim, good neighborhood, or individual merit.[21] To examine the current racial project pragmatically, one must view it in the context of our racial history, then ask how it affects the complementary goals of ending racial hierarchy and moving to racial justice.

The Creation of Race

The precursor to racial categories in the United States was a differentiation between Christian and non-Christian in the English colonies. In some ways, the first "racial benefit" in America was that a Christian could not be permanently enslaved.[22] Because Christianity welcomed converts, however, this distinction proved less than ideal for its primary function. It was too porous: its relationship to slavery gave conversion to Christianity high value, regardless of religious benefit. When substantial numbers of slaves converted, a more immutable characteristic had to be devised. Over the next hundred years, modern race – and racism – would be created in response and would prove much sturdier. There would be no conversion to whiteness by enslaved blacks.[23]

Even so, the racial divide continuously needed shoring up. During the seventeenth century, as racial slavery took hold, more people of African descent lived in Virginia and Maryland than in the other colonies combined, and the patterns set in these colonies determined much of the development of race in this country. In 1662, before racial categories had become deeply entrenched, "any christian" having sexual relations with black men or women faced double fines in Virginia, and interracial marriages were banned in Maryland two years later.[24] Virginia passed an anti-miscegenation law in 1691 that was designed "for prevention of that abominable mixture and spurious issue which hereafter may increase in this dominion, as well by negroes, mulattoes, and Indians intermarrying with English, or other white woman, as by their unlawful accompanying with one another."[25] Massachusetts prohibited the marriage of white men and women to the racial other in 1705.[26]

These early anti-miscegenation laws were harsh. Consider, as a punishment for one's choice of marriage partner, a sentence of slavery for life. History recited by the U.S. Supreme Court in the *Dred Scott* opinion of 1856 includes a 1717 Maryland law imposing such a penalty upon any free black or "mulatto" man who married a white woman, or any black or mulatto woman who married a white man.[27] There was an exception made for a mulatto born of a white woman, who would become a servant for seven years, as would the white partners in the marriages above.[28]

This was an era in which the meaning of race and its supporting laws and practices were still in their initial stages. Some laws approached the issue of interracial marriage and children differently for men and women. For example, if a free white woman had a child with a black man and was not married, she might be ordered to pay a fine. If she could not pay the fine, her services could be auctioned off for five years. Yet often there was no similar provision for white men who had children with black women.[29] One of the implicit goals of these laws was to limit the sexual relations of white women to white men while simultaneously allowing white men sexual liberty, short of marriage. This state of affairs can be traced back to a larger effort to define white women and blacks as property and to afford white men legal protection of that property.

A 1705 Virginia statute demonstrates the power of the jealously guarded control of lawmaking: "All Negro, mulatto, and Indian slaves within this dominion shall be held to be real estate and not chattels and shall descend unto heirs and widows according to the custom of land inheritance, and be held in 'fee simple.'"[30] These laws and social practices were put in place by propertied white men in order to define whiteness generally, as well as specifically, for their own benefit. The regulations included careful distinctions as to who could participate in making the rules, as exemplified in the law above: "Nothing in this act shall be construed to give the owner of a slave not seized of other real estate the right to vote as a freeholder."[31] Similarly, marriage laws were not about interracial marriage per se as much as they were about perceived white purity and white property. There was relatively little regulation of marriage between people of various non-white races.

Sixteen states still had anti-miscegenation laws on the books in 1967, when the Supreme Court struck them all down, in *Loving v. Virginia*.[32] One section of Virginia's law had made marriage between a white person and a person of color a felony, punishable by one to five years' imprisonment; another section automatically voided all such marriages.[33] In the four decades since then, there has been more than a fivefold increase in marriages between people with differing racial identities.[34]

Nearly 15 percent, or one in seven, of all new marriages in 2008 were between people of different races or ethnicities, and more than a third of all adults surveyed reported having a family member whose spouse is of a different race or ethnicity – up from less than a quarter of respondents in 2005.[35] The multiracial movement has become increasingly vocal as the number of interracial marriages and families increases.[36] But the multiracial movement often fails to accept the socially constructed nature of race at all, in contrast to the color-blind movement, which misappropriates the recognition of the social construction of race.

Struggles with Categories

In 2000, the multiracial population of the United States was estimated to be approximately seven million, when 2.4 percent of the population chose to check two or more boxes on the census form.[37] The number rose to nine million in 2010, almost 3 percent of the total population.[38] Individuals are able now to choose more than one race as a result of the adoption of the U.S. Office of Management and Budget's (OMB) 1997 "Revisions to the Standards for the Classification of Federal Data on Race and Ethnicity."[39] The new categories include five racial groups (American Indian or Alaska Native, Asian, Black or African American, Native Hawaiian or Other Pacific Islander, and White) as well as "some other race." There are a total of seven Asian and four Pacific Islander choices, including the "some other" variation of each. The 2010 form also includes spaces to provide more detail. Individuals choosing to write in "multiracial," "mixed," or "interracial" are included as "some other race." The Census Bureau calculates that the form allows for fifty-seven possible combinations.[40]

Groups such as Project RACE (Reclassify All Children Equally) had unsuccessfully advocated the adoption of a separate "multiracial" check box, arguing that the currently recognized categories do not account for the identity or experiences of a rapidly increasing number of multiracial people.[41] Susan Graham, a leader of the multiracial movement, has described her frustration with the fact that her child was assigned his mother's race during his first census count, another race based on his teacher's "knowledge and observation," and the category "two or more races" during the 2000 census.[42] In this way the multiracial position appropriately points out the inconsistency and incoherence of our current categories.[43] It may also reflect a reaction to the intrusiveness of dealing with non-white status in America. For even after the Supreme Court struck down anti-miscegenation laws, there continued to be an assertion of the need to control, if not these marriages, then the children of such families. Concern about the "best interests" of the children are raised, even today, with respect to children from "mixed marriages." Moreover, this concern extends to the adoption of children across racial lines as well.[44]

Certainly there are vital points to be made about conflicts and inconsistencies between the common use of racial categories and the government's classifications, as well as within official classifications. Michael Omi notes that "most of the categories rely on a concept of 'original peoples,' only one of the definitions is specifically racial, only one is cultural and only one relies on a notion of affiliation or community recognition."[45] Few comparable criteria are deployed across all categories. For example, current guidelines define a black person as one "having origins in any of the Black racial groups of Africa"[46] but define a white person as someone "having origins in any of the original peoples of Europe, the Middle East, or North Africa."[47] Black is in fact the only category that is defined with an explicit racial designator, and it is one that is quite problematic. What, we might ask, are the "Black racial groups of Africa"?[48] It's small wonder that we often think that "race" means "black."

A person is considered and classified as Hispanic or Latino not as a race but as an ethnic group. The Hispanic or Latino category is the only ethnicity that the state is interested in explicitly identifying and classifying. That category is defined through cultural designators: "a person of Cuban, Mexican, Puerto Rican, South or Central American, or other Spanish culture or origin, regardless of race."[49] "American Indian or Alaska Native" requires that individuals both have their origins in any of the original peoples of North and South America *and* maintain "tribal affiliation or community attachment."[50] The problems outlined here are not limited to inconsistencies. Some groups are omitted from classification altogether, and, as advocates for a multiracial category point out, those who identify as multi- or mixed-race are either forced to identify themselves improperly or left out altogether.[51]

The question of how to categorize and think about multiracial groups was of serious concern to my friend Trina Grillo, a legal scholar who experienced the difficulty of being multiracial in a society in which identity is organized around very limited concepts of race.[52] She experienced being excluded and miscategorized, yet she continued to question the wisdom of adopting multiracial categories, expressing concern about white mothers who seemed particularly interested in distancing their multiracial children from the societal injury of being black in America.[53]

With her subtle and nuanced thinking, Grillo raised many of the questions that are important to consider in analyzing these complicated issues. In spite of the personal pain she experienced in using the existing categories, she insisted on investigating the issue of multiracial designations at the personal, historical, and political level. She raised the question of how existing categories, and particularly the black category, could be reconceptualized to make a home for the offspring of black and white parents. If this reconceptualization project did not succeed, these children would have to find another home, an issue that can be made more pressing when white parents find they have less interest in raising their children as black after separation from a person of color.

Grillo was determined that a new multiracial category not be just another form of colorism with a strong anti-black subtext.[54] She was aware that such a category, if it developed a strong class dimension, with those of the middle and upper-middle class using their multiracial status to be something other than black, might weaken the black community's political position and strengthen the dominance of whites.[55] Grillo was therefore concerned that if white supremacy were not addressed, the move toward multiracial categories could lead to a more entrenched pigmentocracy, similar to those in many Latin American countries.[56]

Grillo's position was not that new multiracial categories necessarily entailed anti-black sentiment: she understood the need for family and cultural identification. Nor was her concern the greater inclusivity of the category. Rather, she focused on the political and theoretical implications of new racial categories, given the political context in which the multiracial project was taking shape. Without defending our current typology, I embrace many of Grillo's concerns. The descriptive position's call for new categories is based on the premise that multiracial persons are not accurately described by existing categories. Although not universally, advocates for the multiracial category, like the conservative color-blind advocates, often make a political and pragmatic claim: that an increase in multiracial categories will weaken racial hierarchy.[57]

Racial Categories and Individual Identity

The multiracial idea has at least two versions. One is that multiracial people are of mixed blood or mixed genetic material.[58] The other is that multiracial people are those with parents of different recognizable races. On examination, both of these positions present problems. The first is most blatantly tied to the racist science of the nineteenth century. It suggests that a person with both black and white ancestry is not adequately or accurately described as black (or white). This assertion rests on the discredited biological model. To sustain this position, one would have to show not only that bloodlines or genes are the appropriate foundations upon which to classify races, but also that bloodlines or genetic indicators are clear. Stated more strongly, this view implies that pure bloodlines – people who are uniracial – define the current racial categories.

Many of the proponents of new multiracial categories are politically left of center and reject the overt racism of nineteenth-century biology. Yet, a number of the assumptions adopted by these advocates end up relying, unwittingly, on the same discredited science, one of the main assertions of which was that race and racial categories were based on blood or genes. Supposed racial difference cannot be sustained on this basis, however; the majority of white Americans have African ancestry, the majority of blacks have white ancestry, and a substantial number of each have American Indian ancestry.[59] Indeed, under the old hypodescent or "one drop" rule, which asserts that "white blood" is pure and therefore contaminated by even one drop of "black blood," most white Americans are, in fact, African American.[60]

The hypodescent rule emerged from our racist history and from the interest in maintaining white purity.[61] Although we no longer live under a patchwork of state laws with mathematical formulas for determining race, a 2010 study by researchers at Harvard indicates that the power of hypodescent has not entirely dissipated. Researchers asked subjects to view computer-generated "biracial" facial images. The participants found the combination of Asian and white faces to be "white" at lower percentages of whiteness than they required for black with white faces. (The average percentage of "white" required in the composite for white identification was 63 percent when combined with an Asian face and 68 percent when with a black one, in spite of the often greater degree of shared ancestry of blacks and whites in the United States.[62]) The study's authors point out that in evaluating both sets of faces, the inclination was toward placing "mixed" appearance faces into the "lower status" (i.e., non-white) racial category. Overall, subjects presented with computer-generated facial images that were 50 percent white and 50 percent some other race consistently identified the face as belonging to the non-white racial group.[63] The authors conclude that biases in perception and categorization of biracials "have implications for resistance to change in the American racial hierarchy."[64]

Indeed, although most Americans could be viewed as multiracial or mixed, the multiracial movement seems less interested in pursuing this aspect of our racial arrangements, perhaps because it would undermine the implicit position that mixed-race people have a different experience and need their own category. The point is not that we are all genetically mixed – we are. The point is that this fact is generally considered irrelevant to the business of creating racial categories.

Some multiracial advocates have responded to the problems encountered in relying on blood or genes by suggesting that we label people multiracial if their parents are of different recognized races.[65] But if this is the designation, how do we categorize the offspring of the union of a multiracial and a "monoracial" person?[66] If we say that the children are multiracial, we are back to the problem that virtually everyone is multiracial. If we say that the child is the race of the uniracial parent, then we reproduce the problem of forcing the child to deny part of his or her heritage. Despite this difficulty, there is a strong appeal for allowing the child to claim the entire racial and ethnic heritage, though it is not clear that the issue can be resolved this way either. If we categorize children so that they may claim their parents' heritage, how should we categorize a black child who is raised by white parents in a culturally white environment? Of course, a totally different way of thinking about this is to suggest that the white parent who has children with a black person could be entitled to cross over and no longer be white. Black could be reconceptualized, once we drop the "blood" issue, to allow for this move.[67]

This idea comports with another position often advanced by multiracial advocates: that people should be able to define themselves.[68] While this option has great intuitive appeal, it is probably not workable or desirable. Much of the attraction to this position stems from our ideology of individualism.[69] Given the normative structure of whiteness in the United States, the claim of individualism can be little more than a thinly veiled effort to claim the privileges of whiteness. The right to self-definition on individual terms therefore suffers from the failure to embrace the significance of race and identity as socially constructed. This does not mean that we cannot or do not participate in the construction of our identity, but it does mean that the idea that we can define who we are in isolation is a false claim and a flawed hope.

THE POLITICAL PROJECT

The color-blind claim is that the elimination of racial categories will end racism. Multiracial advocates assert that an increase in the number of categories will soften, if not completely destabilize, the existing racial hierarchy. They cite the history of laws prohibiting race mixing, especially between whites and blacks.[70] Because of the threat of contamination of the white race, anti-miscegenation laws took great care to define the racial other, while whites were defined primarily in opposition to the other and as pure.[71] These laws did not stop racial mixing and prohibited it only in certain situations. Under slavery, for example, there was no sanction against the male slaveholders who impregnated enslaved women. In fact, the slaveholders' policy that the child would be the race of the mother allowed these men to enhance their "holdings" by producing such offspring, while maintaining the exclusive nature of whiteness.

After emancipation, the laws that regulated black-white relations expanded in order to continue white dominance outside the state of slavery. For a brief period, racial categories proliferated: the 1890 census included Chinese, Japanese, Indian, Mulatto, Quadroon, and Octoroon.[72] Only those with at least three-fourths black ancestry were classified as black, while those having at least "one drop of black blood" but no more than one-eighth were classified as Octoroon.[73] A person with one white and one black parent was neither black nor white, but "Mulatto."[74] Whites were defined as pure and enjoyed benefits attached to whiteness that were not available to any of the people of mixed or non-white groups.[75]

This intensive use of multiracial categories did little to destabilize the white hierarchy, as the U.S. Supreme Court made clear in *Plessy v. Ferguson,* the 1896 case that declared the segregation of black from white constitutional.[76] This disturbing case was the linchpin of post–Civil War jurisprudence in regard to race. The country had been through the bloodiest war in its history, and the government and the Constitution had been radically restructured to include the concepts of equality, citizenship, and a right to political participation for those freed from slavery. This was, therefore, both a restructuring of the meaning of whiteness and a profound reshaping of the country. Power was to be shifted from the states to the federal constitution for the protection of citizens, and blacks were to be equal.[77]

In spite of the refining of the calibrations of racial categories during this era, white racial purity remained the prerequisite to a person's being classified as white and obtaining the attendant privileges. This was nowhere clearer than in *Plessy,* in which a multiracial group of citizens, the Comité des Citoyens (Citizens' Committee), challenged the Louisiana Separate Car Act of 1890. The Citizens' Committee had correctly identified the potentially devastating consequences of a law requiring that citizens be separated by race in public conveyances. Homer Plessy was "seven-eighths white," and, even though he was classified as black under state law, his appearance allowed him to board the white car undisturbed. He did so and launched the challenge.

One line of argument that Plessy advanced in opposition to the Separate Car Act was that sorting passengers in this way was a re-creation of caste and a denial of equal rights. He and the Citizens' Committee hoped, in protesting the sorting, to also undermine the right of states to arbitrarily create non-white racial designations that denied equal rights just as surely as if the states were allowed to arbitrarily deprive citizens of property. The committee's attorney, Albion W. Tourgée, had raised the question in the inverse in an 1890 novel:

> How much would it be *worth* to a young man entering upon the practice of law to be regarded as a *white* man rather than a colored one? . . . [I]s it possible to conclude that the *reputation of being white* is not property? Indeed, is it not the most valuable sort of property, being the master-key that unlocks the golden door of opportunity?[78]

The Court disagreed, cynically turning its eyes from the possibility of equality:

> It is claimed by the plaintiff in error that, in any mixed community, the reputation of belonging to the dominant race, in this instance the white race, is *property*, in the same sense that a right of action or of inheritance is property. Conceding this to be so, for the purposes of this case, we are unable to see how this statute deprives him of, or in any way affects his right to, such property. If he be a white man, and assigned to a colored coach, he may have his action for damages against the company for being deprived of his so-called property. Upon the other hand, if he be a colored man and be so assigned, he has been deprived of no property, since he is not lawfully entitled to the reputation of being a white man.[79]

The benefits of whiteness, described in this way, throw the disabilities attached to blackness during the "separate but equal" era into sharp relief. For many, being white automatically ensured higher economic returns in the short term as well as greater economic, political, and social security in the long run. Being white meant gaining access to a set of public and private privileges that materially and permanently guaranteed basic needs and survival. Being white increased the possibility of controlling critical aspects of one's life rather than of being the object of another's domination.

Access to these societal benefits connected to whiteness was dependent on statutes and court holdings that determined who was, and was not, white. Thus the legislatures and courts were at the center of a system that routinely and purposefully distributed rights and opportunities along racial lines, as described so poignantly by Tourgée in the passage above. So the proliferation of racial categories left hierarchies in place, perhaps even increasing the dominance of whiteness, uncontested at the top.

Some advocates suggest Latin America as an example of how multi-racial categories can lessen the harshness of racism in the United States.[80] Brazil in particular has been regarded as an example of a multiracially open and tolerant society. Brazil did not, for example, enact formal anti-miscegenation laws, even though it has many more racial categories than does the United States.[81] Recent scholarly work, however, points to pig-mentocracies in Brazil and other Latin American countries, in addition to strong anti-black sentiments.[82] Indeed, a closer examination of these multiracial systems suggests that they leave the extreme poles of white-ness and blackness undisturbed. This closer look also cautions against a backing into a position in which the nearly white lobby for inclusion, rather than for dissolution of the hierarchy.

Both Brazil's current situation and our own history demonstrate that an increase in racial categories does not guarantee movement to-ward racial justice.[83] To avoid an analytical error such as the one my college friends and I discovered in deliberations about the existence of God, I must concede that even if my argument is right, there still might be a need for a multiracial category. One cannot exhaust all the pos-sible justifications. But resting justifications on bloodlines or biology and failing to consider the implications in terms of racism are definitely problematic, especially from a historical point of view.[84]

So is there an argument for multiracial categories that takes the social construction of race into account? In fact, there are several, but one of the strongest is that the life experience or situatedness of those designated mixed race in our society is qualitatively different from that of groups designated as single race.[85] This argument does not rest on genetic or blood composition, nor is it weakened by the insight that virtu-ally all of us are mixed race, based on blood or genetic material. Rather, this argument relies on the socially constructed nature of the experi-ence of people in our society – individually and collectively – and calls, therefore, for a much deeper understanding of our situatedness and how it reproduces race, racial meaning, and distribution of opportunity.

From an anti-racist perspective, one could argue that the way other people of color treat multiracial people should be more important than how whites treat them. One reason for this is to prevent whites from favoring some people of color over others, while maintaining white privilege. Because the racial caste system is based on pigmentocracy, whites, and even some blacks, have a history of favoring lighter-colored over darker-skinned blacks. Perhaps this goes back to the preference of slaveholders for having mixed-race blacks work in their houses.

Given our racial history and practice, especially with regard to hypodescent, it is not surprising that the white community has been less accepting overall of people designated multiracial than has the black community.[86] But acceptance in the black community of both lighter-skinned blacks and those designated as mixed race has been provisional and qualified as well.[87] This mistrust may trace back to a fear that such people may have aligned themselves with whites in important ways. It has been claimed, too, that mixed-race blacks look down on darker-skinned blacks, and some of this uneasiness is not merely internal ambivalence in the uniraced blacks.

From another point of view, there may be good reasons for children of parents with different racial identities to want a designation that reflects their heritage. Related issues may come up in transracial and transnational adoptions. The reasons for advocacy on this issue are numerous and complex, but it is clear that if the existing socially constructed categories cannot provide a home for those designated as mixed race, there may be a need either to reconstruct or add to them. Existing racial categories are not only incoherent and limiting but also often oppressive and exclusive. The problem with the multiracial position is that in addition to failing to acknowledge important insights concerning social construction, it also falls back on nineteenth-century beliefs about biology.

A more productive way of thinking about these issues is to acknowledge the implications of the socially constructed nature of race and simultaneously acknowledge that race operates differently in different spheres.[88] In the larger political sphere, race is not only socially constructed: its meaning and function are also the locus of intense social and political struggle.[89] When people are categorized in ways that disfavor them and favor others, there will be resistance and reappropriation. As people push against them, boundaries will be redefined. After all, the effort to categorize people is not simply a question of getting it right;

the process of racial categorizing is a power struggle with structural, cultural, economic, personal, and political implications.

Because race is a social construction, individuals inhabiting racial categories can be understood only in relation to one another. The lasting effects of our co-creation as raced people must be acknowledged. In this sense we are all multiracial. We are also fractured racially not because of blood, but because we are mutually and continually defining and constituting our race by what we include and exclude of the racial other. Black and white are not only co-dependent (though in different ways); they are also parts of one another, in a fluid and destabilizing dance of consternation.

The fact that there is probably no such thing as racial purity need not take away any special position that might be produced at a site we call multiracial. Nor does it mean that there are no uniracial categories. What it does suggest is that we need to examine the political and power implications of any recategorizations. Because politics and power operate differently in different spheres, it may be appropriate to use differing approaches, depending on the site. We may constitute and define race differently at the family level and at the public or group level. Although these spheres will continue to bleed into one another, we may want to ask how race functions in a given realm and what impact a change might have on racism and power relationships.

Personal identification is and will remain important, but the pivotal issue here is what impact the color-blind and multiracial projects will have on the axis of racism in different spheres. At the family or individual level, there may be space for more personal involvement in racial identification. It is, after all, important for people to be able to claim their full racial and ethnic heritage, especially if collective structures and practices treat people with parents of different races differently from the way people with parents of the same race are treated. As we engage these issues, it is important that we guard against a hierarchy of pigmentation and against exhausting our efforts on racial categories while leaving racism itself unexamined and intact. It is also important that an examination of the white racial category and the privileges associated with it be part of both projects.

To reexamine racial categories in light of the insights of both the social construction of race and an anti-racist agenda, we must always ask what impact a particular effort has on racial hierarchy, at the top of which is whiteness. What work is race doing, and how is it being done? For example, some have called attention to spatial segregation and mass incarceration in the constructed modern race.[90] If we are to take the social construction of race seriously, we must be willing to examine the processes involved. In this examination, we will find an ideation and sets of material practices that must be understood.

To destabilize racial hierarchy, then, we start with whiteness and strengthen our understanding of what it entails and how those terms might be challenged and rejected.[91] If we want to reconstitute blackness, brownness, or any other negatively privileged racial categories, we might consider the way race is discussed in England: all groups that are not categorized as white could be categorized as black, brown, or some other inclusive term,[92] and this non-white group could include those who may have been formally designated as white but who have rejected that "privilege." In other words, race could be a political space.

This possibility exists because some see all of us as racially mixed, not just in terms of blood and genes, but also at a deeper, more psychological level. If we are indeed socially constituted, we are also constituted by multiple voices. In the blood sense and at a deeper level, there is no unitary race. We carry many different racial and gendered voices inside us. While we are not all the same or interchangeable, important understandings and mutualities dwell within each of us. From this perspective, our diversity is both an internal and an external reality. Our differences and similarities are relational, shifting, unstable, and constitutive. If we are willing to drop the claim of racial purity, we may be able to claim our different racial voices. We might be able to think and imagine together in concrete terms.

As we reconstruct racial categories – and this is a job not just for the multiracialists but for all of us who care about a racially inclusive democracy – we must do so in a way that dismantles racism, racial hierarchy, and white supremacy. Whites may want to consider the implications of abandoning the property interests associated with whiteness and to explore becoming traitors to privilege. We may want to seek out different racial voices and see what structures call forth or repress those voices. This effort requires serious work as well as play. And because our project to rethink racial categories is also about destabilizing racial hierarchy, we will reject the new right's color-blind position. Supporters of a multiracial category need not wait until this effort is complete to seek a home, but it is important that they, and we, not use the tools of the master's house unreflectively, or simply move closer to the master's house.[93]

Our efforts may have implications beyond their areas of immediate focus. Advocates of the new racial categories should therefore think and feel carefully, historically, and pragmatically about how to proceed on a multiracial project. Those who would maintain the existing categories need to subject the status quo to a similarly searching examination. Perhaps the answer is to have only two categories of alignment: one supporting racial hierarchy, and the other supporting racial justice and democracy. In any case, in this project of reconstituting racial categories and challenging racism, I hope we will use our hearts, minds, and one another to be more expansive in our thinking than the old categories and discredited methods allow.

THREE

The Racing of American Society

RACE FUNCTIONING AS A VERB
BEFORE SIGNIFYING AS A NOUN

O, yes, I say it plain,
America never was America to me,
And yet I swear this oath – America will be!

Langston Hughes, "Let America Be America Again"

Myth is facts of the mind made manifest in a fiction of matter.

Maya Deren, Divine Horsemen: The Living Gods of Haiti

The color-blind and multiracial issues are but two of the problems we encounter in our efforts to understand race in a consistent and disciplined way. Michael Omi, an important voice in this effort, identifies several others, including the difficulties scientists encounter when attempting to apply ostensibly objective analytical criteria to a concept that has no scientific reality yet a powerful social one – a concept that is instrumental in shaping our individual and collective identities.[1] Indeed, even within particular analytical frameworks, different sets of understandings and beliefs about race abound. Once recognized, these theories can provide useful insights into the nature of the work necessary to come to terms with race and racism in our society.

An important first step is to recognize that race mutates and adapts across sociohistorical contexts and life spheres, rather than existing as a single, unitary concept. An important touchstone must be that the underlying objective of the study of race in society is, as I emphasized in the previous chapter, understanding and addressing racism and racialized structures and hierarchy. If we assert that race is problematic in any of its varying manifestations, then we bring our focus not to race per se (indeed, there *is* no race per se), but rather to what is problematic about the ways race functions in different contexts. Often race is used to create and maintain domination and hierarchy, yet the way it functions varies, just as our concepts of it vary. Remedial efforts therefore must be adapted to the many contexts and manners in which race is used.

THE MULTIPLICITY OF TRUTH

The scientists' dilemma described by Omi is not surprising when we contrast prevailing notions of race with the roles race plays in our everyday lives. As discussed in previous chapters, the U.S. Supreme Court, especially in recent decades, has adopted a color-blind imperative in evaluating race-related legislation and actions. This principle is based on the flawed assumption that race and racial categories are the problem. The color blind Court reasons that the effort should be to make color irrelevant and to consider all racial recognitions suspect, regardless of intent or effect. In this, color blindness calls for blindness to racial stratification and its meaning in our society. Thus color-blind theory as practiced in our courts is a form of racing that helps maintain and reinforce racial hierarchy. Rather than being race-neutral, color blindness further naturalizes the norm of whiteness and white privilege without even referring to race.[2] The Supreme Court attempts to justify this legal analysis by calling on the conventional wisdom that race is reducible to physical characteristics that ought to have no bearing on official decisions.

In *City of Richmond v. J. A. Croson*, for example, the Court reviewed a plan to address the fact that fewer than 1 percent of city construction contracts went to minority-owned or -controlled businesses, in spite of the fact that the city's population was 50 percent black. The Court struck down the plan for lack of proof of direct prior racial discrimination, a new standard at the time. In concurring with the Court, Justice Scalia ignored the historical and social aspects of race, equating the protected class of "race" with "the color of their skin":

> The difficulty of overcoming the effects of past discrimination is as nothing compared with the difficulty of eradicating from our society the source of those

effects, which is the tendency – fatal to a Nation such as ours – to classify and judge men and women on the basis of their country of origin or the color of their skin.[3]

Thus, even as the Court prohibits a city's effort to manage public resources in a more equitable way, it invites us to look past the realities of the situation and into a future in which race will not matter.

Regardless of what we say, think, or feel about race as a physical reality, however, it undeniably plays a central role in our everyday understanding of and interactions with one another and in our lived experience. This seemingly self-contradictory aspect of race has partly to do with the difference between scientific truth and experiential truth. Philosopher and ecologist David Abram points out that the Western liberal tradition's attempt to understand and order the world through objective criteria and classifications fails to grasp the multiplicity of truth:

> Despite all the mechanical artifacts that now surround us, the world in which we find ourselves before we set out to calculate and measure it is not an inert or mechanical object but a living field, an open and dynamic landscape subject to its own moods and metamorphoses.[4]

This metamorphic realm of everyday experience is where race primarily operates. Attempts to establish and define the total reality or unreality of race by quantitative analysis will therefore necessarily fail. Race may be a biological fiction, but it is a social and experiential truth. It is therefore a categorical error to try to reduce its meanings and functions to scientifically verifiable measurements.

Although not susceptible to such measurements, race nevertheless shapes our social world in the same real way that experience shapes our perceptions of self and reality.[5] Once we understand the multiplicitous nature of truth, it becomes clear that the assertion that race is irrelevant because of its weak scientific basis is not just a fiction; it is a dangerous fiction. Truth is relative as well as multiplicitous. Because we perceive the world through a lens shaped by individual and collective experiences, our science is necessarily subjective or intersubjective. We can understand "objects," as Abram explains, only to the extent that they are the "subjects" of our perception:

> [T]he scientist never completely succeeds in making himself into a pure spectator of the world, for he cannot cease to live in the world as a human among

other humans . . . and his scientific concepts and theories necessarily borrow
aspects of their character and texture from his untheorized, spontaneously lived
experience.[6]

The subjective or intersubjective nature of truth does not mean that all
things, or assertions, are of equal value. The role of subjective experience
may be lesser, of course, in the context of measuring and understanding
physical phenomena (the weight of an atom, for example, or the relationships of force, mass, and acceleration), but it looms large in our attempts
to understand the less easily quantified aspects of life that are inextricably entwined with our experience.

Increasingly, scientists recognize both this perception problem and
postmodernism's assertion that reality is subjective.[7] With respect to
race, however, popular discourse has failed for the most part to note this
shift, and notions of scientific certainty continue to be used to draw inappropriate conclusions about race in social and political spheres. Through
the lens of scientific analysis, race constitutes nothing more than skin
color and perhaps a few other physical characteristics, at most. Yet efforts
to support the current racial hierarchy often make dramatic claims with
regard to purported associations with traits such as intelligence or other
aspects of human capacity.[8] Meanwhile, race is also reduced to physical
characteristics by those opposing programs intended to address the effects of racism.[9] This situation is particularly problematic because the
experiential and subjective realities of race have deep implications for
efforts to understand race and racism in our society. Failure to recognize
that race is a function, that "racing" is something we do to one another,
strengthens uninformed popular racial discourses by causing them to
seem natural or accurate.[10]

Once we accept that race is a subjective reality, it does not necessarily follow that its significance exists solely on an individual and attitudi-
nal level. Race is an example of what Abram describes as "intersubjective
phenomena – phenomena experienced by a multiplicity of sensing subjects."[11] Each of us has a unique understanding of race, but its collective
significance causes it to function in ways that have profound structural
significance. For example, unlike a daydream, the experience of which
is entirely individual, race functions in collective ways that we cannot
alter solely through individual will.

RACE AS A SOCIAL CONSTRUCT: THE VERB "TO RACE"

If we realize that race is neither objectively real nor purely imagined, we must define it in a manner that accounts for its socially constructed, mutable nature. Michael Omi and Howard Winant have described race as signifying and symbolizing "social conflicts and interests by referring to different types of human bodies."[12] David Theo Goldberg suggests that we think of the categories as "the various designations of group differentiation invoked in the name of race throughout modernity."[13] Both of these definitions provide key insights into the nature of race that can be captured by the understanding that race operates as a verb before assuming significance as a noun.[14] In other words, before someone can be said to possess a racial characteristic or identity, there first must be a process of "racing." This requires the social creation of racial categories, the assignment to categories, and the determination of the meanings associated with each category. Goldberg dates this syndrome among Europeans to the fifteenth century, despite the fact that Europeans had already had repeated contact with many of the groups that were later to be "racialized."[15]

Racing is largely a top-down process in which the more powerful group first denudes the racial other of self-definition. This is often accomplished by denying the other its language and culture, then assigning a set of characteristics that are beneath those of the more powerful group.[16] The dominant group thus becomes the invisible standard by which all others are (unfavorably) measured. This process defines the racial other, but it also defines the racially privileged: they are not the other. As Martha R. Mahoney describes it, "the construction of race in America today allows whiteness to remain a dominant background norm, associated with positive qualities, for white people, and it allows unemployment and underemployment to seem like natural features of black communities."[17]

The dominant group is never completely dominant, however. The racial other will try to resist the negation of its self-definition and to redefine some of the assigned traits and characteristics in a more favorable manner. There is therefore ongoing contestation in the racing process. When Latinos assert that they are not a racial group and are outside of the black-white paradigm, they can be understood as objecting to efforts to race them. They understand that to be raced is to be subjugated in a particular way. Of course when Africans first came to this land, they were not black or Negro and had not been fully raced either. This is certainly not to suggest that Latinos will have a similar experience. It is rather to point out that racing is not a straightforward taxonomy. The fight about race and racing is a fight about social positioning, status, and meaning, in which Latinos and other groups will engage. And, as Allen observes, "[t]he social death of the subjugated people is followed by social resurrection in new forms from which they take up the task of overthrowing racial oppression."[18] Thus social death is not always complete, and different groups are raced to different degrees depending upon such dynamics as power and the resolve of the racing group. Moreover, because power is always fractured, there will be efforts – sometimes successful – to race the more dominant group. This work may also be carried out by "race traitors," those interested in identifying and destabilizing the invisible privilege of the dominant group.[19]

Omi and Winant refer to this racialization process as "racial formation": the "sociohistorical process by which racial categories are created, inhabited, transformed and destroyed."[20] Because of its socially constructed nature, the meaning attributed to a racially identified group or characteristic depends to a great extent on the sociohistorical context in which the racing occurs, and racial meaning varies across time and space. Who is white, for example, and the implications of this designation, differ across and within societies and historical periods. This insight applies not only to race, but also to gender, the self, and even to God. The way that we perceive all of these concepts is specific to our social and historical contexts.[21] The problem with race, then, is not that it *is* socially constructed, but rather how and why it has been so constructed.

Racialization in the United States

Despite its varying manifestations, the function of race in the United States has remained relatively constant. Groups of people have been "raced" as a mechanism for implementing and justifying domination and subjugation. The defining of racial categories has corresponded with

the distribution of the right to participate in the body politic and to access opportunity structures. Racial minorities have simultaneously been
defined as the other and denied the benefits of membership in American
society. This has caused the adverse effects of exclusion to manifest along
racial lines, and the white majority uses the results as justification for
the original definition and exclusion. Goldberg recognizes the insidious use of this inverted logic in popular explanations of racialized space
in metropolitan America: "The poverty of the inner city infrastructure
provides a racial sign of complex social disorders, of their manifestation,
when in fact it is their cause. . . . [I]dealized racial typifications [are] tied
to notions of slumliness, physical and ideological pollution of the body
politic, sanitation and health syndromes, lawlessness, addiction, and
prostitution."[22] Thus the history of America is replete with what Omi
and Winant refer to as "racial projects" that are "simultaneously an interpretation, representation, or explanation of racial dynamics, and an effort
to reorganize and redistribute resources along particular racial lines."[23]

An examination of the evolution of racial categories in the United
States and the significance attributed to them demonstrates that race has
been primarily a tool for maintaining white, European privilege. As Neil
Gotanda points out, racial categories in colonial America were largely
derived from a person's labor status.[24] Status was originally categorized
as free and unfree, English and non-English, but "[a]s slavery became
entrenched as the primary source of agricultural labor, slaveholders developed a complementary ideological structure of racial categories that
served to legitimate slavery."[25]

Racial categories that seem natural and immutable today have
evolved historically as various groups vied for inclusion in American
society and in the distribution of privilege. Benjamin Franklin's statement advocating continued racial purity for America demonstrates that
many people seen as white today have not always been viewed as such:

> [T]he Number of purely white People in the World is proportionally very small.
> All Africa is black or tawny. Asia chiefly tawny. America (exclusive of the new
> Comers) wholly so. And in Europe, the Spaniards, Italians, French, Russians and
> Swedes, are generally of what we call a swarthy Complexion; as are the Germans
> also, the Saxons only excepted, who with the English, make the principle Body
> of White People on the Face of the Earth.[26]

The metamorphic development of racial categories is more than just a curious historical footnote, however, because being considered white in America has been key to attaining privilege. As noted in the previous chapter, in 1896, the Supreme Court, in *Plessy v. Ferguson,* accepted the characterization of whiteness as a property right to which only those so designated were entitled.[27]

When the Court considered *United States v. Bhagat Singh Thind* in 1923, it noted that the Naturalization Act of 1790 specified that only "free white persons" were eligible for citizenship and its benefits.[28] The Naturalization Act was passed only a few months after the ratification of the Constitution, and every naturalization act from 1790 until 1952 included similar language, restricting citizenship to whites.[29] Thind, an Asian Indian who was categorized as white (Caucasian) by the ethnology of the day, applied for citizenship and was declared ineligible by the Court.[30] In order to deny the privileges of citizenship to Thind, the Court construed whiteness in terms of the understanding of the "the common man," who knew that Asian Indians were not really white – i.e., not *functionally* white – even though they may have been formally white.[31] Roediger points out that "[*Thind*] marked the culmination of a process by which the legal system . . . 'rejected science, history, legal precedent and logic to put the Constitution at the disposal of a legal fiction called "the common man."'"[32]

The Court went on to reconcile its reliance on "common" understanding by pointing out that prevailing notions of whiteness had changed between 1790 and 1923 to include eastern and southern Europeans. According to the Court, these groups came to be considered white because, despite their "dark-eyed, swarthy" complexions, they "were received as unquestionably akin to those already here and readily amalgamated with them."[33] In other words, the Court conceded that definitions of whiteness are predicated upon common acceptance, or rejection, of demographic groups. In the years following this decision, sixty-five Asian Indians had their citizenship revoked as their imposed racial identity shifted from white to non-white, and thus from American to non-American.[34]

Irish Catholics also found themselves, for a while, in a position of ambiguous racial status. During the period of rapid immigration in the mid–nineteenth century, they were portrayed as "simian" and "savage," and there was speculation about black ancestry.[35] What has distinguished the experience of blacks from the Asian Indian and the Irish (as well as southern and eastern Europeans and Jews), however, has been the persistence of their otherness, and the persistence of their exclusion from full societal participation. As Roediger notes, "[t]he duration of 'not-yet-whiteness' [for Irish, eastern European, and various other immigrant groups], as measured against that of racial oppression in the U.S., was quite short."[36]

Hypodescent, as discussed in the previous chapter, decreed that even "one drop" of "black blood" rendered an individual black. Cheryl Harris points out the derivation of this rule as "the law's legitimation of the use of Black women's bodies as a means of increasing property."[37] Harris refers to the fact that the law allowed or even incented white slaveholders to force black women to bear children who were then enslaved, in spite of their patrilineage. The fact that formerly the common law presumption had been that a child's status was determined by the status of the father demonstrates another way that racial categories have shifted in order to maintain and enhance white domination and privilege and exerted profound and perverse effects on multiple aspects of society.[38]

More recently the rule of the hypodescent led to the case of Susie Guillory Phipps. In 1977, a forty-three-year-old functionally white woman traveled to New Orleans to pick up her passport and was informed by the clerk that her self-designation did not match state records classifying her as colored.[39] Louisiana law at the time held that the state could classify anyone who had more than 1/32 "Negro blood" as "colored."[40] Comparing the *Thind* case to *Phipps*, we find shifting legal terrain that alternatively applies functional (the "common man's" understanding in *Thind*) or formal (hypodescent, in *Phipps*) classifications to manage the distribution of whiteness.

Moreover, just as the racing of groups has mutated to maintain white dominance, so have the justifications supporting these identifications shifted to reconcile continued white domination with democratic egalitarianism. Initial efforts to justify slavery, for example, focused on religion and biology: the domination and exploitation of blacks were justified on the grounds that blacks were heathens and less than human.[41]

As supporting pseudo-sciences such as eugenics and craniology were discredited, however, the effort to reconcile racial caste privilege with democracy has taken other forms.

Racialized Space

In the current era of de facto segregation and discrimination, white domination survives without explicit racial discrimination. Blacks' inferior social, economic, and political status is instead justified by a supposed "culture of poverty" and contained within what John Calmore calls "racialized space."[42] Under this rubric, non-white individuals congregate at the bottom of the social ladder not because of group-based discrimination or structural racism, but because each individual has internalized cultural tenets that conflict with the societal norms of hard work and lawfulness – values that enable other individuals to succeed. As Calmore points out, this explanation appeals to conservatives because it adopts and fosters their emphasis on individual autonomy.[43] This focus also absolves those who have "succeeded" in society of responsibility for those who have "failed" by severing any causal connection between successful whites and unsuccessful blacks – or indeed anyone less successful.

Thus when explicitly racist discourse became increasingly discredited, a new discourse consistent with conventional understandings of race arose to maintain white supremacy. The shift away from racial language toward support of racial caste demonstrates the ongoing strength of the white dominance imperative. Many race-neutral terms that are popular today have undiguisedly racist historical underpinnings and practical racial implications: the terms "individualism," "working class," "equal opportunity," and others mentioned in the preceding chapter all hark back to explicitly racist exclusionary practices.[44]

The Enlightenment's exaltation of the individual was adopted in part to distinguish white Europeans from African, Indian, and other non-white peoples who organized their societies around more collective norms.[45] The construction of the individual was in this respect neither natural nor race-neutral but rather a critical part of the development of the racing process. Similarly, the concept of equal opportunity was used early in the Enlightenment to mean that people had an equal opportunity (i.e., freedom) to become Christian. By adhering to the divine law of Christianity, they could in turn gain inclusion into the polity.[46] Those who rejected Christianity – Muslims, pagans, and others – violated this universal morality and were not deserving of inclusion. Thus we find that an unquestioned, seemingly universal norm is grounded in culturally specific norms that furthered – and further – the racializing process.

Today, of course, instead of referring to minorities as inherently inferior, we define the undeserving poor (or "the underclass") by characteristics that are race-neutral in theory, but heavily racialized in practice and effect.[47] John Calmore notes that the traits that separate the deserving from the undeserving are heavily racialized in popular discourse: criminal propensity, welfare dependency, employment status, and so on.[48] When Ronald Reagan condemned the "Chicago welfare queen" as a societal pariah, and George H. W. Bush used Willie Horton to represent the depraved criminal, it was no coincidence that the images evoked were black as well as abhorrent.[49]

As is the case with explicitly racist discourses, current implicitly racialized discourse persists without regard to its failure to accurately describe reality. Thus blacks as well as other minority groups are largely perceived as poor, criminal, and unemployed, in spite of the fact that, for example, in 1991, 67.3 percent of blacks did not live in poverty,[50] and by 2009, 74 percent were above the poverty threshold, even after an increase in the national poverty rate in the midst of a severe recession.[51] This rate of poverty is still far too high, as is the overall number of Americans – 43.6 million – living in poverty in 2009. The point is not that poverty is not so bad; it is that there is an association of poverty and blackness that is a reinforcing, self-perpetuating part of the racing process.

Implicitly racialized discourse mutates to accommodate inconvenient inconsistencies. Popular discourse draws a distinction between blacks in general and "middle-class blacks," and between whites in general and "poor whites." Middle-class blacks are perceived as somehow transcending blackness by virtue of their socioeconomic advances, and poor whites are perceived as somehow less than white because of their failure to live up to the economic and cultural norms of whiteness.

Segregation's racialization of space is a primary vehicle for maintaining the viability of this contemporary form of racial discourse. Martha Mahoney refers to segregation as "the product of notions of black inferiority and white superiority, manifested geographically through the exclusion of blacks from more privileged white neighborhoods and the concentration of blacks into subordinated neighborhoods stigmatized by both race and poverty."[52] Statistics bear this out: despite a 24 percent decline from 1990 to 2000 in the overall number of people living in neighborhoods with poverty rates over 40 percent, and a large drop in the percentages of blacks and Latinos who lived in them, almost 70 percent of the residents of high-poverty neighborhoods in 2000 were black or Latino.[53] The intersection of racial, social, and economic marginalization that this segregation creates in America's central cities legitimizes culture of poverty theories by creating a location simultaneously identified by concentrations of people of color in conditions of economic deprivation: joblessness, low incomes, low asset levels, structural deterioration, and attendant social ills, such as crime.

What is ignored in this scenario, however, is the explicit role that the white majority and the government have played in creating and maintaining this racialized space – in creating a society in which good neighborhoods are defined as white neighborhoods, and positive individual characteristics as white characteristics. White flight, the process whereby whites abandon central cities for suburbs (and whereby metropolitan space became racially defined along the suburb/center-city line), has been fueled by racist fears and facilitated by a host of government policies ranging from home mortgage financing[54] to highway and infrastructure construction, as discussed in the first chapter.[55]

The federal government established the Home Owners Loan Corporation (HOLC) in 1933 to refinance mortgages and provide low-interest loans to address suffering during the Great Depression.[56] The Federal Housing Administration (FHA) was established the next year, with the aim of guaranteeing home loan mortgages. Both agencies adopted the practice of redlining in the administration of their loans, developing uniform appraisal standards that deemed integrated and predominately non-white areas too risky for investment.[57] These governmental practices in turn influenced and legitimated redlining in the private lending industry. Government officials even circulated redlined maps to private lenders.[58] The effect of redlining was to subsidize homeownership opportunities for whites, white communities, and the suburbs, while strictly excluding prospective borrowers in communities of color and mixed-race communities.[59]

The impulse behind white flight was not new: Massey and Denton describe riots in northern cities between 1900 and 1920 in the wake of the migration of blacks from the rural South.[60] But the whiteness of the flight to the suburbs was maintained by an endless array of governmental and non-governmental tactics, including steering by real estate brokers, exclusionary zoning laws enacted by municipalities,[61] mortgage lending discrimination,[62] and refusal to regulate predatory lending targeted at low-income communities of color.[63] These efforts maintain racialized space, with low-income blacks concentrated in easily identifiable locations and low-income whites dispersed among more economically integrated white neighborhoods. A 2003 report by the Civil Rights Project found that in the Boston metropolitan area, only one-quarter of low-income whites lived in poverty areas, compared with half of low-income Asians and two-thirds of low-income blacks and Latinos. Indeed, African American and Latino households with annual incomes over $50,000 lived in poverty tracts at twice the rate of white households with incomes of less than $20,000.[64]

Predatory lending patterns also demonstrate the way that race-blind policies applied to racially discriminatory structures and practices replicate (and exacerbate) underlying inequities.[65] A 2006 report by the Center for Responsible Lending (CRL) reviews a number of earlier studies, including the 1996 study by the Federal Reserve Bank of Boston finding that, controlling for individual, property, and neighborhood factors, Latino and African American applicants in the Boston area were 80 percent more likely than white applicants to be denied a home loan.[66] The CRL paper also refers to a 2000 study by HUD and the Department of the Treasury reporting that, controlling for neighborhood income, the rate of predatory refinance loans in predominately black neighborhoods was 51 percent – five times that of predominately white neighborhoods.[67] The CRL report advocates addressing these patterns by curtailing steering by lenders; holding brokers and lenders responsible for providing suitable loans; expanding disclosure of risk and pricing of loans; enforcing fair lending laws; and providing incentives for better service to African American and Latino communities.[68] Tolerance of existing patterns serves instead to shore up the functional strength of our current "race-blind" racial discourse.

Because racial meaning accrues through historical and social processes, the significance of racial classifications is neither given nor immutable. Racism necessarily carries with it a negative implication about the racial other, but race alone need not and often does not. For although race and racism are closely tied historically, they are not coterminous, and race can be a positive contribution to the ways that people organize their identities.

So although race continues to operate in complicated and multiplicitous ways in society, it is racism, not race, that is the heart of the problem. Efforts to address racism should therefore focus on the manner in which racialization processes create and maintain hierarchy, while also seeking to destabilize and reverse them. In other words, we need to focus on the processes by which white and black are defined, and our efforts should be focused upon racing situations and mechanisms, such as the policies and practices described above that racialize metropolitan space and distribute privilege accordingly.

Focusing on racing and racial hierarchy rather than on racial categories is a necessary approach, but its effectiveness is uncertain. This uncertainty is only made worse by the movement toward "e-racing" any record of the racial mechanisms currently at work in our society. Ruth Frankenberg, a pathfinder in whiteness studies, refers to this color-blind impulse as "color evasiveness" or "power evasiveness"; that is, the tendency of whites, even when discussing race, to avoid consideration of power and hierarchy.[69] E-racing, as practiced by most advocates of color blindness, is nothing more than another quite potent form of racing. It is not necessarily problematic that groups identify with and partially define themselves through racial categories. Race, unlike culture, always entails a relationship to others, but not necessarily a dominant/dominated relationship. Race in and of itself does not entail subjugation. Racing is problematic when it is imposed by others, so that the raced group is stripped of its self-identity and redefined by the racer. Ruth Frankenberg points out that in the context of American race relations, "White/European self-constitution is . . . fundamentally tied to the process of discursive production of others, rather than preexisting that process."[70]

When a group points out race-related issues in order to challenge racial hierarchy and subjugation, racial evasion or color blindness then becomes a tool of the dominant group to deny the challengers an identity that might destabilize racism. In this sense, racing involves both the assigning and the depriving of racial identities. Moreover, much of what is considered racially neutral from a color-blind perspective is merely whiteness hiding behind the invisible norm that its power bestows.[71] What is called for is not the e-racing of society, but the elucidation and destabilization of whiteness. The imperative of anti-racist efforts is to bring a focus to the aspects of race that are most problematic and most abhorrent to our egalitarian ideals – racial domination and privilege certainly, but also the use of racism to sanctify social domination and privilege.

The Uncertainty of Abolishing Racial Categories

Given the fact that race has been socially constructed to create, maintain, and justify a system of white privilege, suggestions that we could and ought to abandon racial categories altogether have a certain logic to them. As I have suggested, however, this response misunderstands the relationship between racism and race on one hand and the meaning of social construction on the other. While race undoubtedly continues to have meanings in our society, the relevant inquiries address how these meanings are obtained and what their relationships are to racism. At any given moment, race has a number of different meanings, and these meanings often interact with one another in complex ways.[72]

This interconnected relationship only touches the surface of the complex nature of race. Race is not just an external trait that allows us to categorize one another; it is also an internal process that can create and destroy internal and external worlds. Even in our internal world, race is multiplicitous, unstable, and subject to change.[73] This is true largely because the self, organized around concepts such as race, gender, and religion, is multiplicitous, dynamic, and unstable.[74] Also, because race is relational, how one experiences one's racial self will vary depending on one's basis for comparison. Zora Neale Hurston captures this idea by describing the day she left her all-black society for school: "It seemed that I had suffered a sea change. I was not Zora of Orange County any more, I was now a little colored girl."[75]

Even if we could eradicate racism in our society, it is not clear that race would cease to have meaning. The historical persistence of racism makes it difficult to envision a United States in which race has no meaning at all.[76] Racial definitions are so inextricably woven into the structure of our society that efforts to change them require fundamental changes in social concepts and organization – what Goldberg calls shifts in "ways of world making."[77] Such a monumental reorientation is problematic because it entails a widespread and thorough reformulation of core social and political beliefs, reaching into and out of individual identities and understandings. For regardless of the origins of racial classification in the United States, racial definitions have played various and changing but central roles in individual and group conceptions of identity.

By its nature, identity needs to develop around things; there is no identity *as* identity. And although racialization has operated as a mechanism of domination, notions of race as a social reality have developed in ways not conceived of or encouraged by the racing majority. Thus, racial identification, although often thrust upon racial minorities, has developed in some positive directions. Gotanda refers to these positive aspects of racial identity as culture-race: the "broadly shared beliefs and social practices" that result from the common sociohistorical experiences of a racially defined group.[78] Efforts to deracialize society therefore have the potential also to delegitimize culture-race and undermine valued aspects of the identities of racialized minorities.

Attempts to deracialize American society are also problematic from a more pragmatic standpoint. Racial projects continue to structure and organize society, so denying racial relevance without first addressing its structural centrality actually impedes efforts to address racial hierarchy. The common view tends to be that the assignment of privileges and benefits ought to be based on "individual merit" as evidenced by indices such as education, performance on standardized tests, or other measures that tend to be distributed (rationed) in a highly racialized way. The current political landscape provides ample evidence of how application of this ideology is used to facilitate the continued subjugation of people of color and other traditionally excluded groups in the name of neutrality. In California, for example, opponents of affirmative action employed color-blind theory to support the California Civil Rights Initiative (popularly known as "Proposition 209"), a constitutional amendment banning public-sector affirmative action programs. In 2006, the same group sponsored Proposition 2, a similar initiative in Michigan, which passed as well.[79] (That initiative was challenged on several grounds, including voter fraud, and was overturned by the 6th Circuit in July 2011.[81]) A law against race- and gender-conscious programs was passed by voter referendum in Washington in 1998, and Nebraska voters amended the state constitution to that purpose in 2008.[80]

Notions of neutrality have been employed in other contexts as well, such as Colorado's use of "sexual orientation blindness," which was little more than a thinly veiled attack on remedial programs aimed at ending discrimination against homosexuals.[82] Indeed, despite the calls for fairness and justice from the proponents of color blindness, contemporary examples in which color blindness or neutrality are invoked for the benefit of a subjugated group are difficult to find.

By focusing on formal classifications rather than the functions of race, moreover, color-blind theorists fail to comprehend, or choose to ignore, the extent to which opportunity in our society is very much affected by one's racial designation. Their decontextualized view of race and "merit" portrays racial differences in the distribution of opportunities and benefits either as the aberrant result of irrational discriminatory individuals or as individual failure on the part of minorities. This analysis serves the ends of racial domination because de facto racial segregation, our racial history, and current racial hierarchies are all ignored, while race-based remedial efforts, such as affirmative action, are considered to be as irrationally tainted as the programs and practices that maintain color-coded systems of privilege.[83]

In portraying formal recognition of race as inherently negative, color-blind theory also fails to consider positive aspects of racial identification. Shared sociohistorical experience has led to the development of rich cultural traditions within racially identified groups. Color-blind theory, combined with majoritarian politics, fails to recognize that in a democratic society, all groups should have avenues for self-expression, and all members of society should have the opportunity to be exposed to one another's views and experiences. Indeed, such exposure is an important step in the process of becoming a more unified and integrated society. In this way, color blindness results in an erroneous lack of support for democracy-building policies, such as meaningful diversity in educational environments.[84]

Color blindness asserts that we live in a deracialized society, despite the fact that societal norms and concepts of what it means to be an American have developed in almost exclusively white political, social, and cultural space. The white Western liberal tradition asserts that we are fundamentally atomistic and individual, and that we gain identity through our selves.[85] This focus on the individual solution proposes merely another form of assimilation, in which racial others are assessed by the values of white culture and, ultimately, by their (in)ability to achieve whiteness.

Positive aspects of race are not accounted for in color-blind theory because of the erroneous correlation asserted between race and racism. An equally flawed assumption of color blindness is that if something is socially constructed, it can be willed away.[86] As discussed in the preceding chapter, however, "socially constructed" means "not individually constructed" – not nonexistent. Even the more modest assertion that much of what we take as fact derives its meaning from language and social structure is sobering. Moreover, if there is such a thing as scientific fact in opposition to social fact, it may be that the social fact is able to make at least as strong a claim on us, because social truths often have at least as much descriptive validity for the individual.[87] The way we think about race and the self will change therefore as a result of psychological and cultural events, though this change cannot simply be willed into existence.

Problems with Retaining "Positive" Aspects of Race

Many staunch proponents of not seeing race show very weak support for anti-racist measures. On the Supreme Court, the justices who most forcefully assert the importance of color blindness continually elect to uphold the interests of white supremacy. Some also view as problematic the fact that attempts to address racial hierarchy must necessarily affect current racial definitions and their relevance for individual and collective identities.[88] Because of the centrality of race in ordering individual and collective experience, destabilizing race must entail the destabilization of entire systems of belief, a very uncertain and daunting undertaking. This task is nevertheless a necessary one, given that racial identities are, to some extent, products of common, racialized experiences as well as of white racial projects.

Celebrating an identity that is significantly defined and shaped by racist oppression without adopting, to some extent, the terms of the oppressor is difficult – nearly impossible. Omi and Winant assert that contemporary America is a racial hegemony in which white privilege is maintained by a combination of coercion and consent – a consent obtained when the subject of racialization adopts and internalizes the terms of racialized identity.[89] This adoption is never complete, and the terms of racial discourse are often appropriated and transformed by the racialized other, but a failure to challenge the discourse itself, rather than its manifestations, enables this hegemony to persist. To effectively address racial hierarchy and domination, we must address racing as a hierarchical process, whatever the implications for racial identities and cultures.

This task warrants less cause for concern when we consider that ideas of race and racialized culture have shifted in the past and will continually shift in the future. To treat black culture, for example, as a static concept is to ignore the fact that race and culture, as social constructs, are constantly in flux. Because there is no inherent essence to these notions – that is, because notions of race and racialized culture are inextricably linked to sociohistorical context – their meanings will necessarily change as the myriad contingencies of their existence change. Our goal in addressing racism, therefore, must be racial transformation informed by the number of different ways that race is used within specific contexts to create and maintain white privilege. By addressing how race functions to dominate, we will transform racial meanings without necessarily destroying racial identity. The result of this effort is uncertain, but no more uncertain than the future in general.

SEEING THE INVISIBLE

Rather than paralyze ourselves by attempting to understand or predict the uncertain, we need to focus on addressing what it is about racing and racial discourse that most violates our ideals and aspirations. Privilege and exclusion have been structured around racially identified groups, so it is imperative that we focus our efforts on race's current function of creating and perpetuating gross inequality. Comparing black and white demographics for opportunity-enhancing indices, such as wealth,[90] homeownership,[91] and income[92] reveals sharp disparities. Moreover, these disparities are the direct result of racial subordination and discrimination, particularly in the housing sector, and have a mutually reinforcing and self-perpetuating nature. One's location within a metropolitan area determines access to opportunity. Income and wealth, determined by job status and access to lending institutions, largely determine one's ability to choose a residential location within a metropolitan area, and suburban municipalities engage in exclusionary zoning practices that prohibit the development of low- and moderate-income housing.[93] The ends of white domination are, therefore, achievable in our era of de facto racism without the previously necessary means of overt, de jure discrimination. This recognition helps to clarify the intentions of color-blind theorists and the insidious effects of color-blind ideology.

There are numerous examples, however, of ways to address whiteness and destabilize current racial arrangements to drive needed change. One way is by reducing metropolitan segregation. Segregation's racialization of space in turn races individuals, by defining blackness as inner-city, unemployed, uneducated, and criminal, and whiteness as suburban, employed, educated, and law-abiding. Addressing this racial discourse requires, as Martha Mahoney notes, "changing widespread patterns of residence and economic development and changing the social meanings attached to these patterns."[94] When low-income communities of color are spatially segregated, with little access to opportunities, such as sustainable jobs, high-performing schools, and quality health care and child care, they are deprived of the resources critical to quality of life, financial stability, and social advancement. Isolation and disinvestment threaten individuals and their families, but they also affect entire communities. Eliminating these patterns of isolation would result in wider distribution of opportunity across metro areas and more flexibility for all in terms of cultural and residential choices.

Another driver of needed change may be pressing environmental concerns and the need for more sustainable development practices in our intensely segregated and stratified society. Acceleration of the current modest movements toward urban infill and public transportation could be increased and targeted to reduce our environmental impact and improve access to opportunity, especially when these goals are taken into account in both planning and implementation.

Exposing the incongruity of racial classifications in America can provide useful insights and raise critical issues for those committed to pursuing true democracy. Recognizing that race is a social construct is helpful for efforts to address racism. Dismantling the racial hierarchy that was built into the foundations of this nation will take more than recognizing that all people are genetically more than 99 percent the same, however. It will take looking seriously at the work that race does and why. It will take confronting the resistance to change of those who unduly benefit from that work.

Cheryl Harris has insightfully observed that, as the Court acknowledged in *Plessy*, whiteness is a property interest.[95] Harris explains:

> Property is a legal construct by which selected private interests are protected and upheld. . . . When the law recognizes, either implicitly or explicitly, the settled expectations of whites built on the privileges and benefits produced by white supremacy, it acknowledges and reinforces a property interest in whiteness that reproduces Black subordination.[96]

The characteristic of whiteness thereby becomes a sort of reputational interest by which individuals are deemed to be deserving of certain opportunities and benefits.[97] This reputational interest in turn shapes individual identity and an individual's sense of worth and entitlement.[98] Theodore Allen points out that for immigrants, whiteness in America meant that "however lowly their social status might otherwise be they were endowed with all the immunities, rights and privileges of 'American whites.'"[99] Until the mid–twentieth century, calling a white person black was considered defamation: to deprive people of their whiteness was to deprive them of a legally protected interest in their reputation and status.[100] Not surprisingly, the laws did not recognize any harm in calling a black person white.[101]

Accepting whiteness as the American norm without addressing the underlying privilege is a particular problem given our tradition of Western liberal thought. That tradition is premised on the notion of nature and experience as orderable and objectively knowable. When we deny the fact that individual experience is necessarily filtered through the subjective lens of perception, the power to define "objective" truth resides with those whose perceptions are valued and validated. Thus, in our society, the subjectivity of white Europeans, shaped by their perceptions, culture, norms, and ideology, has been exalted as objective, and they have been empowered to determine what is normal and natural.

Attempting to address racial hierarchy without addressing this backdrop of whiteness achieves the "assimilationist ideal" while devaluing the positive aspects of race.[102] Non-white groups gain a semblance of equality, but on conditions that are predetermined by a white-majority society, and without a critical evaluation of what aspects of whiteness are shaped by historical and contemporary racisms. Furthermore, failing to address the privilege that has shaped whites' settled expectations creates a sense of meritocracy in which the concentration of whites in the upper ranks of society is seen as the well-earned result of individual effort. Given the depth and power of this reality, changing our expectations about race is a formidable task.

Addressing racial hierarchy by focusing on whiteness is a peculiar proposition in our society. Most people are accustomed to speaking of racism in terms of the burdens it places upon people of color, without recognizing the benefits it confers on whites.[103] Conventional wisdom seems to ignore that both whites and non-whites occupy racial categories – instead assuming that only non-whites have a racial identity. Whiteness thus takes on the property of invisibility in the everyday experiences of whites. This is understandable, given that throughout American history, non-whites have been excluded from those political, social, and cultural institutions that define what is American. Consequently, American identity is defined as white, and whiteness is used to examine, without being examined.[104]

The invisibility of whiteness in a white-dominated culture is similar to the invisible presence of the narrator in a story told from the third-person point of view. The ever-present subject (i.e., the author, or racer) has the power to name and define the object without ever calling explicit attention to his or her presence or perspective. This perspective then becomes the unexamined framework by which objects are described and defined. John Berger, in *Ways of Seeing*, makes a similar observation with respect to photography: "Every image embodies a way of seeing. Even a photograph. For photographs are not, as often assumed, a mechanical record. Every time we look at a photograph, we are aware, however slightly, of the photographer selecting that sight from an infinity of other possible sights."[105]

Trinh T. Minh-ha has noted how the other, in this case the female writer, is colonized, and thus defined, when forced to use language that has developed within her male-dominated society:

> She-her has always conveyed the idea of a personal and gender-specific voice. In order to be taken more seriously, she is therefore bound to dye this voice universal, a tint that can only be obtained through words like man, mankind, he-him. ... Such a convenient way to generalize and to transcend the sex line. One must practice to forget oneself.[106]

Similarly, Frantz Fanon noted how colonial and non-colonial powers define blacks as the objective other. Fanon refers to colonialism as the "systematic negation of the other person and a furious determination to deny the other person all attributes of humanity."[107] The invisibility of the related "white gaze," as well as of whiteness itself, enables whites to simultaneously recognize that non-whites have been denied opportunities and resources and yet to assert that whites have achieved their own societal status through personal merit. By failing to critically examine their identity and status, whites also fail to connect the denial of opportunities for minorities with the greater access to these opportunities of the majority.

While the story of race has been discussed primarily in the context of whites and non-whites, with whites in the privileged space, there are a few alternative ways of retelling this story that are important. One is that we are moving from a white and non-white society to a black, non-black society, in which everyone who is not functionally black has a sense of belonging to society while those considered black do not belong. This is

what George Yancy sees as evolving.[108] Yancy's story is about the possibility of a future in which even those who are phenotypically black
need not be black, and some who are not phenotypically black may be
functionally black. Those in this functionally black group become the
racialized non-human other.

Steve Martinot offers another story, by looking at the past. He asserts that race has never been a binary system, and that the construction
of race was by elites who did not see themselves as white.[109] Through
this lens, race was about both social control and the creation of new
identities. In this system, whiteness was just a middle stratum, in which
whites were given the right to help define policy and control the lower
stratum non-whites in exchange for maintaining allegiance to the elite,
but without membership. Those above expected and demanded this allegiance without any reciprocal acceptance of responsibility.

Martinot argues that we still live with shades of this structure and
that understanding it helps explain the disdain and fear of those in the
white space toward the racial other, as well as their blind attraction to
elites. Under these arrangements, calls for alliances between those in the
white space and the racial other will almost always be an incomplete, if
not failed, strategy. If we also consider the fact that whiteness continues
to be such an important element in the ontological grounding of many
Americans, then the perceived interest in maintaining this inherited
alignment with elites calls for a different project to achieve racial justice
than one that might succeed in a true racial binary.

As race continues to adapt, we must be careful not to become too
distracted by change without a critical eye toward what the change entails. One can imagine a new racial order that continues to exclude and
subjugate but in a different way. The goal is not simply to do the sorting
correctly or to describe our racialized system more precisely: the goal is
to foster a just society. This requires not only that we move beyond black
and white but also that we move beyond human and less than human.
This project will require the participation and the involvement of all. The
hard edge of this system has been both the role of the elites and its ontological grounding in whiteness. What is needed then is a new grounding
that is not based on disassociation from the racial other or on allegiance
to the elites that created and control whiteness.

PART TWO

White Privilege

FOUR

Interrogating Privilege, Transforming Whiteness

Blacks are made visible and invisible at the same time under the gaze. For example, when Black youth are seen it is often with a specific gaze that sees the "troublemaker," "the school skipper," or the "criminal." Thus they are seen and constrained by a gaze that is intended to control physical and social movements. The purpose of the gaze is that it should subdue those who receive it and make them wish to be invisible.

Frantz Fanon, Black Skin, White Masks

Whether or not we understand ourselves through lenses of identity, we still make ethical choices about how to live with those identities. It is the choices that require critique.

Mari J. Matsuda, "I and Thou and We and the Way to Peace"

Seeing and naming the whiteness of whiteness, then decentering whiteness from its position as the universal norm, is an undertaking with enormous potential for liberating our society. The necessary first step is acknowledging that there is indeed white privilege, or what I prefer to call white supremacy or white racial hierarchy. I endeavor here to consider the nature and function of this privilege as it has been articulated in order to determine how we should think about it and how best to end it. This work presents some difficulties, the first of which is defining privilege and its relationship to otherness, at least rhetorically. This includes examining the ways that the rhetoric of white privilege contributes to its invisibility and corroborates the myth of white innocence. In order to more fully state the problem and make the case for a transformative approach, I will draw here upon the debate of sameness and difference. I question the long-term usefulness of valorizing difference, as well as of assimilationist approaches to power structures. I advocate a communicative ethic, informed by the relational nature of difference.

I also want to emphasize the importance of the participation of both marginalized and privileged groups in jointly confronting exclusionary ideas, practices, and structures. One of the most powerful and eloquent voices in such work is that of Stephanie Wildman, whose penetrating analysis exposes privilege that is often viewed as an objective norm hiding within the language of the dominant discourse of our society. Wildman's work demonstrates that once we learn to look for this privilege, and how to look for it, we start to discover it in virtually all aspects of our lives. Her effort is not simply to name privilege but also to destabilize and change it. I want to contribute to that effort with an examination of some of the complexities and difficulties, in the hope of deepening and strengthening this effort.

THE PROBLEM OF DEFINING PRIVILEGE AND DEFICIT

The relationship between privilege and non-privilege, or "deficit," is difficult to describe. Wildman defines privilege as a "systemic conferral of benefit and advantage," triggered not by merit but by "affiliation, conscious or not and chosen or not, to the dominant side of a power system."[1] In other words, privilege is a system by which groups of people actively acquire or passively attach to reward without earning it, simply by membership in privileged groups such as whites, heterosexuals, males, ablebodied persons, or a combination of these or other categories. Individuals and groups can be privileged in society without being all of these, a point which complicates recognition of privilege. For example, a black female heterosexual can access structures of privilege as a heterosexual, even if she may not be privileged by her status as a member of a racial minority or as a woman.

If privilege is relatively simple to define, its relational other is not. This difficulty casts doubt on the validity of a definition of privilege, as well as on the lived meaning or social construction of the term. French structuralists would seek the meaning of privilege in opposition to other meanings: the significance of a word is located through contrast.[2] But an opposite to privilege is not readily available. Until recently, most dictionaries did not contain the terms "aprivilege," "nonprivilege," or the term Margalynne Armstrong employs, "unprivileged."[3] The definition problem is more pronounced when approached from a postmodernist or poststructuralist orientation.[4] Instead of a spectrum of terms to express the nature of groups that access systems of privilege at multiple sites, few sites, or no sites, there is only the term "underprivileged."

"Underprivileged" functions problematically as a linguistic companion to privilege; it unfortunately reifies the notion of privilege as normal and unquestionable. In indirect contrast to privilege, underprivilege is

> a kind of special case, to indicate those falling below an assumed normal level of social existence. It is the assumption of what is normal that is then the problem, given the verbal continuity of privilege, which in its sense of very specific and positive social advantages underprivileged can have the effect of obscuring or canceling.[5]

There is continuity to privilege, but the absence of a discrete set of descriptive terms often makes it difficult to examine it, and its relational other, from either structuralist or postmodernist perspectives. The lack of a vocabulary limits dialogue and action. The dearth of terms has not, however, eliminated the creation of definitions for the other in the privilege dialogue. From the conservative perspective, which is a place of power in this context, the privilege holder is "normal," and the groups that cannot access or attach to privilege are "aberrant," "alternative,"[6] or "deficit holders." But none of these definitions fully conveys the complex implications of otherness.

The Function of Privilege

In illustrating how privilege normalizes the situation of the privileged, Wildman offers the example of the workplace. Although the term "workplace" seems neutral, it is exclusive of many locations of work, such as child care and informal economic structures, where women and people of color, rather than white males, predominate.[7] "Workplace" does not contemplate these types of work and is indeed exclusionary of them, but the term survives because it has a semblance of neutrality. Looking beyond language, Wildman points out that the behavior expected at workplaces, from social interactions between employees to collective practices, is white and male. Laws governing discrimination in the workplace serve only to compensate the other for the deficit held. They may create or protect access to the white male work structure, but they do not transform the workplace.[8] One is expected to adhere to the unstated male norms.

At the systemic level, privilege serves to normalize such power structures. At the level of the individual – the level at which we can almost see privilege – it advantages members and disadvantages nonmembers. Members access privilege and receive rewards both actively and passively. As described by Armstrong, "white privilege involves advantages and options that are available merely because one is white. A white person need not be a bigot to benefit from racial privilege; simply having white skin means having access to neighborhoods and jobs that are closed to people of color."[9] At another level, this access may be gained with a socially valued whiteness that may not require white skin. As Wildman puts it, "the characteristics of the privileged group define the societal norm" so "privileged group members can rely on their privilege and avoid objecting to oppression."[10] This insight sheds more light on how "color-blind" jurisprudence preserves ongoing structures of racial hierarchy and white privilege, so much of which was acquired through exploitation, exclusion, and subjugation of non-white others.

White Innocence and Racial Subordination

In "Innocence and Affirmative Action," legal scholar Thomas Ross challenges the color-blind idea that whites are innocent if they do not actively discriminate against people of color or otherwise act in a racist manner. Ross points out that now that the "dominant public ideology" is at least ostensibly non-racist, whites know that they must avoid overt discrimination; otherwise, how could they fully separate themselves from the "historical figures or aberrational and isolated characters" who represent racism in the popular imagination today.[11] In spite of the general distancing of the society from its cruder manifestations, however, "the culture continues to teach racism," Ross says, in a belief system perpetuated with stereotypes and preconceptions that pervades society and dictates behavior that subordinates people of color. These biases are part of social schemas and associations that exist in all of us, privileged or othered and that are often reflected in our behavior and policies. Addressing such bias is a collective and structural project more than an individual and psychological one. To this extent, personal culpability inhering in the indictment "racist" is reduced, though it does not make the individual innocent.

It would be a similar mistake to try to locate privilege solely in the white psyche, because the operation of privilege does not demand the conscious participation of whites. Privilege is distributed and mediated through structures, language, power, and institutions that always outrun the control of any given individual. In fact, I would also suggest that having unconscious bias and stereotypes should not be labeled racism. Having these biases is certainly not innocent and requires action, but it is misleading to call them racist when they are formed without conscious intent. Whites are implicated in the arrangements that support these unconscious attitudes: most are willing to see others as deficit-holders while wearing the benefit conferred on them by whiteness as if it were their due. But interrupting the negative feedback from structural arrangements is perhaps the most critical part of freeing all of us from unwanted attitudes, conscious and unconscious. It is not the bias that most implicates whites in this system, but their possessive investment in the benefits and spoils of the system and their willingness to act on the purported unworthiness of the racial other.[12]

Other whites go further, of course, supporting and engaging in a rhetoric, as in the affirmative action dialogue, that casts white non-recipients of contracts, school admission, and jobs as innocent "victims." In contrast, non-white recipients of these assets are cast as "takers"[13] of something rightfully belonging to whites, or to white society. By failing to challenge the unthinking propagation of negative views of the racial other, accepting the racialized distribution of benefits, and portraying non-whites as usurpers or even would-be thieves, whites assert their innocence and demonize the other. They hoard and protect their spoils from a deeply racialized system. This conceptual perpetuation of systems of privilege translates into very real subordination of people of color and other nonholders of privilege. Each of these methods also has insinuated itself into court decisions, with grave implications for efforts to protect civil rights.

The Damaging Effects of Privilege on Privilege Holders

An important benefit of recognizing and confronting privilege is addressing its effects on not only the "deficit" holders but also the members of the privileged group. In her now classic working paper on privilege, Peggy McIntosh writes of her realization that acknowledging privilege means accepting that comforts and gains are not necessarily the result of good work, and that rewards are not always deserved.[14] Recognizing the necessity of confronting privilege is a difficult task for privilege holders. As McIntosh puts it, "the pressure to avoid it is great, for in facing it I must give up the myth of meritocracy."[15] This means giving up the view of oneself as innocent as well as the material advantages and status not earned.

McIntosh reminds us that a privilege holder's participation in the myth of a meritocracy is more complex than could be reversed by any single act of self-reflection. Awareness and confrontation of the myth are, in fact, traumatic, not only because they provide an imperative to undo present circumstances and avoid automatic attachment to privilege in the future but also because they require exposure and recognition of the problems caused by the legacy and values of the world of privilege holders. McIntosh writes about white privilege in particular but not in isolation:

> We need more understanding of the ways in which white "privilege" damages white people, for these are not the same ways in which it damages the victimized. Skewed white psyches are an inseparable part of the picture, though I do not want to confuse the kinds of damage done to the holders of special assets and to those who suffer the deficits.[16]

Indeed, a frequent question in discussions of white privilege is, Why should whites give it up if it is so good? Toni Morrison encourages us to examine the way the history of slavery and racism have marked and scarred white people.[17] Holding on to unearned skin privilege means alienation not only from the racial other but also from oneself. In this sense, white privilege comes with baggage: fear, anxiety, and dissociation. As Roediger and others have demonstrated, whites have at times also consciously worried about being consumed by the racial other. This anxiety may be expressed in terms of white purity, as captured in the "one drop rule" of hypodescent. There has long been a fear, sometimes conscious, sometimes not, that the whiteness of this country would be lost to the racial other. Whites have consequently been able to demand and have often received express material and social benefits in support of whiteness.[18]

The conundrum for many whites, however, has been that such benefits were doled out (or withheld) in a non-democratic system that forced them to align themselves with powerful interests that were, ultimately, acting against their interests as workers. When whites protested that their conditions constituted "slave labor," they might be given the vote, for example, increasing their separation from, and negative perception of, blacks, which increased their white anxiety. In the carefully maintained competitive context of threatened scarcity, however, the acceptance of the bait was rarely questioned. The resulting false attachment to whiteness, and to its need to dominate and exclude, have poisoned and ruined our democracy, to paraphrase Du Bois.[19] Indeed, racially disparate disenfranchisement continues, as in the new Voter ID laws, which inhibit both registration and voting among non-white and younger voters, that have been passed in thirty states since the 2008 election.[20] When the wages of whiteness decline, we often see not an increase in democracy or freedom but rather a decline of both. So one practical reason whites might decide to give up white privilege is that it is not all it is made out to be and is, for many, truly a losing game. Yet today, even as the material and social benefits of whiteness diminish, more attention is paid not to the elites who regulate these benefits but instead to a loss of control, loss of "Americanness," fear of diversity, or contempt for the public sphere.

There is also strong social support, especially in the United States, for seeing privilege and deficit as organic outcomes of individual behaviors and talents. This support leads privilege holders toward denial and a search for other reasons for their status, inhibiting confrontation and recognition. Moreover, that path is paved and tended by stories from the courts. Martha Minow describes the normalization of privilege that is constantly reified in the courts:

> There is an assumption that the existing social and economic arrangements are natural and neutral. If workplaces and living arrangements are natural, they are inevitable. It follows, then, that differences in the work and home lives of particular individuals are because of personal choice. We presume that individuals are free, unhampered by the status quo, when they form their own preferences and act upon them. From this view, any departure from the status quo risks non-neutrality and interference with free choice.[21]

This naturalization of what is also attempts to protect elites from a more critical gaze. We are willing then to accept that they, like middle class whites, have earned their power and wealth. Moreover, an assumption of the neutrality of what is doesn't just support the notion of white innocence; it also suggests that those who would challenge these arrangements are blameworthy. It is a short step from this position to one that sees whites as racial victims and the racial other as an undeserving perpetrator. Attempts to reconcile the notions of otherness and free choice have thus resulted in only limited, compensatory models of altering power structures, such as affirmative action programs, rather than structural change.

Working against Privileging Systems: A Critical Approach

Because the system of white privilege is inscribed into our relationships, language, and law, undoing it may seem an impossible task. The enterprise, moreover, is riddled with questions and fear: If systems of privilege are undone, will this dismantling obliterate useful components of the social structure? When a system is so pervasive and entrenched, how can the bad be distinguished from the good? Does the recognition of privilege require the complete razing of existing structures, or is access to these structures by marginalized groups enough? Several critics offer approaches to privilege that stop short of entire disassembly of existing structures. These approaches, alone or in combination, seem to address the ill fit of the other into the systems and structures designed to exclude it without promoting either assimilationism or relativism.[22]

Minow, for example, advocates a critical position characterized not by mere tolerance or celebration of multiple perspectives but instead by attention to the tensions between different systems.[23] One would not describe the system of slavery, for example, as a difference in perspectives. Minow asserts that a critical position is therefore ultimately a more productive one:

> Some say that moral relativism results if we solicit and celebrate the view of those who have been excluded, degraded, or oppressed. Surely, this celebration of multiplicity topples the hierarchy that canonized one set of experiences as the norm. Yet the demand for that kind of pluralism does not and should not suspend the critique of power relationships that motivate it.[24]

The need is not for pluralism that makes all perspectives equal; the need is to look critically at the dominant white perspective and understand it through relationships, power, and history. The multiple perspective may seem progressive, but often it is in fact conservative and supportive of much of the status quo. By bleeding out any consideration of power, it suggests that all interests and concerns of whites are on equal footing. Under this approach, we would give equal weight to demands for and against segregation. This false symmetry is organized around a neutrality with respect to process that makes it more difficult to see and address racial subordination and hierarchy.

The more helpful approach is to make power relationships – privilege – visible. Rebecca Aanerud calls this exposure of racial dominance the "interruption of whiteness"[25] and advocates its use in reading both texts that omit race in assumption of whiteness and those that approach race uncritically. Ruth Frankenberg also recognizes the utility of the visibility approach as a first step toward confronting privileging forces, hegemony, and seemingly monolithic whiteness. In regard to textual analysis, Frankenberg argues that this confrontation will expose the ways in which whiteness is continuously reinforced as the norm, as neutral, and as common belief.[26] If the seeming normality of whiteness is not questioned, Frankenberg says, it will continue to be the dominant, subordinating actor.

Wildman emphasizes that making privilege visible is only a first step. "Once the hierarchy is made visible, the problems remain no less complex, but it becomes possible to discuss them in a more revealing and useful fashion."[27] Our efforts to make these processes more visible must be tempered by the realization that many of our mental processes can never be completely available to us at the conscious level. This does not mean we should not seek a greater level consciousness in this realm, only that we must be aware that it is an important but necessarily limited strategy. The complexity of the problem and of the theoretical discourse surrounding it should not result in stasis, however. Responses to the power structure are available and should be implemented, even if they do not represent a complete solution, because incremental steps taken in confrontation of whiteness will help uncover deeper aspects of the problem and suggest further appropriate responses.

DECENTERING WHITENESS

*Reason and Individualism: Civil Rights Ideals
or Exclusionary Mechanisms?*

The white gaze described by Frantz Fanon changes the dominated group into the racial other without emphasizing how that action also helps to constitute whiteness. This move normalizes whiteness and places upon the racial other the impossible burden of becoming equal by becoming like whites – that is, raceless.[28] This transparent norm has a seductive appeal. As blacks and others have been excluded, subordinated, and marginalized for being apparently different, there has been a powerful pull on both the excluded and the privileged group to address these issues by making blacks just like whites.[29] Of course, the language of sameness is expressed in terms of being treated the same as everyone else. Until recently, it was hardly noticed that the sameness that is being held up as a universal norm is in fact a specifically white norm.[30] The specificity of this white gaze has been hidden in the language of Enlightenment ideals of objectivity, rationalism, and universalism. It is not surprising, then, that challenges to the universal claims associated with whiteness are attacked as undermining objectivity, reason, and standards.

Critiques of the Enlightenment's perspectiveless story have been leveled almost since its emergence. For the role of reason, and other foundational claims of universality, were not just philosophical issues: these claims were bound up with the way society rationalized the exclusion of women, racial minorities, and other groups. Often, however, as the language and justification for the inclusion of each of these groups took hold, arguments were cast in the same rational discourse. These arguments could take on absurd forms. One example is the discussion as to whether slaves, as property, were capable of human reasoning and therefore able to form the mens rea, or guilty state of mind, that distinguishes certain crimes, such as murder. Also debated was whether women could participate in society as public figures without male supervision.

The argument about the place of these subordinated groups in society often was framed on the sameness/difference axis. One position was that if indeed women and blacks were different from the universal norm of the white male, they were appropriately limited in terms of societal participation. Those who championed the inclusion of marginalized groups often did so, therefore, by asserting that members of these groups could perform the tasks or had the traits requisite to or identical to those who were already included in the dominant society.

This reasoning, a vehicle for inclusionary practices, was a direct counter to earlier efforts to explain who was not included in the apparent universalizing reach of equality at the founding of the nation. In *White over Black*, Winthrop Jordan argues that it was the need to justify slavery and the exclusion of blacks contemporaneously with the spread of the rhetoric of equality that helped the ideology of racism and of the racialized other coalesce so powerfully in the United States. The simultaneous process of inclusion and exclusion was not only descriptive of how members of society functioned or were to function – it was constitutive as well. The Enlightenment project that rhetorically championed the equality of white males thus also inspired justifications for the subordination of others. The "othering" of blacks, American Indians, and women was essential in the making of white males.[31] The challenge to whiteness, then, is more than an aberration requiring marginalized groups to tinker at the edges of an otherwise rational, free society.

The Sameness/Difference Debate

The sameness and difference of dominant and marginalized groups is an area of contention that continues to hold a central place in public and private discourse. The consequences of the argument have been extraordinary. Those who support inclusion have been forced to argue that members of the disfavored subordinated group are the same as everyone else.[32] As Frye and Minow have noted, however, this means being the same as, or different from, some assumed norm.[33] This unstated norm through most of our history has been one based on whiteness and maleness, though of course the norm is not necessarily the same as any actual white man.

The logic of the sameness/difference discourse under the prevailing meaning of equality is that people who are the same should be treated the same, or equally, and people who are different should be treated differently. The liberalizing role of this schema is that as we come to accept that we are all apparently the same – reasoning, autonomous, rights-holding individuals – then we can all make claims to equal treatment.

Given the powerful, damaging function of the rhetoric of difference, it is certainly unsurprising that the rhetoric of sameness has appeal. But I have argued that in our society the sameness/difference debate is predicated on white supremacy.[34] One who is not the same as the white norm is both different and inferior and therefore can be excluded. On the other hand, if one wants to, one can seek sameness by being like the white norm. The sting of this position becomes clear when one realizes that the very whiteness that the other is called to emulate is constitutively un-black, anti-black, and indeed exclusive of blackness.[35] The position has a relationship to blackness, and that relationship is both hierarchical and oppositional.

What if individuals and groups are different? The sameness/difference approach implies that it is appropriate that the different be excluded or in some other way subordinated. To treat people the same who are, in fact, different would be to give them special treatment, thereby violating the requirement of equality that is fundamental to the logic. Society at large has failed to address the sameness/difference dilemma. Part of the racing process is taking language and culture away from the dominated group, subjecting its members to what Allen and others have called social death.[36] The dominated group is then left to try to reclaim its humanity through the language and social practices that have defined it as less than, or inferior to, the empowered group. In response, some call for assimilation. While the "passing" of the late nineteenth and early twentieth century has fallen out of favor, the passing of today takes the form of the assertion of "pure" individualism, stripped of race and gender. But this notion of the individual is an ideological fiction, reflective of the image of male whiteness, and still situated in the assimilationist position.

In *Racist Culture,* David Goldberg explores how the ideological concept of the individual was used in derogation of the collective social arrangements of Irish immigrants, indigenous people, and blacks in the United States. The concept was used against those groups as part of a process of white-making and other-making that racialized the concept of the individual. It is not surprising, then, that women and racial minorities may experience the weight of their femaleness or blackness and long for the seeming weightlessness of white maleness or the freedom to be "just" an unencumbered individual. Robin West provocatively states that women are not human beings if "human being" means a rational, autonomous individual.[37]

One could go further and argue that no one is human as it is conceived of by the Enlightenment project. The effort to be so cuts whites off not only from the other but also from themselves. Some have recognized the project of whiteness as being built around dissociation from and fear of the other, but one might add that the dissociation and fear is ultimately experienced in relation to oneself.

Is Valorization of Difference the Answer?

If maleness and whiteness are normative, those who are neither may choose between rejecting what is apparently white as well as calls for assimilation (which in its current form can only be understood as a form of both passing and self-denial) or accepting and valorizing perceived difference.[38] The dilemma attached to sameness is also a dilemma attached to difference and is not easily resolved. The heart of this dilemma is that the other is still caught in the dominant discourse and structure, whether embracing the assimilationist/sameness side of the paradigm or the separatist, self-determinist/difference part. Indeed, many of the apparently more radical members of marginalized groups have adopted the latter stance, claiming and valorizing the "deviant" characteristics that the dominant discourse names as both other and negative.

I remember receiving the message as I was growing up that to be black was negative. Part of the message of the Black Power movement was that we should claim and reclaim the positive aspects of being black. But even after tentatively accepting the positive possibilities of blackness, there was still the negative connotation of Africanness. The move to rename black Americans as African Americans was a further effort to both redefine and reclaim an identity in opposition to the dominant discourse. But how does one know which part of the anti-white stance will reflect a positive position for marginalized groups? And how often is the "deviant" behavior a creation of the white observer or institution? Consider the educational setting. A 1986 study by Fordham and Ogbu suggested that a number of African Americans, especially young males, define doing well academically as "acting white" and take pains to avoid the stigma of whiteness, or perhaps the stigma of seeming to separate from the group to win acceptance from an institution perceived as fundamentally hostile or rejecting.[39]

This theory on black failure continues to have proponents, including some who attribute the problem to school desegregation.[40] Researchers Tyson, Darity, and Castellino have shown, however, that black and white students' attitudes about school were essentially the same: they understood the importance of education and wanted to succeed. These researchers also found that the stigmatizing of high-achieving students of any race (as "brainiacs" and the like) was similar. What differed by race was the response of teachers to typical high school behaviors. The researchers found that some "oppositional attitudes appear to be connected to everyday experiences of inequality in placement and achievement" – indicating that the expressed resentment is at least partly rooted in anger at being denied access to higher-quality learning environments and other opportunities because of race.[41] Even when not expressed, the assumptions at the root of these denials continue to operate in our structures as well as the collective unconscious. Roslyn A. Mickelson and others have documented the problem in studies of within-school segregation, or "tracking."[42] Others have written about the increases in achievement levels and decreases in racial segregation associated with opening higher-level curricula to all students and creating the structures needed to ensure success for all.[43]

In some situations, of course, profoundly marginalized groups do experience a liberating effect in asserting qualities for which they have been urged to bear shame, even if the effect is transitory. The embrace of the word "queer" in the gay and lesbian community, for example, is more than a renaming;[44] it and other such moves are political and cultural attempts to create space not presently available in the dominant discourse.[45] As discussed in the previous chapter, for much of our nation's history, whites, and white males in particular, have been the subject that has "raced" the other. Oppositional efforts to valorize what has been denigrated are a challenge to the racing, or othering, process. Attempts to claim a voice as subject, however, are often trapped within the unexamined language and symbols of the dominant group from which freedom is being sought.

The oppositional approach, even though it may not be as destabilizing of whiteness as we would like, nonetheless evokes strong reactions from those adopting an assimilationist stance. Public conversation about new names and the right to name is littered with statements such as "Why do they want to call themselves black? They aren't really black." Such resistance has even come from black civil rights leaders, including Justice Thurgood Marshall, who for some time refused to embrace this shift.[46] The renaming strategy is associated with an anti-assimilationist stance as well, and sometimes an explicitly separatist stance. The anti-assimilation position was and still is often confused with an anti-integrationist movement. In much of the popular debate, these terms are used interchangeably. But true integration is not the same as assimilation.[47] As Iris Young points out, one can think of assimilation either from a transformative perspective or from more narrow perspectives. The confusion of these terms has made the discourse on these issues unnecessarily acrimonious at times.

Marginalized groups may explore any or all of these approaches, but if these strategies are not part of a larger plan or are seen as ends in themselves, they ultimately will fall prey to the sameness/difference dilemma. To the extent that groups only remain oppositional, or only try to assimilate, they remain dependent on the very discourse they seek to challenge. And to the degree that either approach fails to include engagement with underlying issues, its results will be of limited value.

The Deficit Story Told about Blacks

The decentering of whiteness and the exposure of the white gaze must occur either prior to or concurrently with a strategic effort to separate from or assimilate into society. There may be resistance to the decentering process, as it may appear that it would require that marginalized groups refocus on white people instead of on themselves. But what I am suggesting is that the dominant language is not language that only whites use; it is the language we all use. The dominant language is both the black and the white language. Focusing on the failure of blacks without considering the privilege of whiteness and whites and the relationship between black and white status in society leads to the locating of the race problem in blacks. While blacks may indeed have problems, the heart of the problem is the dominant discourse itself – both the deficit story it tells about blacks and the innocence story it tells of whites.[48]

The deficit story essentially says that there is nothing wrong with the institutional and structural arrangements of society and certainly nothing wrong with whiteness. In fact, there is hardly an acknowledgment that we have a structural arrangement. To the extent that such a structure is acknowledged, it is to be considered neutral and fair. By fair, it is meant that all have an equal opportunity to achieve; that is, that what white males have, they deserve by virtue of individual commitment and hard work. Those who don't have what white males have lack those advantages because of personal failure. Indeed, they have what they deserve.[49] For policy makers to consider race, then, is both wrong and violative of liberalism and the civil rights goal of being treated as an individual.

Peggy McIntosh has described the invisible knapsack of "special provisions, maps, passports, codebooks, visas, clothes, tools and blank checks" that whites are given.[50] I envision in that knapsack versions of stories that allow whites to rationalize and feel innocent in the face of racial oppression and exclusion: "If only blacks would change their family structure." This story is augmented by claims that other groups who started at the bottom, such as Jewish or Irish immigrants, have made it without special dispensation, as discussed in the previous chapter.

Despite the telling and the retelling of these stories in schools and churches, on television, in the popular media, and in public and private discussions, cracks do emerge. The stories are challenged by a counterstory of privilege, whiteness, and relationalism. In law, legal realists were some of the first to challenge the claim of objectivity. In politics and philosophy, late modernism and postmodernism continue to interrogate and point out the dubious assumptions of these claims. As people of color and women have gained political voice, many have begun to assert counterstories to autonomy, reason, and individuality. Even as liberalism tries to accommodate challenges to the Enlightenment without relinquishing core principles, the challenges persist and are likely to intensify. These struggles are not contained within the limited domain of philosophers. The culture wars show that these issues are touching increasing numbers of people in our political community, as more and more citizens notice their absence from or low status in prevailing social and political discourse. Although it is not yet clear what the result of these challenges will be, it is probably safe to say that the disembodied, rational, transcendent, and autonomous "individual" is behind us.

Those of us who have taken the counterstory by Wildman and others seriously must then ask not whether unjustified white male privilege exists, but – having caught a glimpse of it – how it should be discussed and addressed. We must refuse to be trapped in the deficit story, even one that calls for asserting the positive aspects of deficits. The project is not to decide on a rejection or an embrace of what is considered the norm; rather, it is to develop an understanding of what our relationship to these norms should be and thereby to change them.

Understanding Difference as Relational,
Embracing a Transformative Model

Merely accepting or rejecting the terms of the sameness/otherness dilemma reinscribes the norms of whiteness. Marginalized groups fighting to assimilate into the existing power structure – to give everyone an
equal right to live the white male norm – are therefore likely to reinforce
and legitimate the existing structure of privilege. Valorizing otherness
ignores that otherness is bound up in the rejected norm as well; in this
way such valorization feeds that norm in a profound way. Addressing this
dilemma requires that sameness and difference be viewed not as bipolar
and oppositional, but instead as relational and mutually constitutive.
From this viewpoint, a transformative model, rather than assimilation-
ist/conformist or separatist/oppositional model, seems most effective
in addressing privilege.

My concern therefore lies with clarifying the dilemma and starting to move beyond it. Iris Young and Genevieve Lloyd have dealt with
some of these issues with great insight, as in their description of these
problems as distributional in nature. If structures, practices, and norms
are reflective of the favored and disfavored status of members of society, however, accessing these distributive structures does not in itself
disestablish hierarchy or privilege.[51] Another way of thinking about the
problem is as a constitutive one – that the language, norms, and culture
that generate the current hierarchy are creating and sustaining not only
the privilege and marginalization of specific groups, but also the groups
themselves, as Genevieve Lloyd notes in *The Man of Reason.*

Iris Young begins by naming and critiquing the assimilationist
model. She acknowledges that even under this model there has been
substantial progress toward an emancipatory ideal, especially in opposition to exclusion based on natural inferiority. Young distinguishes between what she calls the conformist model and a transformative model
of assimilation. The latter "recognizes that institutions . . . express the
interests and perspective of the dominant groups. Achieving assimilation therefore requires altering many institutions and practices in ac-
cordance with neutral rules that truly do not disadvantage or stigmatize
any person, so that group membership really is irrelevant to how persons
are treated."[52]

The transformative model of assimilation importantly recognizes that distributing benefits based upon institutional practices in which hierarchy and group norms are embedded merely reproduces domination at deeper and more subtle levels. This is the point missed in many "universal" or "color-blind" programs and remedies. Yet even transformative assimilation remains flawed, because it is based on the assumption that there is no space in our legal or political system for recognition of positive difference that could support different treatment.[53] Young's transformative assimilation does not assume that the other must become like the norm; instead both would participate in the creation of new norms and institutions. The weakness of this model as Young sees it is that it still does not leave room for groups and group differences.

Young calls for the mainstream culture of liberal individualism to make room for other values, including the roles of groups. She advocates a more relativistic outlook as an embrace of what she terms the "politics of difference," noting, however, that by positively claiming difference, one may be backing into the sameness/difference dilemma:

> Analyzing W. E. B. Du Bois's arguments for cultural pluralism, Bernard Boxill poses the dilemma this way: "On the one hand, we must overcome segregation because it denies the idea of human brotherhood; on the other hand, to overcome segregation we must self-segregate and therefore also deny the idea of human brotherhood."[54]

Similarly, as previously noted, treating everyone "the same" can result in worsening inequality, where structures are created and maintained in support of white male privilege. This happens, Young continues, because

> the privileged groups are neutral and exhibit free and malleable subjectivity, [but] the excluded groups are marked with an essence, imprisoned in a given set of possibilities. . . . Difference in these ideologies always means exclusionary opposition to a norm. There are rational men, and then there are women; there are civilized men, and then there are wild and savage peoples.[55]

Anti-Essentialist Struggles

The efforts of women and people of color to break out of the entrapment of the universal gaze of a white-male-defined culture run the risk of transporting the sameness/difference dilemma into the individual essentialism debate. Daniel Ortiz argues that many legal theorists who

have critiqued the sovereign, or individualized, subject have done so in-
completely, leading them to transpose the errors of liberal individualism
to the level of community. As an alternative to "metaphysical individualism," he says, they posit "monolithic and discrete" communities, of which
individuals are expressions.[56] Ortiz notes the failure in such a move to
recognize the "multifaceted, complex, and highly provisional" – indeed
fluid – nature of identity.[57]

> [C]ommunity *does* matter to identity in a way traditional liberal legal theory
> cannot well account for. Community *does* at least partly constitute the
> individual and is not wholly reflective of unencumbered individual choice.
> Unfortunately, however, . . . [j]ust as much legal liberalism rests its analysis on
> autonomous, free-standing individuals, the critics rest theirs on autonomous,
> free-standing communities. . . . Only the size of the unit – the person or the com-
> munity – is different.[58]

In essence, we can't rescue the essential individual stance without also
reconfiguring the community stance. For just as none of us is "just" an
individual, none of us can be fully defined or contained by any group
with which we are affiliated, whether that affiliation is by choice or by
social construction or convention.

Given the importance of groups, in terms of both community and
social and political activism, Ortiz recommends recognizing the multifaceted nature of identity, in which we shift among "complex" identities, both creating and being created by the groups with which we associate ourselves.[59] It is true that this acceptance of complex identities
and, therefore, diversity (and dissension) in groups can make for a less
streamlined presentation in terms of advocacy, but whatever is lost in
that way should be more than made up for in the opening up of new perspectives and connections that reflect the complexity of fully realized beings engaged in building a society that reflects their common aspirations.

Young underlines the importance of the recognizing difference as
contextual and "more or less salient depending on the groups compared,
the purposes of the comparison, and the point of view of the compar-
ers," with group differences "conceived as relational rather than defined
by substantive categories."[60] This perspective on difference means that
"whites are just as specific as Blacks or Latinos, men just as specific as
women, able-bodied people just as specific as disabled people."[61] This

shift would also function to reduce limitations imposed on both groups and individuals and would open up new possibilities for identity. Young points to the example of people who use wheelchairs, who have often faced limitations not only because of inadequate attention to accessibility but also, Young reminds us, "because the differences between the disabled and able-bodied were conceptualized as extending to all or most capacities."[62]

This specific and relational conception of difference does not wholly avoid the tendency to focus almost entirely on personal relationships – a common problem in discussions of white privilege. Our personal relationships are mediated through power and institutional structures; privilege therefore cannot be adequately addressed at the personal level.[63] But this approach to difference provides a framework for the acknowledgment of both common cause and situatedness, without falling into the individualism trap.

This issue arises when blacks and other racially and culturally subordinated groups push for acceptance as individuals without confronting the historical construction of individuality in opposition to them.[64] Genevieve Lloyd sees the positing of individualism as oppositional to blacks as analogous to transcendence as oppositional to women. Lloyd's warning about sameness and assimilation lays the foundation for a constitutive stance on difference and otherness. In *The Man of Reason*, she recognizes the dilemma of accepting either the universal claims of the dominant group or the limitations associated with a flat rejection of them. Unlike Young, however, Lloyd focuses her attention on the inutility of the undertaking.

Noting the role of reason as marking and justifying the domination of the gendered other, Lloyd successfully makes the case that "reason," as we understand it, is a male-centered process that is neither universal nor central. Yet "reason," this universal consciousness, is perceived to be a prerequisite for membership in public life. Those lacking it – specifically women and people of color – are justifiably excluded under the Enlightenment and modern models.[65] It is not the white male characterization of reason to which attention is drawn, it is the purported lack of it in the other: woman's immediacy, and her lack of the transcendence deemed necessary for reasoning, are alleged to make her a hazard to public life.[66]

Through a discussion of the work of Simone de Beauvoir, Lloyd highlights the problems associated with trying to reconstitute the other without a related and similarly penetrating questioning of the supporting discourse. The challenge is not primarily one of material redistribution, she concludes, but rather of reconstitution of both the dominant self and the subordinated other. Lloyd does not try to define the models of the self that de Beauvior employs, mostly drawn from understandings of the work of Hegel and Sartre. She focuses instead on de Beauvoir's use of them. While challenging the claim that women, because of the bodies they inhabit, are consigned to the Hegelian netherworld and unable to transcend the specific, de Beauvoir nonetheless seems to accept the idea that the immediate, the body, must be transcended.[67] Lloyd sees de Beauvoir as being aware that the body, as experienced by women, is a social construct. But she also sees her as trapped by the assumptions of the discourse against which she argues, retaining the language of transcendence without seeming to recognize its male – indeed, anti-female – perspective.

So can marginalized groups claim the positive aspects of their differences without slipping back into the sameness/otherness dilemma? With respect to the female as other, for example, can immediacy be claimed and the need for transcendence eschewed? Young believes that through the recognition of difference as relational, rather than oppositional, this type of claim is possible. But as Lloyd reminds us, the otherness of the other is itself constituted in the discourse and defined as inferior.[68] Lloyd rejects the simple assertion that women should be viewed as having the same capacity as men to participate in the dominant structures, including the structure of reason – as does Young. But Lloyd also argues against simply accepting as valid what constitutes the otherness of the other, even if one tries to reevaluate it as positive:

> Unless the structural features of our concepts of gender are understood, any emphasis on a supposedly distinctive style of thought or morality is liable to be caught up in a deeper, older structure of male norms and female complementation. The affirmation of the value and importance of "the feminine" cannot of itself be expected to shake the underlying normative structures, for, ironically, it will occur in a space already prepared for it by the intellectual tradition it seeks to reject.[69]

Lloyd's observation about gender applies with equal weight to other excluded groups, including racial minorities: "The content of femininity, as we have it, no less than its subordinate status, has been formed within an intellectual tradition. What has happened has been not a simple exclusion of women, but a constitution of femininity through that exclusion."[70] This process of constitution of the other through subordination and exclusion also constituted the included, dominant group.[71] The distorting effect of subordination and privilege thus marks the "normal" group as well as the denigrated one.

Whites are often willing to concede that slavery and racism have marked blacks, but they usually assume that whites have remained largely untouched. This error or denial underlines the need for a much more questioning appraisal not only of otherness, but also of the structures and institutions that support what we currently see as normalcy. In challenging these norms, it is important to be agnostic about the norms of excluded groups, many of which would have been assigned to them – as Lloyd reminds us – in the process of constituting them as other. To that extent, asserting that what was negative is now positive does not resolve the difference dilemma but may just reinscribe the prescribed characteristics and roles.

Lloyd argues not only against trying to claim the positive nature of one's otherness, but also against summarily rejecting social norms. While being critical of the maleness of reason, for example, she wishes to avoid relativism or a facile rejection of reason. Her solution is to adopt an "ambiguous stance" toward it; its maleness is not an excuse to abandon it or to leave it uncritically intact: "Such criticisms of ideals of Reason can in fact be seen as continuous with a very old strand in the western philosophical tradition; it has been centrally concerned with bringing to reflective awareness the deeper structures of inherited ideals of Reason."[72]

Thus the complexity of the sameness/otherness dilemma does not suggest paralysis. As Young points out, a pragmatic response to the immediate problem would support transformative assimilation as well as positive claims of otherness.[73] As one embraces this dilemma and all of its implications, it becomes apparent that it cannot be addressed in a solitary, unequivocal manner. Solutions require engagement across and

within groups as well as with society more broadly. This work places a
high priority on participation and looks with skepticism on practices,
structures, and norms that exclude identifiable groups.[74] The dilemma
can only be addressed by defining and challenging not only the white
gaze but also the material conditions that support it. This is neither a simple rejection nor an embrace of whiteness or otherness; it is a transformation that disturbs both. For it is not enough for marginalized groups to
claim their voices for their communities or their worlds. They must participate in the making of the whole society and the selves that inhabit it.[75]

CHALLENGING WHITENESS

What about the idea that whites might renounce white privilege? Although it is important to interrogate how privilege is generated and how
it functions, it is not clear that much of what is called privilege can or
even should be given up. There is often a false symmetry: if blacks are
denied something that whites have, then it must be a privilege. If we
define privilege as an illegitimate benefit that injures others, however,
this confusion can be avoided. Consider voting rights, for example, or
being treated fairly in the judicial system, or any number of other benefits
denied in disproportionate numbers to blacks. These are privileges of
whiteness, to be sure, but they are not ones that whites should contemplate giving up. These rights must form the bedrock of any humane society. Thus, although the structures of whiteness often deprive non-whites
of things that we would associate with human dignity, not all deprivation
means there is privilege on the other side of the ledger.[76]

Where whites do in fact possess privileges associated with whiteness, it is not clear that they can give them up. David Roediger and others have pointed out that the phrase "white privilege" is redundant. To
renounce the privileges would be to give up whiteness itself, and this
cannot be accomplished at the individual level. As Martinot points out,
"white people cannot individually abandon whiteness in order to abjure
their white skin privilege because they do not produce that whiteness; it
is bestowed upon them by social institutedness in white society. It will
be continually reimposed by the social institutions that preserve and reconstitute it."[77] While Ignatiev and other proponents of the abolition of

whiteness posit that "the task is to gather together a minority determined to make it impossible for anyone to be White,"[78] it is not clear that this is at all a viable objective. John Warren notes that any attempt to eliminate racial hierarchy and whiteness based on the intention and choice of the white subject makes the implicit assumption that the choice exists. However, "a subject is not accidental but rather a product of historical choices and discursive norms. . . . [W]hiteness . . . is a reproducing of a historical situation . . . a product of time, not individual intent."[79]

This is not to suggest that the interrogation of whiteness and the privileges bound up in it is not useful, but that any particular focus on privilege as something that can be separated from whiteness is likely to leave the structure of whiteness in place, with the reinscribing of a new arrangement of privileges. And any focus on the deconstruction of whiteness through the individual intent of whites risks, as Wiegman notes, "reproducing . . . the White male rebel as the . . . subject of anti-racist struggle."[80] In our increasingly complicated postmodern world, transgression is much more complicated than deciding "not to be white."

Instead, transforming the terms, assumptions, and arrangements that arbitrarily and unfairly diminish the life chances of disfavored groups requires that we name, engage, and challenge those aspects of our society and the claims associated with them. Further development of our understandings of privilege and whiteness is therefore crucial. The failure to make the universal norm of whiteness visible leaves its attendant privileges effectively cloaked both to whites and to people of color. The normalcy of male whiteness, moreover, while obscuring the privilege of whiteness, does not obscure the deficiencies of the racialized or gendered other. Indeed, what this normalized structure does is name the failure of blacks and women as something that has little to do with white males. So the excluded other must suffer material and cultural oppression caused by exclusion and domination while shouldering responsibility for it as well.

While the understanding of privilege and innocence is an important part of the move to a more just and inclusive society, it still remains a project. Many of our efforts to address privilege revolve around the assumption that if we can make it visible, it will cease to operate. There are a number of problems with this assumption. One is the idea that we can become fully conscious of our emotional and cognitive processes and that these processes are produced and controlled at the individual level. This idea reproduces the Enlightenment error of the rational and self-determining individual. Much of what we are learning from neuro-science flatly refutes such assumptions.[81] Certainly we can and should become more conscious, but we should not see the problem of privilege and race as primarily an individual psychological effort.

A second problem is that in describing whiteness, we are describing not just what whites and the racial other get from the current arrange-ments but also the ways that those arrangements determine how our very being is constituted. One can imagine giving up one's things – a car or a house – but not one's being, with its sense of identity and all of its deeply ingrained associations.

Another problem is that whites in the twenty-first century are in-creasingly experiencing a sense of loss, not privilege. It would be tempt-ing to just say that they are wrong, but it is not that simple. Clearly, some of the status and benefits that have been a part of being white are chang-ing. Indeed, they should and must change. But this does not take away from the anxiety, fear, and sense of loss that can be experienced during the transition. Our limited understanding of privilege does little to help us with how to talk about it. Without re-centering whiteness, we must pay attention to this aspect of needed change.

Finally, some of the loss that is being experienced by whites is not in favor of the racial other; it is in favor of the elites. Given the growing and extreme inequality that is reshaping our lives and our society, it would be a mistake to try to understand or address privilege without including the role and function of the elites and the increasing power of the corporations they serve and from which they draw their power. The goal then must be not only decentering whiteness but also transforming whiteness and otherness. This requires a project that gives birth to a new meaning and space for whiteness that is not based on exclusion, internal and external separation, and disaffiliation or power over others.

If we understand the injury that whiteness does, not only to those excluded but also to those inhabiting this white space, we will no longer have to ask why whites would give up their privilege. As suggested above, this is not a project to be carried out through individual will – although individuals can and should participate in the project. Such a project would transform whiteness into a space where interrelationship could be healthy and not hostile to individuality but rather the ground for a true individuality. In short, in transforming whiteness and privilege, whites would get the chance to be humane beings.

FIVE

White Innocence
and the Courts

JURISPRUDENTIAL DEVICES THAT OBSCURE PRIVILEGE

Those whom we would banish from society or from the human
community itself often speak in too faint a voice to be heard above
society's demand for punishment. It is the particular role of courts to
hear those voices, for the Constitution declares that the majoritarian
chorus may not alone dictate the conditions of social life.

Justice William J. Brennan, McCleskey v. Kemp

Oppressive language does more than represent violence; it is violence; does
more than represent the limits of knowledge; it limits knowledge. Whether it
is obscuring state language or the faux-language of mindless media; whether
it is the proud but calcified language of the academy or the commodity driven
language of science; whether it is the malign language of law-without-ethics,
or language designed for the estrangement of minorities, hiding its racist
plunder in its literary cheek – it must be rejected, altered, and exposed.

Toni Morrison, Nobel Lecture

We are differently situated in today's United States, not only as individuals, but also as communities, with respect to history, ability, culture, and
access to opportunity. It is not these differences in our situatedness that
create the dramatic inequalities we see today; it is our societal and structural responses, or lack of response, to the differences. Moreover, we not
only allow inequality, we maintain and reinforce what Douglas Massey
calls categorical inequality,[1] in which resources are distributed with attention to characteristics like gender, race, poverty, or sexual orientation,
creating or exacerbating patterns that diminish or deny the potential of
far too many of us.

Much of the public language that is used to support these patterns is drawn from legal discourse, but the law is much more than discourse – it is also coercive. Its power, moreover, goes beyond even the force of the state, for it is a medium of both rhetoric and myth. It tells a story of individuality, reason, objectivity, and symmetry. I assert that some of the ways the judicial system functions make the problem of building a just and inclusive society more difficult through both language and law, discussed here primarily through the lens of race.

In notable decisions, the U.S. Supreme Court approaches racial hierarchy as if it believes it has a duty to defend and vindicate current arrangements, rather than the communities living under the yoke of those arrangements. Deploying an interdependent set of stories, doctrinal devices, and rhetorical techniques, the Court argues that the Constitution provides no solution for the problem of racial hierarchy. This is a break from the Warren and earlier Courts. The more recent Court often tells stories that lie outside of history, decontextualized stories of assimilation and bleaker stories of the undeserving in a fair system. Relevant facts are minimized or deemed insufficient according to shifting evidentiary standards. There is an insistence that injustice be addressed at the individual level, and specific decision makers must be shown to have acted with conscious discriminatory intent toward specific persons. Group-related conditions of the other, whether defined by color, ethnicity, sexual orientation, disability, or poverty – no matter how striking – can only rarely be addressed. Indeed, rather than acknowledging the realities growing out of our nation's history and continuing today, recent Supreme Court decisions have rationalized, if not enshrined, white racial hierarchy behind a thin veil of the language of neutrality and various other legal fictions.

Here I will discuss some of these stories, offering an explanation of how the intent standard supports the white innocence myth and how the Court's insistence on judging only individual actors and on viewing those actors outside the realm of history (or current realities) are also a poor fit with the ongoing race-based harms that continue to plague our nation. For race-based harms that are so widespread and well documented that they simply cannot be fitted into white innocence patterns, the Court may resort to the threat of the slippery slope. This argument suggests that if we address one injustice, other injustices in comparable or related spheres might need to be addressed as well, possibly leading to unending efforts to adapt our institutions to the service of equal justice under law – apparently a nightmare, fool's errand, or both, in the eyes of some of the justices. The Court seems to worry that racial justice will hurt "innocent" whites without even acknowledging how racial injustice has benefited and continues to benefit them. First I discuss some of the cases that employ these devices and strategies and contrast them with some positive steps taken or ideas advanced by the Court. Then I reflect on how the courts view these matters, how we view the courts, and how policy and activism can help.

THE MYTH OF THE INNOCENT WHITE – THE INTENT STANDARD

In *Washington v. Davis,* the 1976 case that established the discriminatory purpose doctrine, the District of Columbia police department was allowed to continue to use a verbal test that African American applicants failed in disproportionate numbers. The Court listed other contexts – juries, schools, voting districts – in which plaintiffs had been required to prove discriminatory intent, though it did not rule out the possibility that plaintiffs might submit claims demonstrating that "the discrimination is very difficult to explain on nonracial grounds."[2] This intent standard feeds and is fed by an ideal of "neutrality," in which individuals live outside of any social, historical, or political context. This decontextualization is one of the rhetorical devices that the courts commonly use to justify the exclusion and subordination of different groups of people. Implicit in this approach is yet another rhetorical device: arguments and language that draw on dominant norms to convey the impression of objective decision-making. At the heart of the intent standard are deeply embedded assumptions about the nature of identity – namely, that all of us are rational individuals whose decisions depend solely, or at least primarily, on individual moral will.[3]

At this time, advocates continue to challenge the intent doctrine with both new evidence from structural analysis and new understandings of the mind and unconscious bias. Both of these approaches substantially undermine this doctrine. Given the current Court's attachment to prevailing institutional arrangements, however, and its barely disguised hostility to the racial other, there is little likelihood that it will soon become responsive to these findings and developing insights. Indeed, in a recent case involving a test meant to be used in making promotions in the New Haven Fire Department, *Ricci v. DeStefano* (2009), the Court ruled against the city, which had discarded results from a test in which no black firefighters had scored high enough to be eligible for promotion. There were questions about the suitability of the test, and the department had a real interest in maintaining the level of diversity it had achieved in its leadership, especially given its history of almost complete exclusion of black firefighters and officers. But the Court held that the city had discriminated against the white firefighters. Justice Ginsburg wrote in dissent:

> In so holding, the Court pretends that "[t]he City rejected the test results solely because the higher scoring candidates were white." That pretension, essential to the Court's disposition, ignores substantial evidence of multiple flaws in the tests New Haven used. The Court similarly fails to acknowledge the better tests used in other cities, which have yielded less racially skewed outcomes.[4]

Access by formerly excluded non-whites is a limiting factor for whites only in a zero-sum scenario, which expansion of opportunity for all could prevent. Yet the Court's current analytical framework functions, as Cedric Merlin Powell notes, "as a rhetorical myth focusing the affirmative action debate not on the victims of systemic racism and caste, but on a generalized class of 'innocents' who are arbitrarily punished."[5] These innocents discovered and protected by the Court for several decades now are overwhelmingly white. This perspective is notable in the 1978 case, *Regents of the University of California v. Bakke,* in which a white medical school applicant successfully challenged a faculty-designed program created to address significant racial disparities. The program had invited "disadvantaged" applicants to include information about special challenges in their applications.[6] The Court did not find that Mr. Bakke was denied admission because of that plan, but Justice Powell did point to the "measure of inequity in forcing innocent persons . . . to bear the burdens of redressing grievances not of their making."[7]

Of course what Justice Powell and others who would use the shield of white innocence must ignore is how whites collectively, if not individually, were and are the beneficiaries of centuries of racial hierarchy and exclusion affecting other innocent persons, even if they did not personally or intentionally cause those harms. The Court's stance is one of deliberate indifference to even recent history, "when affirmative action was white" as Katznelson describes it. To maintain this position, the Court must also turn a blind eye to the legacies of a longtime racial spoils system, structural racialization, and growing evidence of implicit bias that continues to support these systems without any need for conscious intent.

The Court has adopted what Alan Freeman has called the "perpetrator perspective," which sees discrimination in terms of overt acts, and which Freeman distinguishes from the "conditions perspective," the on-the-ground view of persistent and systemic segregation, unemployment, poverty, and stigma.[8]

In doing so, the Court has twisted the Constitution, particularly the Civil War Amendments, beyond recognition. This approach is reflected not only in the Court and the law but also, increasingly, among an anxious white populace trying to hold back a changing world. The intent doctrine, which is not required in the Constitution but was constructed by conservative jurists, has been used for decades now to reassert a view of the Constitution and a public discourse favorable to corporations and hostile to the federal government and marginalized groups. John E. Morrison has observed that the choice to avoid viewing cases in context "reflects a desire to avoid the painful revelations that may be lurking in an examination of either racial history or the current racial disparities in society" and that the Court's race blindness "draws just as much attention to race as does race consciousness."[9]

Thus the color-blind model embraces a series of convenient, racially coded doctrinal myths, featuring the innocent white. This story told by the courts is about protecting white status and disparaging the racial other. Whites are innocent of the country's racial history. In fact, this history no longer seems to exist. Non-whites, meanwhile, are guilty of their status and condition. And the Court with its own racial history has become an advocate for a pre-civil rights, pre-New Deal, states' rights world. The contradiction is that without our history, race would have no meaning. So in spite of the language of color blindness, the unconscious and our structures refuse to abide by this proclaimed ignorance.

Even some of the Court's more progressive justices have used the white innocence language. *United Jewish Organizations of Williamsburgh, Inc. v. Carey* (1977), for example, concerned a challenge to a redistricting plan under the Voting Rights Act (VRA) in Kings County, New York. The county was subject to Section 5 preclearance to ensure that its plans would not have "the purpose and will not have the effect of denying or abridging the right to vote on account of race or color."[10] Under a plan that increased the percentage of non-whites within certain districts without increasing the number of districts with non-white majorities, a Hasidic Jewish community that had been in one district was split between two. The Hasidim challenged the plan, alleging that the voting power of their community had been reduced by changes based solely on race. Their challenge failed because the percentage of majority-white districts in the county conformed to the county-wide percentage of whites. Concurring in the judgment upholding the plan, Justice Brennan recognized that there would be "individuals within those communities who benefited (as whites) from those earlier discriminatory voting patterns."[11] But he nevertheless urged caution with respect to the fact that "the most 'discrete and insular' of whites often will be called upon to bear the immediate, direct costs of benign discrimination."[12]

A few years later, Chief Justice Warren Burger wrote that a "sharing of burdens" by innocent whites is "not impermissible" as long as it is "limited and properly tailored . . . to cure the effects of prior discrimination."[13] The case, *Fullilove v. Klutznick* (1980), concerned a "minority business enterprise" (MBE) provision aimed at procuring minority contractors for at least 10 percent of a 1977 federal public works project, compared to the 1 percent of all federal procurement in fiscal year 1976, when minorities made up 15 to18 percent of the population. The MBE provided outreach, as well as screening to ensure that "unjust participation by minority firms whose access to public contracting opportunities is not impaired by the effects of prior discrimination" was prevented.[14] Recognition of "costs inflated by the present effects of prior disadvantage and discrimination" was to be applied to MBE bids.[15] The program also allowed for the possibility that its target level of participation might not be reachable. Indeed, the chief justice stressed the "relatively light" burden that would be placed on white contractors by the measure, though the Court was far from denying our racial history:[16]

> Congress had before it, among other data, evidence of a long history of marked disparity in the percentage of public contracts awarded to minority business enterprises. This disparity was considered to result not from any lack of capable and qualified minority businesses, but from the existence and maintenance of barriers to competitive access which had their roots in racial and ethnic discrimination, and which continue today, even absent any intentional discrimination or other unlawful conduct.[17]

Thomas Ross has pointed out the way that the more typical story, of the individual innocent white victim of affirmative action, works to counter the fact that whites "generally have benefited from the oppression of people of color, that white people have been advantaged by this oppression in a myriad of obvious and less obvious ways."[18] As Wildman and Davis note however, "[t]he invisible cannot be combated, and as a result, privilege is allowed to perpetuate, regenerate, and re-create itself."[19] Moreover, even when faced with clear evidence of how systems of privilege are working to reinforce racial disparities, the Court turns a (color) blind eye.

THROUGH THE LOOKING GLASS
– DECONTEXTUALIZATION

In 1983, the city of Richmond, Virginia, adopted a plan based on the federal program upheld in *Fullilove* to address the fact that although blacks made up half the population, minority businesses had been awarded less than 1 percent of the city's construction contracts during the preceding five years.[20] Contractors awarded city jobs would be required to make a commitment that 30 percent of their subcontractors would be MBES, though waivers were available if the goals of the program could not be achieved on a particular project. Local contractors' associations, the membership of which was virtually all white, made their opposition known.[21] After experiencing a series of primarily administrative frustrations, the J. A. Croson Company challenged the plan.

In the Supreme Court's 1989 opinion, Justice O'Connor dismissed Richmond's effort, first by pointing out that no evidence of prior discrimination had been presented in hearings related to it, in spite of an earlier case's holding that the Equal Protection Clause required "some showing of prior discrimination by the governmental unit involved."[22] This assertion about a city that was, a century earlier, the capital of the Confederacy, represents at best a stunning example of decontextualization. Justice O'Connor then explained that Richmond had failed to demonstrate a compelling interest in "apportioning public contracting opportunities on the basis of race," apparently referring to the targets for minority inclusion, not its awarding of more than 99 percent of city contracts to whites.

> To accept Richmond's claim that past societal discrimination alone can serve as the basis for rigid racial preferences would be to open the door to competing claims for "remedial relief" for every disadvantaged group. The dream of a Nation of equal citizens in a society where race is irrelevant to personal opportunity and achievement would be lost in a mosaic of shifting preferences based on inherently unmeasurable claims of past wrongs.[23]

In his concurring opinion, Justice Stevens added that the class of white contractors "disadvantaged" by a set-aside for the almost entirely excluded minority contractors "presumably includes ... some [whites] who have never discriminated against anyone on the basis of race."[24]

Justice Scalia's concurrence spins yet another strand of the innocence story. Applying the intent standard, Scalia would require proof of a particular act of discrimination against an individual before any kind of affirmative remedy could be justified.[25] Justice Scalia shows generalized concern, however, for the white "victims" of affirmative action. "Even 'benign' racial quotas have individual victims, whose very real injustice we ignore whenever we deny them enforcement of their right not to be disadvantaged on the basis of race."[26] Again, this solicitude is for the half of the population receiving 99 percent of the contracts.

Justice O'Connor adds a rejection of anti-discrimination measures by governmental entities other than Congress:

> That Congress may identify and redress the effects of society-wide discrimination does not mean that, *a fortiori*, the States and their political subdivisions are free to decide that such remedies are appropriate. Section 1 of the Fourteenth Amendment is an explicit *constraint* on state power, ... The mere recitation of a benign or compensatory purpose for the use of a racial classification would

essentially entitle the States to exercise the full power of Congress under §5 of
the Fourteenth Amendment and insulate any racial classification from judicial
scrutiny under §1.[27]

A little over a decade later, however, the injury to "innocent whites"
in construction contracts did involve a federal program. In *Adarand
Constructors, Inc. v. Pena* (1995), Adarand had submitted the lowest bid,
but Gonzales Construction, which had been certified as disadvantaged,
was awarded the contract.[28] Here Justice O'Connor applied a principle
of "consistency" to conclude that "any individual suffers an injury when
he or she is disadvantaged by the government because of his or her race,
whatever that race may be."[29] This concept of consistency required that
the Court apply strict scrutiny to determine whether the injury to "innocent whites" was justified by a compelling governmental interest. For
Justice O'Connor, racial classifications could satisfy this test only if used
to remedy past illegal discrimination in the particular context of the
challenged policy.[30] Essentially this was a move to ban efforts to ameliorate racial conditions.

Justice Stevens, in dissent, provided a reality check:

> There is no moral or constitutional equivalence between a policy that is
> designed to perpetuate a caste system and one that seeks to eradicate racial
> subordination. Invidious discrimination is an engine of oppression, subjugating
> a disfavored group to enhance or maintain the power of the majority. Remedial
> race based preferences reflect the opposite impulse: a desire to foster equality in
> society. No sensible conception of the Government's constitutional obligation
> to "govern impartially," . . . should ignore this distinction.[31]

Justice Souter's dissent instead emphasized the innocence of the affected
members of the "historically favored race" and pointed to the "temporary nature" of the policies – a hopeful position in a case in which such
efforts are severely curtailed.[32] This was an attempt to appease whites by
casting racial subordination and deeply embedded systems of privilege
as problems that can be solved quickly, so that innocent whites will not
have to give up their "rights" and their privilege for long.

This nation's history has caused whites and African Americans to be
differently situated, and affirmative action programs must treat them differently, if not to the full extent that our history would command, at least
to the extent that equality demands. As Michel Rosenfeld points out,

"[t]he reduction in the prospects of blacks attributable to official racial discrimination has already produced a windfall in the form of increased prospects of success for all the other competitors. . . . In this sense, affirmative action merely restores the equal-opportunity balance."[33] The disadvantaging of African Americans was systematic on the part of both the elites who profited and the many disadvantaged whites who accepted racial superiority in place of cooperation with other working people to improve their common circumstances. This is a difficult realization for many whites, who often have internalized an idea of racism as a harming of non-white people that did not or does not implicate them. This, as Erin E. Byrnes points out, combined with "[t]he failure to acknowledge, the acquiescence in and the reliance upon, the hierarchical status quo enables whites to argue against affirmative action without appearing inconsistent."[34]

"TOO MUCH JUSTICE" – THE SLIPPERY SLOPE

By focusing on individuals – the individual defendant, case, and decision maker – the Court renders invisible the evidence of injury and bias in our society. This pattern is shown in the 1987 case, *McCleskey v. Kemp*, in which the Supreme Court was presented with compelling evidence of the impact of race on capital sentencing.[35] Warren McCleskey was an African American man sentenced to death in Georgia for the murder of a white police officer.[36] In his habeas petition, McCleskey presented a statistical study – the Baldus study – to support his claim that Georgia's capital sentencing policy was being administered in a racially discriminatory manner. The study showed that murder suspects in Georgia were more than four times as likely to receive the death penalty if the victim in the case was white rather than black.[37] Indeed, prosecutors had sought the death penalty in 70 percent of cases with black defendants and white victims and just 15 percent of cases in which both the defendant and the victim were black.[38]

Confronted with an array of such statistics, the Court chose not to address a glaringly greater impact on African Americans or the far lesser concern with cases in which the victims were black. Nor did the Court take up the question of why race mattered so consistently in the decisions of legislators, police, prosecutors, evidence analysts, witnesses, judges, and juries in Georgia's capital sentencing process. The Court chose instead to focus on the requirement of proof of explicit discriminatory intent in the particular case, the standard established in *Washington v. Davis,* for which it found the Baldus study's evidence "clearly insufficient."[39]

The Court also rejected McCleskey's argument that historical evidence demonstrated discriminatory intent on the part of Georgia's legislature in the drafting of the state's capital sentencing laws. The Court acknowledged that the historical background of a legislative decision is one source of proof, but it held that unless this evidence is "reasonably contemporaneous with the challenged decision, it has little probative value."[40] Moreover, even if Georgia's legislature had been aware that its sentencing policies caused racially disparate impacts, proof of the decision makers' awareness of the consequences would not be enough: McCleskey would have to prove that the legislature selected the policy *because of* – not in spite of – its adverse effects on African Americans. Thus even if the Court had accepted the compelling evidence of racial discrimination as accurate, the defendant would have failed to meet the demands of the intent standard.[41]

In dissent, Justice Brennan pointed out that this decontextualization ignores the fact that

> [it has] been scarcely a generation since [the] Court's first decision striking
> down racial segregation, and barely two decades since the legislative prohibition
> of racial discrimination in major domains of national life. These have been
> honorable steps, but we cannot pretend that in three decades we have completely
> escaped the grip of a historical legacy spanning centuries.[42]

Ironically, the Court's majority criticized the Baldus study for "ignoring the realities" of criminal sentencing, and, in particular, the discretion inherent in the process.[43] It accused the study of taking cases with different results "on what are contended to be duplicate facts" and then concluding that differences in the results were based on race alone. According to the Court, these differences could be explained by the individual characteristics of the individual defendants and the facts of the particular capital offense. The Court maintained this conclusion despite the fact that the Baldus study had taken into account dozens of non-racial variables (such as aggravating and mitigating factors, weight of the evidence, defendant's criminal record) and conducted multiple regression analyses.[44] In fact, in response to criticisms and suggestions by the district court, Baldus conducted additional regression analyses, "all of which confirmed, and some of which even strengthened, the study's original conclusions."[45]

At the same time that the Court used the intent standard to deny McCleskey's showing of racial discrimination, it also made contradictory "slippery slope" arguments. This rhetorical technique recognizes the complexity and pervasiveness of privilege, but uses its recognition of the overwhelming nature of the solution as an excuse to turn away from the problem. In fact, the Court has been drumming in the parade of horribles to undermine challenges to white privilege for nearly a century. As far back as 1896, in *Plessy v. Ferguson,* the Court stated that the objective of the Fourteenth Amendment was not "to abolish distinctions based upon color"[46] but to ensure racial equality before the law. That Court noted that laws requiring the separation of whites and non-whites were "generally, if not universally" accepted as valid (a questionable measure of justice for minorities) and had been enacted in "good faith for the promotion of the public good," not for the oppression of a particular class.[47]

Even when the Court finally overruled *Plessy,* in *Brown v. Board of Education* (1954), the same deference to deeply entrenched systems of white privilege shaped and limited the relief granted. "Separate but equal" was no longer equal, but the Court, acknowledging how widely the impact of its decision would be felt, as well as the fact that desegregation would involve "problems of considerable complexity," ordered an "equitable" approach,[48] meaning that in tackling the obstacles to aligning school systems with constitutional principles, only a "prompt and reasonable" start was required.[49] This repeating narrative – recognizing the indices and impact of privilege, then backing away from the full implications – intertwines with the Court's rhetoric of intent and the stories it tells about innocence. It also shows how racial justice, even in that more responsive Supreme Court, was limited by a concern about disturbing the status of whites.

The Court had invoked the slippery slope in *Washington v. Davis,* the case that established the intent requirement. There the Court justified its holding that a "racially-neutral" policy cannot be held invalid merely because it benefits or burdens one race more than another. The

Court explained that if it invalidated a law that was "neutral" in design because it was disproportionately harmful to vulnerable groups, the impact "would be far reaching and would raise serious questions about, and perhaps invalidate, a whole range of tax, welfare, public service, regulatory, and licensing statutes that may be more burdensome to the poor and to the average black than to the more affluent white."[50] The Court even cited one study to the effect that "disproportionate-impact analysis might invalidate 'tests and qualifications for voting, draft deferment, public employment, jury service, and other government-conferred benefits and opportunities . . . ; sales taxes, bail schedules, utility rates, bridge tolls, license fees, and other state-imposed charges.'"[51] Moreover, "minimum wage and usury laws as well as professional licensing requirements would require major modifications in light of the unequal-impact rule."[52]

These arguments – that constitutional principles cannot be brought to bear to end a specific iteration of subordination because doing so would call into question assumptions that run throughout the legal system – suggest how deeply and concretely embedded systems of white privilege really are. In *McCleskey*, the Court had reasoned that recognizing the defendant's claim would open a Pandora's box:

> First, McCleskey's claim, taken to its logical conclusion, throws into serious question the principles that underlie our entire criminal justice system. If we accepted McCleskey's claim that racial bias has impermissibly tainted the capital sentencing decision, we could soon be faced with similar claims as to other types of penalty. . . . The claim that his sentence rests on the irrelevant factor of race easily could be extended to apply to claims based on unexplained discrepancies that correlate to membership in other minority groups, and even to gender.[53]

Justice Brennan, writing in dissent, responded that "[t]aken on its face, such a statement seems to suggest a fear of too much justice."[54]

The Court also recommends that victims of discrimination seek relief elsewhere:

> McCleskey's arguments are best presented to the legislative bodies. It is not the responsibility – or indeed even the right – of this Court to determine the appropriate punishment for particular crimes. It is the legislatures, the elected representatives of the people, that . . . are better qualified to weigh and "evaluate the results of statistical studies in terms of their own local conditions and with a flexibility of approach that is not available to the courts."[55]

At least two state legislatures have responded. Kentucky passed a Racial Justice Act in 1998, and North Carolina followed in 2009.[56] Both states' laws give those facing a death sentence the right to present statistical or other evidence that race was a significant factor in decisions to seek or impose the death penalty. If a defendant's proof is sufficient, the court will order that a death sentence not be sought in the case. The North Carolina law also applied retroactively: a successful challenge meant that a death sentence already imposed would be vacated and the defendant resentenced to life imprisonment without the possibility of parole. Nearly all of the more than 150 inmates on North Carolina's death row have filed such appeals.

Just before the twenty-fifth anniversary of the *McCleskey* decision, a superior court judge in the first appeal to come to trial under North Carolina's law found that race was a significant factor in jury selection.[57] The judge based his ruling largely on a jury study finding that prosecutors exercised peremptory challenges against black potential jurors in capital cases in North Carolina at more than twice the rate that they used them against whites.[58] The pattern was even stronger in the particular county and case under review. The judge found that prosecutors also "intentionally discriminated" in jury selection and made "irrational" and "misleading" statements trying to prove otherwise.[59] After taking nonracial factors into account, the study had found that defendants charged in murders involving white victims were far more likely to receive the death penalty than defendants in cases involving black victims.[60]

The chief problems, of course, with legislative remedies for racial bias are that they require the support of a white majority and limit the role of the court in protecting discrete and insular minorities. In North Carolina, a new Republican majority quickly introduced a bill to "reform" the Racial Justice Act, "to be Consistent With The United States Supreme Court's Ruling in *McCleskey v. Kemp.*"[61] The bill ignored the *McCleskey* Court's urging that state legislatures are better qualified to respond to the implications of statistical studies and address criminal law accordingly, focusing instead on the Court's demand for proof of either discriminatory intent or discriminatory purpose in an individual defendant's case. That gutting of the Racial Justice Act became law after passing over the governor's veto in July 2012.[62]

As enacted, North Carolina's law accepted statistical evidence that race was a factor with respect to defendants, victims, or jury selection, as was found in the first case tried under the Act.[63] This legislation and the outcome in this case are important milestones in pushing back against two arguments raised in *McCleskey:* the overwhelming nature of the changes needed to achieve justice with respect to race and other group-based disparate results and the individualistic and nearly impossible to meet intent requirement.

TAKING CONTEXT INTO ACCOUNT – SOME
POSITIVE STEPS BY THE COURTS

The Supreme Court has not entirely shied away from exposing the ways in which systems of privilege create racial disparities. Some of the clearest instances of this occur when the Court acknowledges and discusses the disestablishment of white supremacy or rejects acontextual claims by individuals in support of broader solutions that foster the common good. In *Swann v. Charlotte-Mecklenberg Board of Education* (1971), for example, Chief Justice Burger, delivering the opinion of the Court, recognized the complex interaction between continuing racial imbalances in schools and changing residential patterns:

> The construction of new schools and the closing of old ones are two of the most important functions of local school authorities and also two of the most complex. They must decide questions of location and capacity in light of population growth, finances, land values, site availability, through an almost endless list of factors to be considered. The result of this will be a decision which, when combined with one technique or another of student assignment, will determine the racial composition of the student body in each school in the system. Over the long run, the consequences of the choices will be far reaching. People gravitate toward school facilities, just as schools are located in response to the needs of people. The location of schools may thus influence the patterns of residential development of a metropolitan area and have important impact on composition of inner-city neighborhoods.[64]

This recognition of how structural factors interact allowed the Court to imagine broad remedies for racial disparities. The Chief Justice also acknowledged the enormity of the problem of desegregation but reiterated that the objective remained to eliminate from public schools all vestiges of state-imposed segregation. The acknowledgment that residential and other seemingly neutral societal patterns were affected by the remnants of past school segregation and could exacerbate ongoing violations allowed the Court in *Swann* to approve a remedy – the use of racial-balance goals – that directly addressed these patterns by taking difference into account.

During the 1980s and 1990s, the Court's recognition of constitutional solutions, and its understanding of the complexity and long-term nature of entrenched patterns of educational and residential segregation was eclipsed. "Choice" became the mantra, both to explain the problem of segregation and to "solve" it. By 1992, Justice Kennedy wrote for the Court in *Freeman v. Pitts,* affirming a district court's decision to relinquish oversight of student assignments in DeKalb County, Georgia, because the racial imbalance in the schools was the "inevitable" result of housing choices, not a vestige of the system's legally segregated past.[65] *Freeman* also established that school districts formerly segregated by law could be released from court-ordered desegregation plans on a piecemeal basis – transportation one year, faculty the next, and so on. The justice invoked the slippery slope in his argument against continued oversight:

> It is beyond the authority and beyond the practical ability of the federal courts to try to counteract these kinds of continuous and massive demographic shifts. To attempt such results would require ongoing and never-ending supervision by the courts of school districts simply because they were once de jure segregated. Residential housing choices, and their attendant effects on the racial composition of schools, present an ever-changing pattern, one difficult to address through judicial remedies.[66]

In the new millennium, however, both Justice O'Connor and Justice Kennedy seemed more open to addressing racial hierarchy and its troubling manifestations. In 2003, for example, Justice O'Connor wrote for the Court in *Grutter v. Bollinger,* upholding a public law school's policy of considering race as one of many factors in admissions decisions. The justice explained that "in order to cultivate a set of leaders with legitimacy in the eyes of the citizenry, it is necessary that the path to leadership be visibly open to talented and qualified individuals of every race and ethnicity."[67]

In his concurrence in *Parents Involved in Community Schools,* Justice Kennedy also seemed more hopeful about broad-based remedies for school segregation than he had been in *Freeman* and far less willing to give up on the promise of *Brown:*

> The plurality opinion is too dismissive of the legitimate interest government
> has in ensuring all people have equal opportunity regardless of their race. The
> plurality's postulate that "[t]he way to stop discrimination on the basis of race is
> to stop discriminating on the basis of race, " . . . is not sufficient to decide these
> cases. Fifty years of experience since *Brown v. Board of Education* . . . should teach
> us that the problem before us defies so easy a solution. School districts can seek
> to reach *Brown* 's objective of equal educational opportunity. . . . To the extent
> the plurality opinion suggests the Constitution mandates that state and local
> school authorities must accept the status quo of racial isolation in schools, it is,
> in my view, profoundly mistaken.[68]

The justice also expresses strong support for these and other districts still struggling to reach "*Brown* 's objective of equal educational opportunity":

> If school authorities are concerned that the student-body compositions of
> certain schools interfere with the objective of offering an equal educational op-
> portunity to all of their students, they are free to devise race-conscious measures
> to address the problem in a general way and without treating each student in
> different fashion solely on the basis of a systematic, individual typing by race.
>   School boards may pursue the goal of bringing together students of diverse
> backgrounds and races through other means, including strategic site selection
> of new schools; drawing attendance zones with general recognition of the
> demographics of neighborhoods; allocating resources for special programs;
> recruiting students and faculty in a targeted fashion; and tracking enrollments,
> performance, and other statistics by race. These mechanisms are race conscious
> but do not lead to different treatment based on a classification that tells each
> student he or she is to be defined by race.[69]

Here the justice seems closer to the *Swann* Court than to his opinion in *Freeman.* But Justice Roberts wrote the plurality opinion in *Parents Involved,* insisting that the harm to be avoided was racial classification, not segregation. Consistent with the doctrine of color blindness, Rob-erts asserted that segregation without proven government action is *not* segregation and cannot be acted on by the Court. Overriding the time-honored conservative battle cry of "local control" and decades of earlier jurisprudence, the plurality sought to strictly limit the use of race in two school districts' voluntary plans to create and maintain diverse public schools. Justice Kennedy joined the plurality even though he found that there was a compelling government interest in overcoming racial isolation, regardless of whether there is proof of government involvement in its creation.

Unfortunately, Justice Kennedy then found that the means to achieve this compelling interest were not narrowly tailored enough in implementation and that therefore the plans violated the Constitution. Advocates will and must continue to try to meet the evolving hurdles, but the Court's hostility to racial justice should not be underestimated. Through self-referencing the Court will continue to adopt more and more difficult rules if the end goal of protecting the current racial status is threatened. Advocates must also pay closer attention to who is on the Court and to the role the Court could play in a true pluralistic democracy but fails to play today.

At times the Court has acknowledged and discussed the need to transform structures in order to alter the current distribution of social assets, including power, as part of the struggle to overcome racial hierarchy. Justice Brennan, for example, in *Local 28 of the Sheet Metal Workers' International Ass'n v. EEOC* (1986), acknowledged the systemic nature of privilege and the need for a far-reaching remedy: "The purpose of affirmative action is not to make identified victims whole, but rather to dismantle prior patterns of employment discrimination and to prevent discrimination in the future. Such relief is provided to the class as a whole rather than to individual members."[70]

Some understanding of the systemic history and contemporary function of privilege is also conveyed in the 1987 case *Johnson v. Transportation Agency,* in which Justice Stevens, writing in concurrence, quotes Kathleen M. Sullivan's "Sins of Discrimination" (discussing *Wygant v. Jackson Board of Education*):

> Public and private employers might choose to implement affirmative action for many reasons other than to purge their own past sins of discrimination. The Jackson school board, for example, said it had done so in part to improve the quality of education in Jackson – whether by improving black students' performance or by dispelling for black and white students alike any idea that

white supremacy governs our social institutions. Other employers might advance different forward-looking reasons for affirmative action: improving their services to black constituencies, averting racial tension over the allocation of jobs in a community, or increasing the diversity of a work force, to name but a few examples. Or they might adopt affirmative action simply to eliminate from their operations all de facto embodiment of a system of racial caste. All of these reasons aspire to a racially integrated future, but none reduces to "racial balancing for its own sake."[71]

In some cases, addressing white supremacy is not just mentioned in passing but is instead named as the source of problems. In *Adarand,* for example, Justice Ginsburg's dissenting opinion cites *Loving v. Virginia,* which struck down state bans on interracial marriage, as indicative of the fact that "the Constitution and this Court would abide no measure 'designed to maintain White Supremacy.'"[72] And a 1982 case, *NAACP v. Claiborne Hardware, Co.,* had concerned a boycott following a Mississippi community's rejection of the local NAACP's petition, "Demands for Racial Justice":

> Objectives of Negro citizens of Port Gibson and Claiborne County are, simply put, to have equality of opportunity, in every aspect of life, and to end the white supremacy which has pervaded community life. This implies many long-range objectives such as participation in decision-making at every level of community, civic, business and political affairs.[73]

The boycott was associated with some violence, as well as lost income, for which one of the targeted businesses sued the NAACP. Justice Stevens, writing for the Court, put the protest and its dangers in perspective:

> A massive and prolonged effort to change the social, political, and economic structure of a local environment cannot be characterized as a violent conspiracy simply by reference to the ephemeral consequences of relatively few violent acts.... A court must be wary of a claim that the true color of a forest is better revealed by reptiles hidden in the weeds than by the foliage of countless free-standing trees.[74]

Much recent jurisprudence, as we have seen, has represented a shift away from recognizing the structures that maintain white privilege and the measures needed to change them. Indeed, the Court has narrowed its view such that it sees little more than individual harms perpetrated by individual actors. At this point, even theorists are unclear about the type of remedies the Court could most meaningfully advance, but a deeper, more meaningful understanding of privilege and a stronger, more inclusive vision of justice will both be required if we are to achieve the necessary changes in jurisprudence.

ACCESS AND PARTICIPATION IN DEMOCRATIC SOCIETIES

Because our courts and supporting institutions are a social system, interpersonal and structural biases are at play in lawmaking, court procedures, and decisions, even when the legal system is unwilling or unable to acknowledge them. Prominent members of the current judiciary explicitly reject any recognition of their own perspectives, instead preferring to see themselves as umpires who call the plays strictly on the basis of precedent.[75] There are patterns, however, in judges' decisions and in legal discourse, and precedents represent habits or predispositions. Even so, the underlying assumptions of these previous cases are often taken as truth, commanding that the precedent be followed – if, that is, it supports the judge's "objective" view.

If context changes, however, a decision or legal standard must be evaluated for change as well. Attention to context, or situatedness, is a fundamental requirement of any genuine progress toward justice. The courts' "objective" view of policies and laws must incorporate reference to actual conditions; otherwise, it merely reinforces the status quo, using blinders to vindicate the results of the racialized past that most Americans readily repudiate, at least in theory.

Tensions arise when opportunity, often seen as a well-functioning system based on "merit," needs to expand beyond its current boundaries. Affirmative action policies in the United States have had their successes, and there are lines of thought that carry the understandings from those successes forward today, as in Justice O'Connor's opinion for the Court in the Michigan law school case, *Grutter v. Bollinger*. Evidence of high levels of discrimination based solely on race, however, indicates that concrete ways of pursuing affirmative policies in furtherance of diversity and access continue to be needed. These policies simply must include empirical elements, so that they can be adjusted for maximum effectiveness across categorical differences, in order to avoid the failures of past policies.

Group-Based Claims

Individual merit was not at issue when, as the Court in *Dred Scott v. Sandford* (1857) described it, "a perpetual and impassable barrier was intended to be erected between the white race and the one which they had reduced to slavery, and governed as subjects with absolute and despotic power."[76] Yet for decades now – at least since 1978's *Regents of the University of California v. Bakke* – the focus has been almost entirely on the individual (white) "victim" of group-based claims in affirmative action cases. The exception to this is in the voting rights context, in which the power of racial groups is acknowledged, even when, as in *United Jewish Organizations of Williamsburgh, Inc. v. Carey,* a cultural or religious concern is ignored. Compare this with *McCleskey,* in which strong evidence of systemic racial discrimination was dismissed for lack of proof of an individual perpetrator of racial discrimination. My suggestion here is that the courts' current insistence on ignoring context and racial disparities springs from the realization (acknowledged in the slippery slope defense) that recognition of these disparities and their causes would have serious implications not only for our justice system but also for our nation.

When we think about our goals as a society and address access in terms of situatedness, we bring affirmative action back into a framework of targeted universalism, in which the search is for participation, not perpetrators. Current limitations on affirmative action make group-based claims difficult, particularly through the use of the intent requirement established in *Washington v. Davis.* Title VI of the 1964 Civil Rights Act, for example, is intended to ensure that recipients of federal funds do not engage in racial discrimination. The Court has recognized an implied right of action under Section 601 of Title VI for individuals who were excluded "on the ground of race, color, or national origin," though it has also determined that 601 is protective only when intentional discrimination can be proved.[77] Section 602, however, had been available for situations in which federal agency regulations produced racially disparate impacts, regardless of intent, and plaintiffs had successfully challenged such impacts in a number of spheres, from educational to environmental.[78]

In *Alexander v. Sandoval* (2001), however, the Court moved to impose a requirement of proof of intentional discrimination in such claims, while also declining to find an implied right of action for individuals.[79] Derek Black has pointed out that federal agencies may continue to enact and enforce regulations under section 602 to prohibit neutral policies resulting in racially disparate impacts.[80] Black has also suggested, per analogies to recognized causes of action under Title IX (the 1972 law addressing gender discrimination) that deliberate indifference to certain disparate impacts should suffice as a form of intentional discrimination sufficient to bring a cause of action in the Title VI context.[81]

Black has also gone one step further by advocating the use of a modified deliberate indifference standard as a replacement for the intent standard in equal protection cases.[82] Under this standard, a challenged policy's constitutionality would be determined as follows: First, a court would determine whether a governmental actor "was or should have been aware of the racial harm or impacts that its actions caused or the benefits/opportunities denied" and whether other less harmful alternatives were available. If so, the court would inquire as to why those alternatives were not implemented. Finally, the court would consider what, if any, interests the governmental actor had in permitting the harm. This standard would place more responsibility on governmental actors to be alert to and intervene in policies or programs in which racially disparate impacts resulted. It would also require serious consideration of situatedness, rather than a highly theoretical investigation of "intent."[83]

The focus on effects and situatedness in Black's test encourages an assessment of what works and what a best effort would be in a given context: how a decision between an elevator and an escalator (or among various designs for an escalator) looks with respect to people using wheelchairs, for example. It shares the democratic and inclusive stance of targeted universalism, structuring governmental accountability and promoting assessment of outcomes and realities. And rather than imposing stringent levels of proof of bad motives by "perpetrators," it evaluates conditions in context, to interrupt racialization with a problem-solving approach to injustice and inequality.

In contrast, the current Court's focus on individuals ("victims" or perpetrators) in affirmative action cases, combined with its shutting down of paths to group-based remedies, increases the sense of personal threat experienced by whites while doing far too little to address structural problems. Michelle Alexander points out that mass incarceration, failing schools, disproportionately high joblessness, and residential segregation may continue unabated under the individualized approach to affirmative action. In this sense, a push for targeted universal policies, while not "taking" anything from any "innocent" individual, could allow more rapid and effective remedies for widespread social problems and for the underlying problem of structural racism. Admittedly, this requires a government of, for, and by the people that seeks to aid the populace and further the development of true democracy. Thus, interests opposing such developments can be counted upon to counter such moves.

Even within our current arrangements, however, court decisions that have shown a willingness to trace causation and context yield reason for hope. In this effort, it is critical to look not only at what a given program or decision purports to do but also at its results. Congress has been willing to do this in the context of the Voting Rights Act (v r a), in which it has rejected race-blind "universal" policies if they reduce minority voting. The v r a is also an important model in its implementation of the preclearance program, which both provides a way to stay a step ahead of new strategies for reducing minority votes and employs a quantitative approach in evaluating results.[84]

Addressing the Legacy of Racial Caste

The experiences of other societies may shed light on ways of dealing with the problem of removing or ameliorating the effects of race, caste, and gender discrimination.[85] Concerted efforts have followed on the heels of independence or demands for political power in some other nations, and the decisions seem to reflect a recognition of the toll that poverty and exclusion take on societies as a whole, as well as on individuals. In India, for example, such programs were instituted after the constitutional convention following independence. They started with a quota system in which members of the former "untouchable" caste, as well as some geographically and culturally isolated groups, received government-controlled educational and employment opportunities in proportion to their percentage of the population. State governments developed similar programs, referred to as "reservations." The programs were expanded later to include a 27 percent reservation for the approximately 50 percent of the population historically discriminated against by caste who still experienced high levels of need. This was then adapted to target the most economically needy within each of three categories of "backward classes."[86] In Malaysia, after an uprising in 1969, the government developed plans to end poverty and change employment patterns such that race was no longer a marker of social or professional status. Under this program, poverty among Malays dropped from 74 percent at the start to 6 percent in 1994, and the majority Malay population now makes up a majority of the students in the nation's public universities.[87]

These programs take the broader view of the role of society – to ensure, to the extent possible, the well-being of its members, and to share cultural resources in ways that allow as broad a part of the population as possible to develop its gifts and contribute to the whole. In the United States, by contrast, "reservations" and the use of specific numbers reflective of the population in creating goals and measuring outcomes have been banned, as in *Bakke*; struck down as discriminatory overreaching, as in *Croson*; or limited, as in the voluntary efforts by school districts in *Parents Involved*.

I have already attempted to describe some of the constraints on participation rights in our society, including the priority placed on protecting white prerogative. Contrary to the fearful slippery slope arguments we have heard, however, measuring the impact of racial discrimination in various contexts can help increase awareness of the need for race-conscious remedies and address the complacency of many whites as to their status, perhaps helping them to recognize the grievous problems our society must address. In employment context, for example, Devah Pager found that with personable college students with equal credentials representing all "applicants," white applicants without criminal records were more than twice as likely to be called back as were blacks (whites, 34 percent; blacks, 14 percent). But Pager's studies have also shown that testers portraying white job applicants *with* felony convictions and a record of incarceration receive more callbacks (17 percent) than testers representing African American applicants *without* criminal records (14 percent). Testers portraying black felons received callbacks at a rate of 5 percent of the applications they submitted.[88] Further studies by Pager also tracked racially disparate upward and downward steering, in terms of job categories, of potential employees.[89]

Pager's disturbing evidence indicates that prospective employers view white male felons more favorably than they do black males who have no criminal record. Compounding that problem is the fact that black males are far more likely, proportionately, to become involved in the justice system, or to become felons. In 2011 in Dane County, Wisconsin, for example, nearly 50 percent of the black men twenty-four to twenty-nine years of age were in the system – prison, jail, or other state supervision – compared with 3 percent of white men that age.[90] Looked at beside Pager's data from the employment context, these numbers indicate the extent to which race affects assumptions about young men's criminality or "innocence" and the devastating results those assumptions have for men of color.

In *The New Jim Crow: Mass Incarceration in the Age of Colorblindness*, Michelle Alexander gives a detailed and nuanced explanation of the politics behind this trend, including the launching of the "war on drugs" in the 1980s, the face of which was the black addict/dealer; targeted/biased law enforcement; lack of access to timely and adequate legal representation; lack of good jobs and adequate income; and high dropout rates exacerbated by harsh and racially disproportionate school discipline policies. These problems suggest several points of departure: Alexander recommends, among other changes, withdrawing federal grant money that escalates drug enforcement activity, which disproportionately targets non-whites; addressing racial profiling in law enforcement; rescinding mandatory drug sentences; and making drug treatment programs accessible to all who need them.[91]

Alexander also advocates funding public defender offices at the same levels as prosecutors, mandating data collection for police and prosecutors, and developing racial impact statements to increase awareness of what the current prison explosion is costing us in human and societal terms. One of those costs is to democracy itself: Bryan Stevenson of the Equal Justice Initiative speaks of the relationship between criminal justice and the right to vote, noting that 34 percent of African American men in his state of Alabama have been permanently disenfranchised by criminal records that include a felony.[92] Disenfranchisement of African Americans has a long history in our country, even after the Fifteenth Amendment was passed, and consistently, the most severe disenfranchisement occurs where the non-white population is the highest. These practices not only make these targeted populations marginal citizens, they also implicate the legitimacy of our democracy.

We are exceptional among mature democracies in the extreme rate of incarceration, as well as in how we treat the formally incarcerated. As Michelle Alexander notes, the current system of incarceration is a harsh and tragic form of social control and another form of Jim Crow. This is all the more clear when it is realized that although the vote is denied to felons and ex-felons, both during incarceration and upon release, these same citizens continue to count to enhance their community's representation in the Electoral College. This is far too similar to the three-fifths compromise that became part of the Constitution in order to enhance the power of slave-holding states while denying enslaved and often free blacks the vote. When one adds the aggressive vote suppression drive now taking place through Voter ID laws, it is clear that we are describing a system of racialized exclusion and marginalization with Court supervision and approval.

Stevenson also points to the fact that "the United States is the only country in the world where we sentence thirteen year-old children to die in prison."[93] In *The School-to-Prison Pipeline,* Catherine Kim, Daniel Losen, and Damon Hewitt suggest that the problems for these children and for young men like those in Dane County start early, with dramatic racial disparities in school disciplinary actions. Moreover, Kim, Losen, and Hewitt report that nationwide, 2.2 million juveniles are arrested each year and 400,000 enter the juvenile detention system.[94] Each night, these authors tell us, 100,000 children are confined in some type of detention facility in our fifty states.[95] In light of the stated ideals of this country and its tragic history with regard to race, not to mention the increasing encroachment of for-profit jails, this is a situation that must be challenged on many levels.

Indeed what we are discussing here moves beyond a narrow or technical understanding of the law. The extreme practices of stop and frisk in New York City demonstrate the severity of the problem: in 2011, more young black men between the ages of 18 and 24 were stopped (168,126) than there were in the city's population (158,406). Only a small number of these stops produced evidence of unlawful activity.[96] The fear of the racial other and the "law and order" advocated by Presidents Nixon and Reagan continue to pick up steam even as the crime rate falls. What we are witnessing is the containment and control of the "non-innocent" other. After all, how could they be innocent or fully American when they are not white?

Overcoming Stereotypes and Unconscious Racism

Improving understanding of unconscious factors in decision-making can increase access to justice throughout our social arrangements and institutions, but it will take a concerted effort across major spheres from health care and housing to education and employment. Attorneys and advocates have begun to identify practices that can help us make decisions that support our common values – freedom, equality, and human dignity. Unconscious racial bias can otherwise affect judgment in areas from hiring, to the likelihood of being stopped and searched, to capital punishment. Justice Scalia addressed this issue in a memo written prior to the opinion in *McCleskey v. Kemp*:

> . . . I do not share the view, implicit in the opinion, that an effect of racial factors upon sentencing, if it could only be shown by sufficiently strong statistical evidence, would require reversal. Since it is my view that the unconscious operation of irrational sympathies and antipathies, including racial, upon jury decisions and (hence) prosecutorial decisions is real, acknowledged in the decisions of this court, and ineradicable, I cannot honestly say that all I need is more proof.[97]

Justice Scalia's acknowledgment of unconscious racism is welcome; his response, that it is "ineradicable," while it reflects our understanding of some of the developmental processes of the brain, is far from true in terms of what we must demand from our courts and ourselves. Unaddressed, this bias can and does corrupt the work of teachers, employers, lenders, and people at all levels of the criminal justice system. But even if we can convince a majority of the Court that unconscious bias is real and consequential, it does not follow that this would cause the Court to believe that such bias rises to the level of a constitutional violation. The Court has already told us that injury – and certainly injury to the less favored – is not enough to trigger its concern. Indeed, it is this lack of concern that must be understood as hostility and indifference of the Court toward the larger society and the "undeserving."

Jody Armour and others have tackled the work of developing strategies to address bias and unconscious factors in ways that can allow decision makers to shift their responses to race from the unconscious to conscious levels, where they are more able and likely to conform to their best ideas about the proper role of race.[98] Armour draws a distinction, for example, between "racial references that subvert the rationality of the fact-finding process and racial references that actually enhance the rationality and fairness of the fact-finding process," a distinction too often lost on the courts.[99]

In weighing evidence and evaluating circumstances, jurors and justices struggle with their own perceptions amid the beliefs and racial stereotypes that permeate our media and shape so much of our daily lives. The Court has long recognized the role of the media and the importance of who controls its various outlets. In *Metro Broadcasting, Inc. v. FCC* (1990), for example, the Court upheld policies intended to address the dramatic underrepresentation of minorities among owners of media.[100] A federal program used minority ownership as a "plus factor" in proceedings for new broadcasting licenses and considered both racial imbalances and their deeper impacts. Even without the presence of a bad actor with discriminatory intent, the Court recognized that a race-conscious policy was necessary to counter structural barriers to the important societal goal of increasing diversity on the airwaves. Justice O'Connor dissented, writing that "[s]uch policies may embody stereotypes that treat individuals as the product of their race."[101]

The ruling in *Metro Broadcasting* was essentially overturned by *Adarand*, discussed above. But stereotypes much harder to fight than those that troubled Justice O'Connor are heavily featured on broadcast news. In one 2011 study, more African Americans were shown on the news as felons than were even arrested for felonies; stories about violent crime were likely to star African Americans, but as perpetrators rather than victims; and African American experts, achievers, solvers of problems,

and just everyday citizens were notably underrepresented.[102] This kind
of skewing of reality affects policy as well as daily life for all Americans,
not just black Americans.[103] Media in all forms affect racial perceptions
and arrangements to a greater extent than we may realize. Much of what
we see or think we see in the public commons is influenced by what we
absorb from the airwaves; indeed, to some extent, the airwaves have
become the public commons. Increasingly, new media seem to offer the
hope of strengthening our connections to one another for both political
action and for accomplishing shared goals. Yet in some important ways,
much of this commons is in fact corporate, not truly public, space.

Indeed, today we face two common enemies that challenge us at every turn: dramatic economic inequality and increasing corporate control
of our society. Previous chapters included descriptions of the ways in
which citizenship and belonging were stripped away from those in the
black racial caste soon after the Civil War. We didn't talk much about
who *was* granted citizenship rights under the post-war amendments:
corporations. Corporations have been deemed "persons" since the *Santa
Clara County v. Southern Pacific Railroad Company* decision of 1886. But
these entities gained far greater rights in the 2010 case, *Citizens United v.
Federal Election Commission,*[104] in which the Supreme Court insisted that
it was not for the government to decide whether unrestricted expendi-
tures in the context of elections would distort perceptions or opinions.
The Court's action – equating such spending with the political speech
of real citizens – thereby handed over vast power to narrow minority
interests whose survival is based on an insatiable hunt for profits.

When Justice O'Connor wrote for the majority in 2003 in *Grutter,*
she and the Court recognized the value of considering race for the purpose of ensuring participation. She differentiated between stigmatizing
individuals on the basis of race and turning a blind eye to current racial
realities, pointing out that "[j]ust as growing up in a particular region
or having particular professional experiences is likely to affect an individual's views, so too is one's own, unique experience of being a racial
minority in a society, like our own, in which race unfortunately still matters."[105] Perhaps most memorably, the justice affirmed the importance to
a democratic society of deliberate inclusiveness: "Effective participation
by members of all racial and ethnic groups in the civic life of our Nation

is essential if the dream of one Nation, indivisible, is to be realized."[106] The courts have an important role in that work.

In a number of recent cases, however, the Court has extended its support for the status quo, rather than for racial justice and inclusion. The Court has raised the specter of further extension of this line of thinking in recent cases concerning voting and employment, and, as this book goes to press, the Court has agreed to review another challenge to affirmative action in higher education. There are more than a few other troubling signs that the Court intends to pursue these attacks on even limited efforts toward the expansion of opportunity and democracy. It doesn't take a lawyer or constitutional scholar to realize that the Court's hostility to racial justice and inclusion, and its defense of white innocence, is exceeded only by its solicitousness in expanding the rights of corporations, as in the *Citizens United* case. These responses come out of a shared history and ideology, that, if not recognized and confronted, will not only severely undermine racial justice but also ensure that the real winner will be not the "innocent" white but rather an increasingly remote class of people who seem to view the world as a field for exploitation and whose commitment is to profit over people.

PART THREE

The Racialized Self

SIX

Dreaming of a Self beyond Whiteness and Isolation

We are all androgynous, not only because we are all born of a woman impregnated by the seed of a man but because each of us, helplessly and forever, contains the other – male in female, female in male, white in black and black in white. We are a part of each other. Many of my countrymen appear to find this fact exceedingly inconvenient and even unfair, and so very often do I. But none of us can do anything about it.

James Baldwin, "Here Be Dragons"

What men believe to be true is true in its consequences.

Alfred North Whitehead, in David R. Loy, The World Is Made of Stories

Some years ago, I conducted an exercise in a class on the history and nature of the self. Most of the students in the class were white, and most were law students. After reading some neo-Jungian articles about dreams, and dreams in relation to identity, I asked the class how many of them had ever dreamt that they were something non-human: an animal perhaps, or something inanimate. The vast majority of the class affirmed that they had. In their dreams, they had been foxes, spirits, and clouds. Then I asked them how many of them had ever dreamt that they were someone of a different race. Only a couple of students raised their hands. The number who had dreamed about being of a different gender or sexual orientation was only slightly higher.

In some ways, the discussion following this exercise was as interesting as the initial responses. For many of the students, the results were unremarkable; after all, why would they dream they were of a different race or gender? It was only after some prodding that they began to share my sense of amazement. Here we were in a class in which many of the students would identify themselves as liberal or progressive, yet in their dreams, they were more likely to imagine themselves as animals than as people of different races or genders. It was easier for a white man to dream he was a cloud than to dream he was a black woman.

Dreams allow us unrestrained adventures, costless experiments, and some of our most uninhibited states. In them, we have license to experience superhuman powers or ignore sexual taboos. Social constraints and reality have little grip on our dream worlds. Yet our classroom discussion indicated that for many, racial boundaries remain largely intact, even in this realm. How is it that such a line is drawn and policed, even in our sleep, and what does this mean for our waking consciousness?

We returned to this theme many times throughout the course. I encouraged and challenged the students to imagine themselves across these racial, gender, and sexual orientation boundaries in their dreams. Before the semester had ended, virtually all of the students had done just that. They had imagined themselves as the other, and they had begun to question how these boundaries were erected, maintained, and given meaning.

Andrew Hacker conducted a similar experiment with white students. He asked them how much money they would need to be paid to switch their race to black. Even as the imagined amount of money increased, there were very few takers.[1] In a different setting, however, many of these same students might claim that race does not exist or matter. In a moment of intellectual clarity, many would insist that race, and therefore racial boundaries, are not real, but instead are socially constructed, as discussed in previous chapters. Yet even with the license to imagine themselves as anyone and anything, crossing this apparent color line remains unimaginable, whether in dreams or for a price.

BOUNDARIES AND BORDERS

Looking at boundaries and borders in a racial context, we have noticed that these boundaries are collectively and socially constructed. It takes a great deal of work to establish them and a great deal of work to keep them intact. Constant challenges and contestation occur around these boundaries: Do they even exist, and if so, how are they drawn? Who belongs inside or out? What work do the boundaries do? Much of the protestation is not about the boundaries themselves, but about which people should be inside or outside of them. Some have suggested that the white border needs to be made more porous so that more people are allowed to pass as white.[2] Others have asserted that a racially white border does not speak to their life experience and is therefore not pertinent to them. Still others want the border to be a project of self-selection, with no public or social input. None of these perspectives closely examines what the white boundary is and what it does. While it is true that boundary issues are in a continual state of flux, whiteness remains consistent in its valuation. As Derrick Bell reminds us, for all the slipperiness involved in the signification of these boundaries, a stable racial hierarchy continues to exist, with whiteness on top and blackness at the bottom.[3]

In examining racial boundaries, it is useful to situate them in the context of boundaries more generally. Boundaries are designed to keep something in, or out, or both. There must be some difference between what is inside and what is outside, with a different valuation given to each. If there is no differentiation, or if the differentiation is too weak, the boundaries become meaningless. Boundaries and borders are not simply markers between equal spaces. They are put in place for the benefit of one group in opposition to another.[4] Crossing from inside to out and from outside to in will have different meanings and require different energy. If what is valued most is inside, there will be much greater interest in getting in, as well as much greater interest in keeping out those who are designated as not belonging. In addition, it is not just the direction of movement that is affected by the nature of boundaries, but also who is doing the traveling. One has only to think about racial, ethnic, and now religious profiling at national borders to understand how these boundaries are contained within and inscribed on individual human bodies.

Boundaries take on the meanings we give them and the social power we ascribe to them. Even a natural boundary such as a mountain may have meaning as a border in one society or era, but no such meaning in another. When traveling in Detroit, for example, there is little to tell an observer that she has left Detroit and is now in Grosse Pointe. Of course, there are visual differences in the constructed environment, but this is not the result of anything natural. While such an insight may seem obvious, it is often lost on the courts. Richard Thompson Ford aptly demonstrated that courts think of jurisdiction and municipal space as completely natural and transparent on some occasions, and as completely political and opaque on others.[5] These wavering views about boundaries make it difficult for courts to acknowledge the racial work that boundaries are doing and all but impossible for them to disturb these seemingly natural arrangements. The need to constantly police the borders, however, strongly suggests that boundaries are not natural or neutral. Moreover, the greater the inequality between borders, the greater the pressure for migration in one direction, and the greater the need for protection in the other. In other words, the greater the desire for movement on one side, the greater the fear on the other.

The nation-state offers a strong illustration of the concept of boundaries. Our public conversations are full of references to national identity, and by extension, national boundaries. Part of this discourse is also about the invasion of the alien other. Anthony Marx and Michel Laguerre remind us that nation-making is complicated, contradictory, and inherently racial.[6] Membership in a nation-state seldom coincides with the demarcation of the territory, although the identification of territory is an important part of the process. What is being sorted in the making of a nation-state is not just the question of who is in a physical space, but also who is in the psychic space, in the imagined community of that space. It is not just space that is being bounded; both space and being are racialized in this process. Some space becomes white space that requires protection and regulation, and some becomes non-white space that requires containment and regulation. Both spaces exist inside and outside of national boundaries.[7] It is not enough to be in the physical space to be part of the imagined community; one also has to be able to assert that one is part of the "racial state of being" to claim eligibility for membership in white space.

In the context of whiteness and race, then, the primary function of boundaries is to create racial identities and to regulate and sort these identities in racialized space. For example, we can see that the early zoning cases were fairly transparent in their goal of sorting people by race, but even the more recent move to less transparent racial motives has not weakened the function or the desire to sort by race.[8] This sorting of people, however, can occur only after the racial subject has come into being. So the primary privilege (or disability) is racial identity, and membership or lack of membership, in the imagined space of the society.[9]

In addition to just keeping some people out and some people in, boundaries can regulate the movement and status of people on the outside for the benefit of a more favored group. This arrangement may entail having some outsiders inside the boundary, but in a prescribed number and under different conditions from those who have full membership. Many interests have been served by people from other nations working on United States soil since its inception – but not as full members. All of the borders that continue to separate whites and non-whites, Americans and non-Americans, support a series of complicated relationships between groups, with outsiders sometimes placed inside the white space (but regulated).

Aspen, Colorado, for example, passed an inclusionary zoning law in 2003.[10] At first, Aspen might seem an unlikely community to support the inclusion of low and moderately priced housing, as the inhabitants are overwhelmingly white and wealthy. Indeed, Aspen wears the high price of housing as a badge of status and honor. Yet it was clear that many of the beneficiaries of this inclusive housing would be lower-income Latinos. The cost of buying housing in Aspen had effectively maintained a segregated community, but the boundary was actually too effective. Because of the housing prices, many of the service workers for the wealthy whites lived a great distance from the resorts of Aspen and could not get there on snowy days. The absence of these nannies and caretakers was disruptive to the lifestyle that the elite valued. To address this problem, they created an arrangement in which some Latinos would be available to work during inclement weather. This situation is only marginally different from the support large corporate agribusinesses provide for the crossing of the national border by Latinos who work in their fields as undocumented laborers. In that case, the issue is not only whether the workers' presence is desired, but also how their presence is regulated for the benefit of others, while precluding full membership and, in many cases, access to basic services in the community.

CONCRETIZING CASTE

Individuals, groups, and institutions with different and even conflicting interests lie inside and outside of various borders. If the varying interests, especially of those on the inside, are too fractured, however, the ability to police the border will break down. Elites have the greatest role in calling boundaries into being, but they need the support of non-elites to maintain the boundaries effectively, as has occurred repeatedly in what is understood as the divide-and-conquer strategy with respect to poor whites in relation to blacks or blackness. The problem with the divide-and-conquer language is that it presupposes that today's white poor and non-whites have a natural alliance related to poverty. This position seems to make a great deal of sense if we accept that poverty and class are the dominant issues and that race is only an illusory trope employed by elites. There are a number of serious problems with this approach, how-ever. Perhaps the most obvious is that it does not seem to work. Time and time again, the elites have been able to play the race card with a special appeal to whites to break this inchoate bond with the racial other.

Why does this work so well? When we begin to explore this question seriously, two things that become apparent are that race is not just a trope for whites, and that its value is not limited to economic interest. All of us are complex, and none of us can be defined by a single factor, be that race, class, or some other marker. In different situations, different aspects of our being become more important than others: sexual orientation, gender, age, ability, or country of origin, just to name a few. Moreover, we inhabit these defining spaces in multiple ways at the same time. This response may still beg the question, but why is race so salient and effec-tive in public discourse in the United States? Part of the reason is that race is foundational for us as a country and to us as individuals – part of our very being. Much of the discussion about class is about interests, but issues of being will usually trump issues of interest. Finally, race and class are deeply inter-related in our country and cannot be so easily disentangled. Race and class have in fact both been foundational and mutually constitutive in the United States. When the elite play the race card, they are tapping into deep levels of identity that challenge being as well as issues.

In our society, "white" has been a claim of belonging or member-ship, and the racial other has borne the stigma of non-belonging. How do Latinos, Asians, Native Americans, and other non-white non-blacks fit into these questions? This issue comes up most sharply in the context of Latinos. One frequently hears that we must go beyond the black-white binary, and that this paradigm does not speak to either the experience or the situatedness of other groups. These are issues that will be increas-ingly important to explore, as Latinos are now the largest non-white group in the United States. Before doing so, however, we need to have an understanding of what is being challenged. A black-white binary is not the same as a black-white paradigm or hierarchy. For example, in a hierarchy, there might very well be a gradient with white at the top and black at the bottom that could easily situate those who were neither black nor white. One could argue that such a gradient exists not only in the United States but also in Latin America and indeed in much of the rest of the world. There is little doubt, for example, that light and dark complexion is reflected in a hierarchy in much of the world.

Maybe what is being sought, however, is not for non-white and non-black groups to be raced, but for them to be noticed through a different lens. If this is the case, it is similar to efforts by blacks who have also ob-jected to being raced. The point here is that the call to move beyond the black-white paradigm might be a transformative move or merely one that uncritically leaves that paradigm in place even as it raises objections to being stigmatized by race. It is probably too soon to say how this will be resolved, but unless we challenge the boundary itself, we could easily slip into a new sorting of who is in and belongs, and who is not and doesn't. In that sense, it is no surprise that in an era of cuts to education and social programs, law enforcement and related resources are being focused so heavily on identifying undocumented immigrants and fortifying secu-rity and borders.

If boundaries are to do their work, they also must be translated across multiple sites. If each institution had to start from scratch in clas-sifying and giving meaning to boundaries, the cost would be much too high. An easily accessible meta-story about race must be available, which is why these boundaries are constructed along what Charles Tilly would call a "categorical characteristic." Boundaries from site to site must be in a relationship, or aligned with one another.[11] Yet, even this statement, while accurate, may not be adequate. It understates the importance of the social construction of race and the creation of whiteness as a privileged space and identity. In many ways, whiteness is our meta-story about race. Because it is inscribed in the self, it can easily be carried and transformed as needed across multiple spheres.

Groups with different interests often draw boundaries differently. It is in the interest of those who benefit from the boundaries to keep them coherent enough to be stable, even as various groups try to maximize their interests and transfer the costs to others. If this shuffling process breaks down, it can escalate into open conflict and even violence, at which point it becomes necessary for elites to overtly reinscribe the boundary. Perhaps the most important example of this dynamic in American history is *Dred Scott v. Sandford*, a case that set clear parameters for membership and opportunity in the fracturing United States of 1856.[12]

Scott had continued to be subjected to enslavement during four years living on free soil. When he returned to Missouri, a slave state, he challenged the right of Sandford, a new claimant to his life and service, to continue to hold him and his family in involuntary servitude. Scott prevailed in district court, but the U.S. Supreme Court concluded that because he was of African ancestry and therefore unable to be a citizen of Missouri, he could not bring a case before the courts. He was excluded from membership in the imagined society because at the time that the Constitution was created, blacks were denied the rights, privileges, and immunities of citizenship.[13] This, as Chief Justice Taney explained in the decision, was a permanent status. Taney – and the U.S. Supreme Court – viewed Scott and other blacks as "beings of an inferior order, and altogether unfit to associate with the white race, either in social or political relation."[14] This sweeping and permanent state of exclusion based on race thus applied to all blacks, emancipated or not.

While we may decry Chief Justice Taney's opinion, in some ways he was merely reiterating the underlying logic of whiteness. If whiteness was freedom, defined negatively as not slavery,[15] then blacks could never be free. They could be slaves, or they could be emancipated, but they could not be free. In fact, the lives of emancipated blacks were extremely regulated, and in white space they were denied many ordinary rights, which were associated with whiteness. In the claim that no black could ever be a citizen of the United States, the Court constituted citizenship as a salient feature of whiteness, and vice versa. In this sense, Chief Justice Taney and his brethren were active participants in the social construction of white identity.[16]

Chief Justice Taney was doing more than limiting black interests, however; much more important for whites, he was defining and distributing white interests. He was expanding the interests of slaveholding whites while limiting the interests of whites who wanted free states.[17] He was saying to these whites: You cannot regulate your space to keep slavery out; slavery is a property interest protected by the federal government and beyond the prerogative of wage-earning whites to regulate.[18] Whites feared that if enslaved or even emancipated blacks were brought into free states, they would drive down wages and expose whites to slave-like conditions. Part of the reason they could think this is that they could not imagine solidarity with blacks.[19] With few exceptions, most northern and southern whites suffered from this inability to imagine blacks as full members of society.

The Civil War and the Civil War Amendments were intended to overturn *Dred Scott* by redrawing the boundaries of citizenship and of whiteness. The Thirteenth Amendment abolished slavery, and the Fourteenth conferred citizenship and its privileges and immunities upon all blacks, including those who had been enslaved, bringing blacks into the state as full members.[20] This achievement, however, threatened an end to whiteness, at least for non-elites. After all, if the other has everything that I have, in what sense is he or she other? Today, especially in the legal community, many view the Equal Protection Clause as the most important part of the Fourteenth Amendment; but the Privileges and Immunities Clause – with its much greater and more explicit promise of full membership for blacks – had the potential to have far greater effects.

This newly gained ground would be lost all too soon, however, to the construction and reconstruction of racial boundaries and to attacks on aspirations for racial justice and democracy. Indeed, the country began to weaken almost immediately on its promises of equal citizenship for blacks as well as on the promise of full membership. With a deft sleight of hand just five years after the Fourteenth Amendment had become part of the Constitution, the Supreme Court asserted in the *Slaughter-House Cases* that while the amendment had given blacks the right to national citizenship, the basic immunities and privileges of the citizen rest with the states; the Fourteenth Amendment would not disturb the states' authority to dispense those rights.[21] This troubling pattern would repeat itself many times over the next century and into the present. Boundaries would be redrawn, or in some cases removed, but new boundaries would be created or old boundaries given new meaning in order to persistently deprive blacks of full membership.[22]

The promises of the Civil War and Reconstruction thus died quickly, as whites in the South staunchly resisted changes that would make blacks and whites equal members of society. In their struggle to regain control, white elites typically structured the redrawing of racial boundaries in ways that diminished the rights of non-elite whites. By impressing the myth that "black progress means white loss" upon non-elite white communities, elite whites were often able to redirect the resulting anger over these changes away from themselves and toward blacks.[23] Casting themselves as the South's "Redeemers," these whites also further isolated blacks with a range of violent tactics directed against them and their white allies, from the burning of schools to the murder of leaders.

The tension between radical Republicans and these angry elite whites rose to such a fever pitch that some feared another civil war. This important struggle was ended, however, with the brokering of the Hayes-Tilden Compromise, which resolved the deadlocked presidential election of 1876. Southern Democrats won an end to Reconstruction and reestablishment of white control of the South in exchange for agreeing to support Rutherford B. Hayes as the winner of the election. Both Anthony Marx and Derrick Bell observe that the end of Reconstruction was largely a compromise between the disenfranchised whites who were reeling from the loss of an explicit racial status above blacks and a northern elite that feared another major white confrontation – and wanted to win the contested election. White boundaries and privilege were remade through the promise of democracy and fairness to white members on the backs of people only recently, one might say partially, released from slavery.[24]

Not surprisingly, after the North agreed to withdraw troops and return rule of the South to southern racists under the rhetoric of states' rights, blacks were systematically terrorized and disenfranchised. This compromise was, after all, nothing short of a redrawing of white boundaries with blacks outside: the South explicitly reinscribed white supremacy with the blessing of the North. Intra-white conflict was diminished, and a post-slavery, post-Reconstruction white identity was born, even as a new pact for black subordination was sealed. That pact would survive until the 1950s and the struggles of the civil rights movement.

ANTI-MISCEGENATION LAWS AND POST–CIVIL WAR JURISPRUDENCE: NATURALIZING RACIAL HIERARCHY

Anti-miscegenation laws, supported by a deeply naturalized conviction that race was fixed and that the mixing of races was absurd, have provided some of the strongest and most enduring protection for white identity and privilege. When Lincoln's detractors attacked him, for example, they often claimed that by supporting the expansion of free states and the end of slavery, he was laying the foundation for the amalgamation of the races and even interracial marriage. Lincoln responded that this was ridiculous. No one would support either of these propositions: there were enough black women for all of the black men. The idea of interracial marriage was seemingly beyond the imagination even of slavery's opponents.[25]

The scare of interracial marriage (and its progeny, mixed-race children) would resurface in the context of integrated schools. It is interesting to note how many whites assumed that this ultimate black "penetration into" the white space/body would mean the destruction of whiteness.[26] Legal regulation of this boundary affected both blacks and whites and limited the personal behavior of white men and women in service of the broader goals attained by defining a coherent scheme of whiteness/blackness. Historian Peter Wallenstein and others have observed that there is an interconnected series of boundaries that serve both to define identities and create and distribute opportunities and burdens. Anti-miscegenation laws were part of such a larger, mutually reinforcing system of citizenship, voting, and property rights. As recently as the 1940s and 1950s, supporters of these laws asserted that they were necessary to prevent interracial marriage, lest the boundaries become too amorphous and the racial caste system fail to function.[27] The need to maintain white purity only hardened as blacks attained greater levels of freedom.[28]

Racialization in the United States has been a long, conflicted, and anything-but-natural process.[29] Yet, as racial boundaries became stronger, the courts began to explain them as something determined by natural law and "individual preference." *Plessy v. Ferguson,* on which much of the system of "separate but equal" racial segregation was based, is at the root of many of these explanations. It is not surprising that *Plessy* allowed for the construction of new racial boundaries. The definition of whiteness was being narrowed with respect to blacks during this era, even as it was being expanded for new immigrants.[30] What is surprising about *Plessy,* and quite telling as to the quick reification of these racial boundaries, is the discourse about naturalness that the Court relied on for justification.

In the blazingly circular logic of racism, the Court's opinion uses the social and economic inequality caused by racialization to enforce separation based on race.[31] Noting some of the segregation imposed by various state courts as proof of the naturalness and legal soundness of that condition, the Court cites the widespread use of anti-miscegenation laws and the legal acceptance of school segregation.[32] Even Justice Harlan, in his trenchant dissent from the ruling, accepted the naturalness and logic of white superiority and did not see the Civil War Amendments or the Court as having a role in disturbing it:

> The white race deems itself to be the dominant race in this country. And so it is, in prestige, in achievements, in education, in wealth, and in power. So I doubt not, it will continue to be for all time, if it remains true to its great heritage and holds fast to the principles of constitutional liberty.[33]

In essence, the Court posited in *Plessy* that, given the pervasiveness of segregation and racial boundaries, it was not reasonable to assume that the Civil War Amendments were intended to change them. This logic – that if addressing an injustice would require action across multiple different sites, it must be unreasonable – is still applied by the Court to issues involving race, as discussed in regard to *McCleskey v. Kemp,* the case addressing race and the death penalty.

The very presence of racial borders, as well as their pervasiveness, makes them seem natural and inevitable, yet the history of the development of these boundaries and of racial hierarchy is full of contingencies and contradictions. Social upheaval has challenged and upset the logic underlying racial meaning and the boundaries of whiteness throughout their creation and imposition. Anthony Marx notes that there were at least three major opportunities for racial restructuring: the Revolutionary War, the Civil War, and the civil rights movement.[34] Indeed, these periods, especially the latter two, did reformulate racial understandings and boundaries. While there was progress, however, there was also a rearticulation and retrenchment that reestablished racial boundaries and continued to forestall the creation of a racially just democracy.[35]

SPATIAL RACISM

How is it that whiteness and racial hierarchy endure, despite the official end of Jim Crow and in spite of the stunning achievements of the civil rights movement, including, essentially, the end of what many considered to be the ultimate boundary, racial restrictions on marriage? White identity and black subordination were reconstructed through the rearrangement of metropolitan space, policies, and governance. The way we organize our metropolitan areas, especially through persistent segregation, plays a large part in maintaining a racialized system of distributing benefits and burdens and provides the necessary space and boundaries for whiteness to continue to flourish. It is clear – and increasingly accepted by contemporary geographers – that the spatial and the social are mutually constitutive.[36]

Historically, Jim Crow laws had been most heavily developed in the South. The North, however, had long used ways of inscribing whiteness that were only rhetorically more benign. While the South was using specific laws that separated whites and blacks more by caste and status, the North was more likely to use spatial separation. At the time that blacks began to demand an end to Jim Crow laws and started moving northward, the country was creating, on a massive scale, a new place called the suburbs. From its inception, this place was explicitly white space.[37] When Dr. King directly challenged this space in Cicero, a Chicago suburb, by leading a march against housing discrimination, he was attacked by angry whites, and northern support for civil rights began to be withdrawn. Indeed, in many respects the civil rights movement in this country was about the South – an attack on the ways that the South had constructed white space. The northern form was not successfully attacked; in fact, it was subsequently expanded to protect and extend white privilege.

Today, our arrangements of metropolitan space – persistent segregation, concentrated poverty, and fragmented governments – sort people and opportunity in a racialized way.[38] All three branches of our government have had a role in creating this landscape: the executive and legislative in financing white flight through transportation spending, subsidies for suburban development and homeownership, and other measures; and the courts in developing legal barriers that facilitated the exclusion of blacks and, to a lesser extent, other non-whites.[39] For years, blacks and other marginalized groups fought to get into public space as full members, in part to have access to opportunity, but also to change the rules around space. What happened in the fifty years following the dismantling of Jim Crow is that rules related to public space changed and shifted, and white space became quasi-private. Now the suburbs are treated as private, with the implicit right to exclude, and cities are treated as public.[40]

Blacks are moving to the suburbs in record numbers, trying to take advantage of well-financed, high-functioning schools and to gain access to emerging job markets and other opportunities. Often their efforts are frustrated by the protections that the law and public policy have extended to this white space. At one point, the Court treated regulation of local space as a function of the states. As blacks began to move into these spaces, however, there was an important shift, and local autonomy became constitutionalized.[41] What we are seeing today is a devolution not just back to states' rights, a concept that always was bound up in the right to regulate blacks and create white space, but also a devolution back to local rights, which are increasingly being used to draw boundaries around white space.

In short, the civil rights movement succeeded in opening up public space just in time to see power and privilege shift to private space. Blacks gained power in the cities as opportunities left. This is why Winant can note that "the elimination of Jim Crow did not really occur" and that civil rights laws fail to address "the deeper logic of race in U.S. history and culture."[42] This situation is not about individual preference on the part of whites. Whites did not and could not create this space without the economic and legal support of the government.

This realignment caused another major shift in political alliances in this country. Northern suburban whites have realigned with southern whites, a move facilitated and exploited by the Republican Party. The restructuring is based on maintaining white space by preying on white fears, rather than through the explicit use of Jim Crow laws. Even though this process was complex, President Lyndon B. Johnson predicted some variation of it when he signed the Voting Rights Act of 1965, reportedly declaring afterward that he had just handed the South to the Republicans for fifty years.[43] It was not long after this that the Republicans began to develop what became known as the Southern Strategy. Initially pushed by Goldwater and implemented by Nixon and every Republican president since, the strategy was to appeal to southern whites by adopting anti-black and anti-civil-rights policies and rhetoric. The trick was to do so without the explicit racist references that had been discredited by the civil rights movement and rejected by more moderate whites. The success of the strategy is apparent in election maps: in 1964, the Democrats won all of the traditional southern states, but as recently as 2000 and 2004, every southern state was listed in the Republican column.

Nearly fifty years after President Johnson's remark, Barack Obama carried Virginia, North Carolina, and Florida in his presidential victory.[44] In spite of that victory and other important changes both before and after *Brown* – lunch counter sit-ins, marches on Washington, civil disobedience, speeches, hundreds of civil rights laws, and considerable gains in terms of racial attitudes – we continue to live in racially segregated neighborhoods, send our children to racially segregated schools, have transportation and health care systems that are highly racialized, and distribute future opportunity through racialized wealth, all with virtually no reference to race or racism. Spatial racism helps explain why the striking down of anti-miscegenation laws and other earlier white boundaries did not bring about the destruction of whiteness as a social category.

In addressing these results of racialization, too often we tend to focus on particular borders or boundaries. This limits our understanding of the fluid and relational nature of the sources of the hierarchy. There is no standard, consistent way of arranging institutions and structures to preserve whiteness and recreate racial hierarchy. A focus on what was, and its demise, may therefore obscure what is, and more importantly, what will be. After all, at the same time that Jim Crow laws were being attacked and dismantled, the country was restructuring with new boundaries that would facilitate a new form of racial hierarchy.

Federal judge Robert Carter, a key member of the legal team in *Brown v. Board of Education*, noted that "[t]he mistake we made was that segregation was the evil. . . . It was the symptom. The evil is white supremacy. . . . [T]hat evil is marring this country."[45] I agree with Judge Carter, not out of pessimism or to downplay the roles that segregation and white space play in creating whiteness, but simply to urge that even as we fight to change specific racial boundaries, we remain alert to new and transformed structures, institutions, and arrangements that may be emerging to shore up a system of white supremacy.

WHITENESS AND THE SELF: MODERNITY, BACON'S REBELLION, AND THE EMPTINESS OF WHITENESS

For years, the challenge to those working for racial justice has been how to think about a new racial arrangement. Our success in that effort has been limited partly by our failure to fully understand whiteness – its pervasiveness, its qualities of both apparent instability and apparent permanence, and why it is seemingly so easy for whites to consistently realign in ways that exclude and punish non-whites, particularly blacks. Much of the writing on whiteness has focused on whiteness as privilege. To the extent that whiteness is equated with privilege, and privilege is racialized, there is a push by those concerned about racial inequality to eliminate white privilege. While this has been and continues to be a useful intervention, it is also limited. It often fails to look at the non-material aspects of whiteness and doesn't necessarily answer the question implicit in James Baldwin's statement: "As long as you think you're white, there's no hope for you."[46]

What is lost in being white? Why is there "no hope" for whiteness? To better understand this, we must look at what might be the clearest case of racial formation in American history and examine the ways that it contributed to the creation of white identity in the early colonial period and to the embedding of whiteness/blackness in the modern sense of self.

In the early seventeenth century, when the English came to this continent, many of them were indentured servants or poor workers. An elite class ran the government, the industries, and the economy. At this point, Africans were brought to the new world, most of them by way of the Caribbean, where they were prepared for work in the colonies and where most of them learned to speak English. The concept of race had not yet been developed. Being English, or Christian, or African might have meaning, but hardened racial boundaries had not been established. Few laws regulated relations among the Africans, the English, and the Indians – groups we would now define as races. There was some amount of cooperation between English workers and blacks, a solidarity born of common experience. That group of workers joined forces in 1676 in a rebellion directed toward both the English elites and the indigenous people, with the goals of securing democratic reform and more land. Called Bacon's Rebellion, this uprising created a great deal of fear among the elites, both because of its temporary successes and, more importantly, because of the cooperation it revealed between the growing number of Africans and poor English.

At the original hearing on Bacon's Rebellion, there was no mention of African or English, because social divisions along these lines were not yet salient. What was salient was the need to prevent cooperation between these different groups against the propertied classes. The rebellion is cited by a number of authorities as the wake-up call to those classes to begin constructing barriers to separate the poor English from the Africans. Allen, in *The Invention of the White Race,* cites this rebellion as an important development in the racial plan that would be developed over the next several decades.[47] At its inception, then, the creation of whiteness was a deliberate strategy to keep poor Europeans, mainly English, and Africans from uniting. This turn to whiteness yielded important property and membership rights to the group that affiliated by color with the ruling elite, along with – most importantly – the right never to become a slave.

Bacon's Rebellion was subsequently retold to the general English public as a story of armed rebellion against English Christians by African slaves, not as a rebellion of workers against the elite. This framing engendered a need among the Christian and English (soon to be white) to unite and police the slaves. Martinot points out that while the other, the black African, was clearly identified from the beginning, it would take some time for the top of the binary to crystallize into a stable racial category. That category would come to rest in the cloudy concept of whiteness, defined, from the very start, in opposition to the dangerous African other. As Martinot states, "The effect of setting aside the African population as a juridicially ostracized category was to construct a social consciousness on the part of all English of a commonality against the Africans."[48] Often the main purpose of excluding and stigmatizing the other into an out-group is to give meaning and membership to the in-group. Part of the insecurity of whiteness was, however, not just the insecurity of defending against the racialized other, but what Malcolmson describes as the uncertainness contained in the negative ontology of the state of whiteness.[49]

Later, Africans were sent to the colonies without the transition time in the Caribbean, so they arrived without knowing English or being otherwise acculturated. This made it easier for colonists to imagine them as alien and dangerous, which in turn supported the racialization of otherness. The governing councils further refined the realignment of poor whites by forming them into patrols with the power to police the slave system. This action was a victory for the elites on all levels: poor whites did not have the ability to create laws, which undermined the original democratic and egalitarian impulses of Bacon's Rebellion, but they did now have enough of a stake in the system to begin to think of themselves as white. Whites would return to this theme – the need to regulate and literally police dangerous blacks – again and again. It is critically important therefore to remember that what made blacks "dangerous" in the colonial period was their desire for freedom and full membership in a newly forming democratic society.

A Fearful Self

Today many policies and practices reinforce the notion that blacks are dangerous and that black space must be regulated and policed. A racial profiling report by the Institute on Race and Poverty, for example, looked at self-reported police practices in Minnesota and found that as one moved from the Twin Cities into extremely white areas of rural Minnesota, the disparities in traffic stops and searches greatly increased for blacks and Latinos as compared with whites.[50] Even though these were predominantly white areas, and even though the rates of found contraband were higher in searches of whites in most jurisdictions, the rates of searches of blacks and Latinos were egregiously high. This suggests not only prejudice but also the regulatory role the searches have in maintaining the present racial boundaries. The more a geographic space is defined as white, the more that others who enter it on their own terms – not working for or directly serving whites – will be suspect. This pattern is nothing new. It was the case with respect to slavery and was pointed out by the plaintiff in *Plessy* with respect to the exception for non-white servants of white passengers in contrast to non-white passengers traveling on their own.[51] And it continues in the special provisions made for household workers in Aspen.

When one considers the timing of the racialization process in colonial America, the powerful impacts of the racial structuring of the collective and individual self become even more pronounced. In many respects, current ideas of the self were born during this period. The self that was being shaped in this context had any number of potential growth trajectories, and this was particularly true for the residents of the new world colonies. Concepts of freedom, democracy, liberalism, citizenship, private property, the modern nation-state, and individualism all were developed and propagated then and there. The self that formed in this cauldron was a new and modern self that continues to be the bedrock of our experience today. That it was so deeply marked by the emergence of whiteness and racialized hierarchy during its formation is exceptionally significant. Inasmuch as we are inheritors of the modern self, born in the Enlightenment, we are inheritors of a racialized self.

Many of the Enlightenment theorists, such as Locke, Hume, and Hobbes, share a vision of a separate and isolated self. Hobbes provides the most extreme example. Hobbes's self is filled with fear and dread. Hobbes sees the self entering society with his things, scared that others will try to steal them. The State, for Hobbes, is called into being to police those predatory other selves and ensure harmony. This self is perpetually at risk of war with the other fearful selves. If such selves come together, their connection is tenuous at best. Many of our laws and structures are designed to protect this self, which, by institutional reinforcement, they also call into being. Other Western theorists, such as the Romanticists and Rousseau in particular, viewed the self as interrelated both with other selves and with their cultures and communities.

Unger has suggested that there are dangers with either extreme. He asserts that the paradox of modern society is that "we present to one another both an unlimited need and an unlimited danger, and the very resources by which we attempt to satisfy the former aggravate the latter."[52] We desperately need each other, but our longing exposes us to a heightened vulnerability. Goldberg suggests that many of the things we value are bound up with the racial self, and that the white racial self in particular is bound up with a process of violence, exclusion, and fear – particularly a fear of the black other.[53]

This fear is increased by the co-dependence of the white subject and its other. As Shannon Winnubst notes, "the more a subject realizes his dependence on the Other, the more vehemently he rejects all connection to and distances himself from that Other."[54] This is the hard edge of white space, the inherent fear of the Enlightenment's isolated self. Importantly, blackness is bound up with whiteness: it is already and always present in the white self. It is because whiteness is empty and derivative that it needs the constitutive other for the grounding of its being. This is how I understand Baldwin's remark. This is why Roediger, Ignatiev, and others assert that there is no such thing as white culture.[55] At its core, whiteness is vacant.

One may object that this emptiness is equally true of blackness, or of any other racial categorization. This objection is partly true, but substantially wrong. Blackness is also inherently devoid of meaning outside of contextual relationships and hierarchies of privilege and oppression, but it is different from whiteness in that the yearnings of blackness largely have been a crying out for liberation and equality. These cries often have been distorted into a mimicking of whiteness, including wanting to be seen as just an individual (in a color-blind world), or at times as trying to hold a space alternative to whiteness or an identity struck as the reverse or opposite of whiteness. But the history of blackness in this nation has been a struggle to escape subordination and achieve membership, while the history of whiteness has been overwhelmingly concerned with providing a space where exclusion, exploitation, conquest, and violence could be rationalized and normalized.

Note that I am not speaking here about individual people called black or white, nor is it my intention to demonize whites or romanticize blacks. There is a history to whiteness that is not very attractive, however, just as there is a history to the space associated with maleness in relationship to femaleness that is not very attractive. That history of maleness does not describe my personal history or aspirations, but it does affect me and the world I inhabit. In a similar way, these characteristics are embedded in the design of the racial categories that continue to organize and regulate our society.

QUESTIONING INSTITUTIONAL ARRANGEMENTS
THAT SUPPORT WHITENESS

The question of whiteness is ultimately a question of humanness: more specifically, can non-whites, and particularly blacks, be considered part of the political community, with all the rights and privileges of membership? Consider again the role of the white patrol to capture and police blacks engaged in a struggle for freedom. And consider *Dred Scott*, perhaps the definitive case on black/white relations in this country: Chief Justice Taney reasoned that it was not possible to consider blacks as part of the political community.[56] He asserted that the only rights that blacks, free or enslaved, could have were those rights that whites granted them. In many ways, this is still the operative norm. Whiteness is the field in which social and political power operates. Despite the Civil War, the civil rights movement, and *Brown v. Board of Education*,[57] the question remains: Can blacks be full members of this society?[58]

When we look at racial boundaries and ask ourselves again what problems they are trying to solve, we can answer that they are solving the problem of how to create and maintain racial hierarchy. I have suggested that these boundaries are designed to regulate status and behavior, constitute being and non-being, and distribute benefits and burdens. As we have seen, these boundaries are also part of the process of creating whiteness itself. It may appear that there are only a limited number of boundary arrangements that will maintain white space and racial hierarchy, which explains why they are so strongly defended (as in the almost manic flight of whites from neighborhoods or schools once a critical mass of blacks is reached). This view, however, although it is held by those who support racial hierarchy as well as those who oppose it, is erroneous.

Throughout history we have seen that whiteness can be constituted in a multitude of different ways, and that even when structures seen as key to maintaining it fall apart, whiteness remains – sometimes through the replacement of overt discrimination with structures that seem benign in intent but that still regulate white space, sometimes through the devaluing of social space that is no longer white. For example, the prowess of white boxers was once seen as a testament to whites' inherent superiority in strength, skill, and intelligence. As Jack Johnson rose in prominence in the early 1900s, many white social critics worried that if a black man were to become heavyweight champion of the world, it would represent a significant loss of value for whiteness. Jim Jeffries, the man who challenged Jack Johnson after he had first gained the title belt, became the Great White Hope. Jack London spoke for millions of whites when he wrote in the *New York Herald*, "Jeff, it's up to you. The White Man must be rescued."[59] Jeffries lost, Johnson won, but whiteness remained dominant: boxing became an irrelevant social space – no longer a sport of skill and strength, but a savage sport of brute aggression.

At times, whiteness is able to embrace token integrationism and other complexities: some of the policies advanced by the George W. Bush administration and its "multicultural" cabinet, for example, or the fact that southern segregationists who had supported anti-miscegenation laws also supported the Supreme Court nomination of Clarence Thomas, whose wife is white. The problem is not the ever-changing structures that form and defend whiteness. The problem is whiteness. We therefore need to tug at the deep relationship between whiteness and the self and return to the question with which we began this chapter. Why is it that white law students would be more likely to dream of being foxes than to dream of themselves as black, and what exactly is policing that racial boundary?

A reading of Foucault is useful here, as I assert that it is the students' internal gaze that is keeping the boundaries in place. Foucault describes a subject internalizing regulatory norms:

> He who is subjected to a field of visibility, and who knows it, assumes respon-
> sibility for the constraints of power; he makes them play spontaneously upon
> himself; he inscribes in himself the power relation in which he simultaneously
> plays both roles; he becomes the principle of his own subjection.[60]

This monitoring occurs both within and without: the subject becomes the one who subjects and the one who is subjected. We police ourselves in concert with social norms and the sanctions for crossing prohibited racial boundaries; this is, in fact, the definition of the racialization process. The overarching reason we internalize racial boundaries, the reason that whites cannot bear to transgress the color line even in their dreams, is that the self constructed from whiteness is in constant fear of being contaminated by the racial other that is always present in absentia.

The fear, moreover, is not just of contamination, but also of the destruction of whiteness. Because whiteness is bound up with the sense of self and gives meaning and value to the self, its destruction equals the destruction of the self. Orlando Patterson's research shows that the Greeks considered slavery worse than death.[61] If one is bound up in the imagined space of whiteness, leaving that space does not take one into nothingness – as scary as that is – but into blackness, into a self that is owned, dominated, and regulated by others. In this blackness one is alive, yet there is a social death. It is a negation that remains present. It is a self that one would not dare to be, even in one's dreams.

MOVING BEYOND BOUNDARIES

The fear of the racial other, then – the black other – is not only about the loss of a job, or property values, or other material privileges; it is also fear of the loss of the self. Conversely, the self that is being so violently protected is at the heart of the problem at the individual level. Ending this policed consciousness will not occur spontaneously. There is an alternative, however, and part of that alternative is a recognition of the inherently compounded nature of the self. When the tight boundaries of self/non-self can become loosened, so can other boundaries.

Before turning more directly to the outlines of a prescription, I would note a few caveats. The recognition that we are contextual and multiple does not deny individuality or imply assimilation. We are individual as a matter of convention. Our connectedness will allow something called "individual expression." This is particularly important in the context of race, given the inclination either to reduce everyone and everything to me or to make the other infinite and unreachable.

We will not eliminate racial hierarchy simply by having people cross problematic boundaries in their sleep (or in their waking lives, for that matter). Some have suggested that the solution to the racial boundary issue could be found in the increasing number of people passing for white, as "white Latinos," for example, become white, in much the same way that the Irish and Italians did. Lani Guinier and Gerald Torres refer to this suggestion as "the racial bribe."[62] Even if more and more people are allowed to pass – and notice the connotations of the words "allowed to pass" – this does nothing to transform the meaning associated with the boundary. The inherently problematic category of whiteness remains intact. The very need to pass indicates the continued salience of racial hierarchy. There is a similar problem with an uncritical notion of inclusion. I am not arguing for exclusion, but it is important to consider the terms on which inclusion is offered. What exactly are people being included into? To paraphrase Baldwin: Who wants to be integrated into a burning house?[63] It is also appropriate to consider what the costs of inclusion will be in terms of potential loss of cultural diversity.[64]

To strike at the core of white privilege, we must address the ontological question. This strategy is not a retreat from the possible or a retreat to the interior. It is a recognition of the fact that it is not only race that is socially constructed; so, too, is the self.[65] We must better understand and address how this self is constructed and what maintains its attachment to whiteness. As noted earlier, this self, particularly the white self, has a history and is constantly being made and remade. This process generally goes unnoticed and hides behind a veil of naturalness, but it would be a serious error to see the study of the self as only an internal undertaking. This is part of the myth of the individual subject – that the self is internal and private. We must expose the social nature of the subject, a subject held together not only by other subjects but also by our norms, practices, and institutions. This subject is related to other subjects and to the world, creating a context in which the subject lives both externally and internally, but this fix is never perfect. The context always denies some possibility that yearns for expression, and that yearning is one source of hope.

As we think about institutional arrangements, we must consider what they mean for routine expression and for the experience of internal space. Unger reminds us that the way institutions are arranged can either mutilate or provide space for the emancipation of our being.[66] Those of us with privilege must therefore use the privileges we cannot reject to better understand, expose, and destabilize the structures and cultural norms that support and reinscribe whiteness. We must raise the cost of maintaining whiteness by seeking strategic interventions that reduce racialized disparities across multiple areas – but still seek to better understand and challenge whiteness. We must begin to work for a new set of arrangements that will support a new way of relating, a new way of being.

Part of the answer, then, is in the material world, the arrangements of structures and institutions – not only because we need to address material needs and disparities, but also because material intervention has great potential for interrupting the circular reasoning that perpetuates racism and the stereotypes that support it. Moreover, structures cannot be viewed as entirely separate from the self. We must also keep an eye on the self that we are trying to call into being. Without working on the internalization of whiteness, we cannot solve the problem of whiteness. Although there has been some development in this area, the ontological question of whiteness remains largely undertheorized.

There is an emerging concern in whiteness studies that the field itself could serve to recenter whiteness or reify racial categories. I share that concern, but the examination of whiteness that I am suggesting is not simply about the study of white people or whiteness as something that can be separate from blackness, but instead about the study of race, racial hierarchy, and the linchpin role of whiteness in maintaining that structure. Whiteness and race must be deconstructed together. From this perspective, the work of critical race theorists, feminist theorists, and queer theorists all becomes essential. The purpose of the pursuit of this understanding is to end the performance of whiteness, not so that whites can be non-white or uncolored people, but so that we can all be human, with all the social amalgamation and complexity that has so long been dreaded and denied.

Feminist theory has developed a view of the self as radically relational. It is this relational self that whiteness is created in but afraid to acknowledge. How can we create communities of kinship that allow us to explore these connections? Another part of the answer is in interior work. Ken Jones reminds us that "[w]ithout the inner work we become part of the problem rather than part of the solution. . . . As Mahatma Gandhi observed, 'the belief . . . that we can devise a social system so perfect that no one will need to be good, is one of the great delusions of our time.'"[67] Similarly, interior work cannot be cut off from the work of transforming structures and arrangements. As Jones notes, "without the outer work, the inner work cannot be socially manifested on the scale that is now required."[68]

Sometimes the inner and outer work can combine to spark changes of which we are only partly aware. A recent series of experiments on perspective-taking and bias demonstrate the value of even minimal efforts to take such steps. Researchers measured the responses of mostly white, Asian, and Latino subjects, predominately female, who were asked to briefly take the perspective of a black male to whom they were introduced by means of a photograph or a film clip. Some subjects were asked to write a short essay about a day in the young man's life.[69] In one film clip, racial discrimination against the black male was made explicit; in others, it was not.

Following one such session, these perspective-takers were asked if they would help a (fictitious) lab assistant who ostensibly needed to practice his interviewing skills. When asked to set up for an interview with a lab assistant whose name was chosen to suggest that he would be African American, the subjects who had engaged in perspective-taking placed the chairs considerably closer together than did those in the control group. They also placed the chairs closer to this "assistant" than they did for another fictitious lab assistant with a "white-sounding" name.[70] (No interviews with lab assistants took place.)

The researchers also noted an "automatic interracial reaction" among perspective-taking subjects during an actual interview. A black interviewer (during an interview on another topic) scored the subjects on "approach-oriented behaviors," such as smiling, leaning in closer, and engaging in eye contact.[71] The group that had previously performed the perspective-taking exercise was rated significantly more positively than the control group. White and black coders who later reviewed videotapes of the same interviews also scored the perspective-takers more positively. The researchers express the hope that this work will lead to "intergroup relations programs" to help address and overcome unconscious forms of racial bias that "continue to thwart the realization of genuine racial equality."[72] The work also seems to suggest how rich and broadly shared the real-world rewards can be from even short journeys across conscious or unconscious racial boundaries.

This does not mean that the needed work can be completed merely by crossing the boundary between the conscious and unconscious, however, as there is much in the unconscious to which we never will have direct access. What we might be able to do is loosen our racial censorship of our consciousness. What becomes important to us consciously and unconsciously is deeply social and is reflected in and fed by our structures and spaces. We must be careful, therefore, not to abandon critical work related to racial justice by focusing too much on colorblindness or on redefining who is in or outside of current boundaries. Race and racial hierarchy have been and continue to be paradigmatic foundations of this country. We can't allow the goal of dealing with this to be hijacked by claims that the racial paradigm is not real, claims of post-racialism, or professions of race blindness.

Moving beyond a view of the self as separate and unconnected is a profoundly spiritual project. It is the urge and yearning for connection that lies within us all. Often we are not comfortable mixing our spiritual yearnings and our secular work for social justice, but this is a false and problematic separation. Perhaps, then, we must end by talking about love. We must draw on love's power to free us from separation and its accompanying sense of loss. Who are we when we are free from the illusions of a separate self? I am talking about bringing something new into being, but I do not know exactly how this space can be created. While I think I see some possibilities, they remain vague. Our present condition of separateness, however, should be – must be – put to rest if we are to have a future that is worth living. Can we imagine a self beyond isolation and whiteness? Can we imagine Dr. King's beloved community? Perhaps we can start this imaginative process in our dreams.

SEVEN

The Multiple Self

IMPLICATIONS FOR LAW AND SOCIAL JUSTICE

I am linked, therefore I am.

Kenneth J. Gergen, The Saturated Self: Dilemmas of Identity in Contemporary Life

I frequently have difficulty sorting out how to think about a number of issues in my life. The problem is not so much that I do not know what I think and feel. Instead, it is that I think and feel many different and conflicting things.[1] Sometimes I let the different voices engage one another in dialogue and find intrasubjective solutions. At other times I simply allow the discord to exist. Often I engaged my friend Trina Grillo in the discussion. Trina was, and is, not just a good friend; she is a part of the multiple aspects of which I am constituted. Trina did more than help me to identify existing voices. She often helped me create new voices that somehow made deep claims upon me, upon us. She helped create the spaces where the silence laced between and within the voices could be heard.

The dominant narrative of Western society would find what I have just written problematic, perhaps unintelligible. This dominant narrative – purporting to be a meta-narrative – denies that we are or can be multiple and fractured and still remain "normal."[2] It makes many claims upon us regarding the nature of the individual. It is an ideology in the sense that Iris Young defines the word: a set of ideals that "helps reproduce relations of domination or oppression by justifying them or by obscuring possible more emancipatory social relations."[3]

Over the course of the twentieth century, the modernist notion of the self as unitary, stable, and transparent was increasingly challenged.

Although rumblings of dissent had been building for more than two hundred years, the advent of postmodernism in general, and the insightful criticism of feminist thinkers in particular, sounded the death knell for this concept of the self.[4] By positing a contrasting anti-essentialist, intersectional self, Trina Grillo and her contemporaries Angela Harris, Kimberlé Crenshaw, Patricia Williams, and others, have made great strides in pushing the dialogue on identity beyond traditional concepts, including those of early feminists, that functioned to marginalize and subjugate oppressed groups. This rejection of the unitary modernist self has in turn supported vast and fundamental criticisms of our legal system – predicated as it is on the individual, autonomous self. These criticisms assert that, by grounding legal doctrines in a conception of the self (or subject) that at best describes only the imaginary white male, our legal system has consistently functioned to create and perpetuate the privilege of white males.

At the base of the criticisms made by Grillo and other feminists is the reformulation of the self as a site constituted and fragmented, at least partially, by the intersections of social categories such as race, gender, and sexual orientation.[5] Thus, far from being a unitary and static phenomenon untainted by experience, one's core identity is made up of various discourses and structures that shape society and one's experience within it. Many feminists and postmodernists have taken this argument one step further and asserted that the self is by its very nature fragmented: an illusory form commonly seen as static and unitary, but in reality completely fluid.[6] Note that while much of the literature speaks of a fragmented self, "multi-self" might be a more appropriate term. Fragmented could suggest that there was once a unitary self that subsequently became fragmented, but there never was such a self. I will continue to use the term fragmented here, but not to suggest a prior unity.

Other presentations share the postmodern and feminist assertion that the self is constructed and fractured, but not the claim that all is constructed, leaving nothing essential or unconditional. Although these presentations are numerous, two – broadly speaking – are particularly germane: the psychoanalytic self and the Buddhist theory of the self and the unconditioned. A third challenge to the modern legal self has started to emerge from neuroscience, in findings showing not only the importance of the unconscious but also the multiple, sometimes conflicting, nature of mental and emotional processes. Some have suggested that the self is nothing but an illusion. While others in the mind sciences may stop short of that claim, there is near unanimity about the view that the self is very different from the modern conception of it as unitary.[7]

My goal is not to advocate any particular notion of identity, but instead to demonstrate the existence of a consensus among those who think critically about the self that the modernist self – the Western, unitary, autonomous self – is ill conceived, or just an illusion. From a jurisprudential standpoint, the implications of a rejection of the unitary self are immense. Indeed, it is impossible to know the myriad impacts this rejection will have upon the law, though we can be sure that the implications will extend to its very foundations. This change represents a paradigm shift that will move us beyond the Enlightenment project.[8]

THE MODERN SELF

Before the Renaissance and Enlightenment, Western society defined the self in relation to both the secular and the divine.[9] The center of premodern epistemology was "the great chain of being," in which all members of society had a proper place.[10] With the rise of Renaissance humanism and the Enlightenment, the individual began to be conceived of as sovereign and epistemologically central.[11] This reconfiguration, spurred by historical events such as the Protestant Reformation and the scientific revolution, ultimately led to the systematic creation of the modern self. Given that the discoveries of the scientific revolution fueled the modernist belief that humans could order reality, it is worth noting that many of the fundamental "truths" of the scientific revolution are now considered incorrect. For example, as Dunning points out in this context, the linearity of time, one of the so-called "dimensions" of reality, is now in disrepute, as linear concepts of time create "boundaries that breed contradictions in the laws of science."[12] Although many participated, Immanuel Kant, René Descartes, John Locke, and, more recently, John Rawls were among the more influential theorists.

Kant asserted that the definitive characteristic of the human self was its capacity for reason. Reason allowed the self to understand and order the world with certainty. According to Kant, "Reason is the faculty which supplies the principles of a priori knowledge,"[13] and "pure a priori principles are indispensable for the possibility of experience, . . . for whence could experience derive its certainty, if all the rules, according to which it proceeds, were always themselves empirical, and therefore contingent?"[14] In defining humans by their capacity for a priori reasoning, the Kantian self reveals that its essence is individual and impervious to experience (that is, static). Kant deduced further that this self was unitary:

> The thought that the representations given in intuition one in all belong to me, is therefore equivalent to the thought that I unite them in one self-consciousness, or can at least so unite them; . . . For otherwise I should have as many-coloured and diverse a self as I have representations of which I am conscious to myself.[15]

Here Kant considers and quickly dismisses the multiple self as inconceivable. He proceeds from the notion of self-consciousness governed by a capacity for reason unaffected by the particularities of experience. There is a subtle difference between the notion of the self and the notion of self-consciousness. It is a difference that is not always recognized and attended to in liberalism. It was Descartes's epistemology that asserted that self-consciousness was proof of a self. Kant felt that "pure reason" both enabled and compelled humans to construct a transcendental philosophy that articulated the structure and order of the experiential world: "transcendental philosophy is only the idea of a science, for which the critique of pure reason has to lay down the complete architectonic plan."[16]

Descartes had preceded Kant with a similar view of the self, in which the capacity for reason was the definitive characteristic: "As to reason or sense, . . . it is that alone which constitutes us men."[17] Furthermore, Descartes saw this essential characteristic as "by nature equal in all men."[18] Thus, all differences among humans were trivial, because "the difference of greater and less holds only among the accidents, and not among the forms or natures of individuals of the same species."[19] Like Kant, Descartes believed that reason contained the capacity for knowing and ordering the world. He constructed his epistemology on the foundation of his awareness of his own existence via the maxim, "Cogito ergo sum," or more familiarly, "I think, therefore I am."[20]

Locke shared with Kant and Descartes the belief that humans were essentially individualistic and defined by a capacity for reason: "It is the understanding that sets man above the rest of sensible beings."[21] Moreover, Locke posited that society ought to be ordered along the lines of a social contract. All men, by virtue of their reason, would assent to this contract insofar as it governed social relations in a manner that enabled them to most freely pursue their individual ends. Locke was also a theist whose humanism led him to conclude that "the law of nature stands as an eternal rule to all men, . . . and the fundamental law of nature being the preservation of mankind, no human sanction can be good or valid against it."[22]

The late modern theorist John Rawls provides an explicit example of this social contract theory in practice.[23] Proceeding from the modern conception of the self as essentially autonomous and a priori – independent of circumstance – Rawls sought to articulate a process for ordering a just society. It is a theory that does not address the nature of the self, remaining neutral on the ontological question and advancing a political theory that would accommodate various notions of the self.[24] The key to this process is the notion of the "original position," from which individuals could consider principles of justice in their essence, without the bias acquired through awareness of social constructions.[25] From this hypothetical position, Rawls believed that one could ascertain those principles that are most fair, because they would be created without regard to any "arbitrary contingencies."[26] Rawls referred to this exercise as a collective one.

Thus, in Rawls we see the reflection of the modern jurisprudential ideal that the law should proceed from fundamental truths about the essence of humans, and need not – in fact, ought not – take account of the particularities of various individuals. It is this view of the self that places individual rights ahead of societal good in deontological liberalism.[27]

Although the modern conception of the self aspires to a universality independent of experience, it is at least in part a response to earlier sociohistorical views. Moreover, even as these universal claims regarding the self were defining the modern era, they were subject to critique. David Hume, for example, argued that the self was nonexistent, an imaginary referent constructed to order an incessant stream of sensations:

> But self or person is not any one impression, but that to which our several impressions and ideas are suppos'd to have a reference. If any impression gives rise to the idea of self, that impression must continue invariably the same, thro' the whole course of our lives; since self is supposed to exist after that manner. But there is no impression constant and invariable.[28]

Hume maintained that this illusion of the self was only made possible by certain artifices of the mind: "Tis, therefore, on some of these three relations of resemblance, contiguity[,] and causation, that identity depends; ... our notions of personal identity proceed entirely from the smooth and uninterrupted progress of the thought along a train of connected ideas, according to the principles."[29] Hume believed that causation created a sense of identity by ordering sensations, and "as memory alone acquaints us with the continuance and extent of this succession of perceptions, 'tis to be consider'd upon that account chiefly, as the source of personal identity."[30]

Building on the skepticism of Hume, Georg Hegel broke with the universal notions of reason proffered by Kant, Descartes, and Locke, to suggest that reason and identity are not transcendental, but instead need to be viewed in historical context.[31] Because Hegel contextualized reason, one commentator has described him as an "idealist" who "does not understand human character or identity to be some fixed, immutable 'reality,' but rather conceives of human beings as actively producing their character and identity in history."[32] The implications of this critique of the universality of reason are profound. Because reason was viewed not only as the essence of human beings, but also as the primary tool that enabled them to understand and order the experiential world, the conclusion that it is relative inherently undermined modern conceptions of the world as objectively ordered and knowable. In other words, the modern project of "self-making" provided the analytical premise for its project of "world-making." If we reject the notion of the self in possession of universal reason, then we must also reject those insights regarding the larger world that reason supposedly allows.

VOICES OF DISSENT

As the modern essentialist conception of individuals informed governmental and jurisprudential theory, a need arose to construct an ideology
to justify certain practices, such as slavery and colonialism, that clearly
violated norms emanating from the equal and essential self. Yet the very
manner in which modernists defined the self justified those practices. By
construing the essence of the human self as individual and autonomous,
European thinkers deliberately excluded from selfhood members of non-
white societies that were organized around non-individualistic norms.[33]
Similarly, the adherence of modernists to Christian beliefs[34] justified
the conquest and subjugation of non-Christian (that is, non-white) "infi-
dels."[35] Other complementary ideologies have been employed as needed
to provide scientific (for instance, eugenics[36] and polygenic effects[37])
and, more recently, cultural (as in the "culture of poverty"[38]) explanations for the inequalities of Western society.

Given the exclusively defined "essence" of identity, it is unsurprising
that criticisms of the Western self have arisen mainly from the groups
that Western society has marginalized. Writing at the beginning of the
twentieth century, W. E. B. Du Bois articulated his anguish as an African
American trying to attain a sense of self-unity in a society that defined
him in ways that contradicted his own sense of identity:

> The Negro is a sort of seventh son, born with a veil, and gifted with second-sight
> in this American world – a world which yields him no true self-consciousness,
> but only lets him see himself through the revelation of the other world. It is a
> peculiar sensation, this double-consciousness, this sense of always looking at
> one's self through the eyes of others.... One ever feels his two-ness.... The
> history of the American Negro is the history of this strife, – this longing to attain
> self-conscious manhood, to merge his double self into a better and truer self.[39]

Du Bois's reflections suggest the postmodern, intersectional self, the self
of "others" fragmented by society's dominant discourse.[40] Importantly,
Du Bois demonstrates that those whom society has marginalized and
dehumanized experience the unitary self not as an essence, but as an
aspiration – a "longing" for coherence and self-satisfaction. As I will argue later, it is an unattainable ideal, not just for the marginalized, but for
all. The unitary self is an illusion that the dominant white male is able to

maintain because of his centrality in modern discourse, which operates to make incoherent any other claims.

Zora Neale Hurston also challenged the idea of a unitary and static self, recounting how her experience of possessing a racialized identity was not an essential one, but rather largely a product of her placement within a societal framework:

> I remember the very day that I became colored. Up to my thirteenth year I lived in the little Negro town of Eatonville, Florida.... [Then] I was sent to school in Jacksonville. I left Eatonville, the town of the oleanders, as Zora. When I disembarked from the river-boat at Jacksonville she was no more ... I was now a little colored girl.[41]

This reflection portrays Hurston's experience of herself as both "Zora" and a nameless "little colored girl." Experience created her identity, which changed as her context changed. Concerning her sense of racial identity, Hurston wrote, "I feel most colored when I am thrown up against a sharp white background."[42]

In such a white context, we can envision either Du Bois or Hurston struggling to reconcile an internal sense of self with the foreign, even subhuman, notion offered by society. Frantz Fanon, writing about the colonizer and the colonized, articulates this conundrum that the modern self creates for marginalized groups: "Because it is a systematic negation of the other person and a furious determination to deny the other person all attributes of humanity, colonialism forces the people it dominates to ask themselves the question constantly: 'In reality, who am I?'"[43]

Hurston's metaphor of the white background also illustrates how it is that white males may not have a similar experience of fragmented identity. Despite the normalcy of whiteness, however, white males are fragmented as well. Against a white background – within a theoretical framework that defines them as coherent and human – individual whites are free to choose the manner in which they distinguish themselves. Confident that those aspects they find most central to their identity are legitimate, white males are free to cultivate their "arbitrary contingencies" with little fear of loss of humanity.[44] There is no dissonance between societal definitions of humanity and whites' personal experiences of humanity. Thus the smooth fit between societal norms of whiteness and the constructed identity of whites creates an illusion of coherence and racial invisibility or neutrality – of "normality."[45] By attaining this sense of racial neutrality, white males are thus able to adhere to notions of the essentialized modern self without problematizing their own sense of identity. Or so it would seem.

The false unity and transparency of whiteness and maleness leave those who are not white males futilely seeking the sense of unity they perceive in a white male self that is in reality neither unitary nor transparent. Like Du Bois, Fanon expresses the view that it is the experience of racial subjugation that fractures the self of the colonized: "I am being dissected under white eyes [that] objectively cut away slices of my reality."[46] Thus the pull to be an individual, especially by blacks and other others, is an effort to claim a humanity not marked by race, gender, or other considerations. It is an effort to become, or pass for, the white male. In a subtle way this error of normalizing the unstated marker of the dominant discourse shadows some of the language of intersectionality.

The Intersectional Self

As noted in the discussion of white privilege, contemporary feminist theorists have made a significant contribution to the rejection of the modern unitary self by asserting that if such a separate and autonomous self exists, it is certainly not the female self.[47] Indeed, they propose an alternative description. Early attempts at creating a separate theory of the self, by white feminists in particular, fell prey to the same essentialist problems inherent in the modern self.[48] As critical race theorists noted, common concepts of male and female could more accurately be described as white male and white female. By accepting the prevailing concept of the unitary, autonomous self as applied to white males, and supplementing it with an essentialist female foil, early white feminists replicated the exclusionary tendencies of the modern self. Put another way, they offered a very modern conception of the female self by acceding to Western society's demand for total, not partial, explanations.[49] Some white feminists were aware of the problem but misunderstood its nature. They assumed that they could delineate the effects of sexism by looking at the experiences of white women "unmodified" by race.[50] They failed to see that white is as much of a racial modifier as black and further assumed that black women's experiences and ontological space could be captured by adding the "race" and "gender" categories together. As Angela Harris notes, this new framework "reduced the lives of people who experience multiple forms of oppression to addition problems: 'racism + sexism = straight black woman's experience,' or 'racism + sexism + homophobia = black lesbian experience.'"[51]

To extend the mathematical metaphor, these early white feminists believed that, in their experience, they could "isolate" the variable of sexism from the variable of racism, and so better understand it. Similarly, the paradigmatic racial experience became that of the minority male, in whom experiences of racism were isolated from sexism.[52] Using this theoretical framework, it was possible to construct the experience of minority women without even considering them. Hence, this conceptualization of the female self functioned to exclude, rather than include, all but the "typical" white female. This essentialized conception of discrimination also informed the manner in which the law addressed racism and sexism.

Feminist women of color developed the theory of the intersectional self in reaction to this flawed analysis, proposing that "women of color stand at the intersection of the categories of race and gender, and that their experiences are not simply that of racial oppression plus gender oppression."[53] Kimberlé Crenshaw provides an explicit account of the unique difficulties and contradictions experienced by women of color in the legal and political spheres. These systems of oppression combine in synergistic ways. Furthermore, because all categories exist in relation to other categories, the intersectional self is descriptive of all individuals, not only those victimized by multiple systems of oppression.[54] In this way, intersectionality subverts the notion of the modern self. As Angela Harris describes it, "we are not born with a 'self,' but rather are composed of a welter of partial, sometimes contradictory, or even antithetical 'selves.'"[55] The significance of each of these fragmented selves for one's sense of identity shifts as a result of both external and internal stimuli and experience.[56] Thus, race's role in Zora Neale Hurston's sense of identity depended on her environment.

Other Postmodern Reflections on the Self

Many postmodern and late modern theories of the self echo the assertions of the intersectionality critique, agreeing that the self is fractured
and multiple. Katherine Ewing, for example, writes that anthropologists have typically viewed the self through a unitary Eurocentric lens
as "a symbol or cluster of symbols that they identify in their writing as a
culture's characteristic concept of self or person ... which they contrast
with *the* Western concept of self."[57] In contrast, Ewing notes, several
"recent studies by anthropologists of the 'self' are grounded in a relativ-
ist paradigm which, if not altogether denying the existence of universals
in human experience, is intended to demonstrate that there is much less
that is universal than we might have supposed."[58]

Ewing posits that "in all cultures people can be observed to project
multiple, inconsistent self-representations that are context-dependent
and may shift rapidly"[59] and that it is these individual self-representations that create the illusory sense of wholeness that people perceive:
"Each self-concept is experienced as whole and continuous, with its own
history and memories that emerge in a specific context."[60] Furthermore,
challenges to the individual's sense of wholeness are a challenge to our
"integrative capacities," testing our ability to preserve the illusion of
wholeness through synthesis and integration.[61] Applying this framework to the experiences of marginalized groups, one would think that
the fragmentation felt by "others" arguably results from the difficult task
of integrating the dominant discourse into an individual experience of
separation or isolation.

Other postmodernists have expressed similar views. For instance,
consistent with intersectionality's assertion "that 'identity itself' has
little substance,"[62] Donna Haraway "skips the step of original unity"
and states that "there is nothing about being 'female' that naturally binds
women."[63] Gender is constructed and is thus an "artificial" determinant
of identity. Postmodernists tend to agree with the notion of the self as
relational, fluid, and dependent upon context. Susan Stanford Friedman
offers an analysis of the self akin to the intersectional critique. She calls
it the "script of relational positionality"[64] and defines it as "[a] feminist
analysis of identity as it is constituted at the crossroads of different sys-

tems of stratification . . . acknowledging how privilege and oppression are often not absolute categories but, rather, shift in relation to different axes of power and powerlessness."[65] Given the shifting crossroads each individual experiences, Friedman maintains that the self is constructed by a "multiplicity of fluid identities defined and acting situationally."[66]

The Multiracial Self

One insight of postmodernism that has valuable implications for how we confront oppression is the notion of the self defined in relation to both its context and its relation to other selves. William V. Dunning advances a "new concept of identity, one which is never fixed or determined, but is forever shifting because it is generated by the individual's perception of the difference between himself or herself and others within a particular system."[67] Given this fluidity and relationality, one's own sense of identity is inextricably entwined with, and dependent upon, the identity of "others." This recognition has led to a new way of understanding racial identity: the multiracial self.[68]

The power of this modern discourse has had fundamental ramifications for the construction of selves. Crenshaw describes how "racist ideology" arranges "oppositional categories in a hierarchical order; historically, whites represent . . . the dominant antimony while blacks came to be seen as separate and subordinate. . . . Each traditional negative image of blacks correlates with a counter-image of whites."[69] Harris notes that for "othered" groups the "experience of multiplicity is also a sense of self-contradiction, of containing the oppressor within oneself."[70] James Baldwin takes this insight a step further and asserts that the experience of the white male is similarly contradictory, if not similarly problematic: the white male self contains the oppressed within it.[71] Ruth Frankenberg points out that "White/European self-constitution is . . . fundamentally tied to the process of the discursive production of others, rather than preexisting that process."[72]

In addition to its effects on self-perception, the multiracial self also has vast implications for how we understand racism and how the law should analyze and address it. Toni Morrison, in *Playing in the Dark: Whiteness and the Literary Imagination*, explores the ways in which the construction and invocation of the "Africanist" identity in white American literature has been central to the development of an American ethos. Morrison chronicles how the creation of the "New World" depended upon the overcoming of the ills of the "Old World" by Americans. She observes that "the desire for freedom is preceded by oppression; a yearning for God's law is born of the detestation of human license and corruption; the glamour of riches is in thrall to poverty, hunger, and debt."[73] Morrison contends that European Americans constructed the racialized and polarized identity of blacks as concrete proof of their own transcending of this oppression, corruption, and destitution, for "nothing highlighted freedom – if it did not in fact create it – like slavery."[74] For white American writers, this oppositional identity became a convenient and vital literary device: "Through the way writers peopled their work with the signs and bodies of this presence – one can see that a real or fabricated Africanist presence was crucial to their sense of Americanness"[75] – that is, to their sense of whiteness.

THE LEAP TO ANTIESSENTIALISM

Despite the postmodern consensus that the self is multiple and relational rather than unitary and static, theorists have not paid enough attention to the internal functions of the multiple self – to the issues of to what extent, and for what reason, the multiple parts are integrated or separated. For example, structuralists tend to see the role of language and context as primary in the structure of the self.[76] Haraway, who identifies herself as materialist, places a similar primacy on the role of language and information systems and claims that the key to displacing the modern project "rests on a theory of language and controls."[77] As James Boyle demonstrates, however, this view is problematic: "The structuralist critiques portray the epistemology of subject and object as a real fantasy, that is to say, something which is already out there, which we need only to criticize. By doing so they ignore or minimize the act of choice."[78]

This deemphasis of agency is an understandable consequence of the rejection of the essentially autonomous and rational self, manifesting itself in an absence of discussion about why the self organizes experience in the manner that it does. For example, although Ewing explains in great detail the shifting, multiple functions of the individual, she does little to explore the internal impetus for these functions, asserting that "these selves are highly context-dependent and mutually inconsistent. There is no overarching, cohesive self that is identifiable to an outside observer."[79] Ewing offers little, however, that might explain what it is about the self that leads to the construction of these multiple identities. She also fails to address the tensions among differing self-conceptions, asserting instead that each distinct self-conception has a set of memories that gives it a sense of wholeness.[80] Although such fluidity of the self may at times be effortless and smooth, the painful experiences of multiplicity and self-contradiction typifying the narratives of subordinated groups make clear that this is not always the case. There is a direct interaction among the multiplicitous aspects of the self, and failing to recognize this interaction threatens a return to the essentialist "math problem" discussed earlier.[81]

If we are to benefit from postmodern criticisms of the modern self, we must address the difficult questions relating to agency, and the seemingly integrated nature of the multiple self. It is also important to consider other conceptions of the self that retain some degree of essentialism. Amy Mullin cautions that "we need to speak with more clarity when we refer to selves as unified or divided. . . . It is important to avoid assuming that effectively unified selves must be homogeneous or integrated to the point that harmony is rarely threatened."[82] She seems to be suggesting that even if one holds on to the notion of a unified she, it does not require a uniform self. A unified self can be conceived of as having many heterogeneous parts. Mullin criticizes the leap from a unitary to an entirely multiple and nonessential self[83] as overly quick and flawed by the modernist need for certainty that postmodernism purports to reject:

> The understanding of the person as a composite of personlike parts expresses
> a conception of the person as ideally a harmonious integrated whole, a concep-
> tion so powerful that, when the unity is not found at the level of the person as
> a whole, it is postulated of the "parts" of the person, [each] associated with a
> community that is seen as itself harmonious and unfissured. Hence while the
> impact of social relations on the formation and the personality of the self is
> acknowledged, it is also simplified and fixed once and for all.[84]

Mullin advocates that rather than insisting that the self is either unitary or multiple, we instead develop "new ways of understanding the unity of the empirical subject as a matter of the degree, pattern, and effectiveness of its organization."[85] A necessary corollary of this viewpoint is that we "at least attempt to understand what shapes and continues to shape our preferences, fears and values."[86] She cautions against overzealousness in moving away from the modern self. Recognizing that the self is multiplicitous does not require the conclusion that there is no essence to it. Given the ramifications of reconceptualizing the self, we must consider whether there is some alternative to the modernist version that does not rest upon social construction. To this end, I briefly offer two conceptions of the self that recognize its multiplicitous and constructed nature but leave room for an essentialist understanding of at least part of the process of consciousness: psychoanalysis and Buddhism.

The Psychoanalytic Self

The idea that unconscious processes affect our functioning is generally accepted, but few have used this insight to enhance understanding of the self and identity. Perhaps this can be explained by postmodernists' distrust of theories that attempt to provide universal explanations for the self. Ewing expresses this sentiment in her statement that "a single model of self or person is not adequate for describing how selves are experienced or represented in any culture."[87] Nevertheless, she recognizes that the psychoanalytic (or "Freudian") self, essentialist in some respects, still has descriptive capabilities that are not necessarily inconsistent with the notion of a multiple and relational self. Ewing claims that "the phenomenon to which the psychoanalysts are alluding when they speak of a cohesive self – that is, the experience of wholeness that derives from a symbolic constitution of the self and the phenomenon of rapid shifts in the content of that experience – may be universal."[88]

Some have not been so accepting of psychoanalysis. Jane Flax criticizes Freudian theory on the ground that it "assumes that individual humans all share an essence with a common developmental pattern and that this pattern is or should be rational, sequential, purposive and additive."[89] Others have embellished upon Freud's theories of internal functionings to propose much more radically situated selves. Carl Jung, for example, maintained that the self was composed of a multitude of daimons, archetypal historical figures of varying genders, races, and even species that all functioned to constitute the individual self.[90]

Psychoanalysis, however, focuses on "the individual in his capacity to generate a sense of 'I-ness' (subjectivity)."[91] Freud saw this sense of unity as a function of the two basic facets of the mind, the conscious and the unconscious.[92] The conscious mind is generally logical and consists of those mental processes of which we are aware, while the unconscious mind consists of processes that escape our awareness but nevertheless shape identity and actions. The unconscious mind tackles the "desires, wishes, and instincts that strive for gratification."[93] Thus, Freud relocates the self from the conscious mind, where modernism places it, to somewhere in the interactions between the conscious and unconscious.[94] Because it consists of the interplay between the conscious and unconscious, the Freudian self is "fundamentally dialectic in nature."[95]

According to Thomas Ogden, this interplay of the conscious and unconscious is a "dialectic of presence and absence."[96] What is present in conscious experience "is continually negated by that which it is not, while all the time alluding to what is lacking in itself."[97] What is absent from the conscious mind's experience is often present in the unconscious mind, and the Freudian mind uses this dialectic to maintain a sense of wholeness and placidity. When there is tension between the context-dependent values of the conscious mind and incongruous thoughts or desires, the subject employs "defensive mechanisms such as repression, denial, introjection, projection, reaction formation, sublimation, and reversal [to] resolve the conflicts between the primary and secondary processes by disguising forbidden wishes and making them palatable."[98]

This dialectical process also has an intersubjective aspect: how we define ourselves and how we define others are interdependent functions of our interactions with others.[99] Psychoanalyst Melanie Klein asserts that the self is actually "decentered from its exclusive locus within the individual; instead the subject is conceived of as arising in a dialectic (a dialogue) of self and Other."[100] Through the process of "projective identification," the subject is able to resolve internal conflicts by projecting those aspects of the conflict considered negative onto others:

> Projective identification ... is not simply an unconscious phantasy of projecting
> an aspect of oneself into the Other and controlling him from within; it repre-
> sents a psychological-interpersonal event in which the projector, through actual
> interpersonal interaction with the recipient of the projective identification,
> exerts pressure on the Other to experience himself and behave in congruence
> with the omnipotent projective phantasy.[101]

Thus, the psychoanalytic subject is contextual and relational in at least two key respects: (1) the formation of the conscious self and its ethos, and (2) the stability of the subject as internal conflicts are resolved through the defensive mechanism of projection.

The Freudian account of the self is in many respects consistent with postmodernism's assertion that the self is relational and contextual. The conscious self is largely defined by social interactions. Consequently, it experiences incoherency and multiplicity as individuals in any socio-historical context do. To this extent, psychoanalysis does not assert an a priori self in the manner that modernity does. Furthermore, the dialectical self of psychoanalysis offers an explanation of how the subject seeks to construct wholeness or unity out of multiplicity and how "others" play an integral role in this process. Yet Freudian theorists believe that these processes of the mind, the interplay of the unconscious and conscious involving drives and instinct, exist in everyone.[102]

The Freudian theory of self provides valuable insight into the way that racism and other systems of oppression function in our society. The dialectic of consciousness and unconsciousness helps us to under-stand the persistence and pervasiveness of "unintentional" racism in our society despite the general disavowal of explicitly racist ideologies. In a society such as ours, where racialized meanings are pervasive, the ostensibly anti-racist individual is consistently confronted with con-flicts between a non-racist ethos and internalized racist attitudes. In his groundbreaking explanation of unconscious racism, Charles Lawrence explained that in order to resolve this conflict, the individual resorts to the aforementioned "defensive mechanisms":

> The human mind defends itself against the discomfort of guilt by denying or
> refusing to recognize those ideas, wishes, and beliefs that conflict with what
> the individual has learned is good or right. ... When an individual experiences
> conflict between racist ideas and the societal ethic that condemns those ideas,
> the mind excludes his racism from consciousness.[103]

This exclusion helps to explain the pervasiveness of actions that contain racist meanings but are not driven by the actor's conscious "intent" to behave in a racist manner.[104]

Psychoanalysis may also provide useful insight into the multiracial self discussed earlier. Through the process of projective identification, the subject is able to maintain a sense of self consistent with its value system by projecting those traits considered undesirable onto the other. Lawrence notes how the two prominent racially stereotyped narratives – the instinctive other who is lazy, overly sexual, and out of control and the other who is conniving, overly ambitious, and materialistic – correspond to two of the most common types of internal conflict: "that which arises when an individual cannot master his instinctive drives in a way that fits into rational and socially approved patterns of behavior, and that which arises when an individual cannot live up to the aspirations and standards of his own conscience."[105]

Because this psychoanalytic process involves the subject actively pressuring the other to behave in a manner consistent with the projected trait,[106] the success of projection in resolving an individual's conflict depends on his or her ability to control the other. As our history of racism makes explicit, control is a key element of the racial project. In some respects, then, the psychoanalytic account of the self is a useful and instructive alternative to the modern/postmodern debate about the self. If correct, psychoanalysis has fundamental implications for our current jurisprudence.

Another view of the self, emerging from social psychology built on neuroscience, views the interaction between the unconscious and conscious mind very differently from the Freudian psychoanalytical model. The unconscious is not seen mainly as a place of unresolved dreams, and conflict, and animal drives. Instead, it is seen as really the major player in our lives, with the conscious mind both much smaller and much less important. Nor is the conscious mind a place of logic and reason divorced from emotion: motivating conscious reasoning is only one of the many important functions of the unconscious. In our discussion here, it is equally important to note the role that bias and stereotype have in the development of intelligence. We make associations that are short cuts and that help us organize a complete world. Some of these associations and stereotypes are negative, but stereotypes and bias in and of themselves are neutral. The associations we make and the value we give to them are social, not just personal. And although problematic when left unexamined – at least in a diverse society – they are part of our evolutionary path and part of what makes us human.

Our increasing ability to see into mental and emotional processes opens this examination to us at accelerating rates. Unlike the Freudian exploration of the unconscious, which was largely indirect and speculative, neuroscience is based on both simple and sophisticated observations, including the visualizations available through magnetic resonance imaging (MRI). Neuroscientists can now stimulate and observe unconscious processes that Freud could never have dreamed of. The modernist view of the self appeared to withstand challenges from feminists, postmodernists, and Freud. It is not likely that it will so easily ignore or accommodate the revelations of neuroscience. This nascent field is already producing robust results that not only challenge the modern Enlightenment self but also totally undermine the modernist view of it. As our knowledge base from neuroscience expands, holding on to the unitary stable rational view of the self will become increasingly difficult. We will again be faced with the question of agency. However that question is resolved, we can be sure that it will reshape how we think of race and our selves.

The Buddhist Self

Buddhism also offers a theory of subjectivity that is both essentialist and nonessentialist. A number of writers have suggested that postmodernism derives from and depends on modernism and that the very attempt to disprove modernism is based on modernist assumptions.[107] This suggests that modernism and postmodernism are conceptually and culturally related: they reflect a common, specific, cultural and historical perspective. This insight also suggests that there may be ways of thinking and talking about issues of the self that do not fit within either the modernist or the postmodernist structure. If those two structures do not exhaust the possibilities, Buddhism may be an alternative structure. Anne Carolyn Klein makes clear that the current focus in the West upon the constructed nature of the self is in part caused by the failure to take seriously the interconnectedness that has always informed Buddhism:

> From a Buddhist perspective, the contemporary fascination with the incoherent and incapturable multiplicities that construct self and knowledge suggests an intellectual history that never took sufficient note of the interdependent, constructed, and impermanent nature of things in the first place. Recognition of constructedness does not, for Buddhists, devalorize the unconstructed.[108]

The conditional and the unconditional, the essential and the unessential, are not contradictory for Buddhism but are always present together.

One of the central tenets of Buddhism is that there is no permanent self.[109] Rather, Buddhists assert that the self and all phenomena are constructed and lack permanent inherent existence. This lack of inherent existence is also described as emptiness. Indeed, the emptiness of inherent existence means that the self and all phenomena are constructed and conditional – that is, put together and unessential. This emptiness of inherent existence is often referred to as the unconditional. But emptiness is not the opposite of, or separate from, phenomena; indeed, phenomena are both unconditioned and conditioned. As Klein notes, the unconditional and conditional coexist and are compatible in Buddhist theory:

> Middle Way Buddhist philosophy emphasizes what I call ontological nondualism, meaning that emptiness and dependent arisings are indivisible. In other words, the play of differences, the process of conditioning, is an insufficient description of how things are. Moreover, the conditioned and unconditioned can be experienced simultaneously because conditioned things and unconditioned emptiness are intrinsically compatible.[110]

The self and all phenomena are put together, compounded, and conditional. While this process of constitution or construction occurs very rapidly, there are gaps nonetheless. In this sense, Buddhism supports structuralist, postmodern ideas about the self by asserting that self-consciousness is largely achieved through language.[111] This assertion of the nonessential self is more persuasive coming from Buddhism, because it is based on a wholly separate tradition, rather than a reaction against modernism.

Hume and others of the postmodern tradition have been compared to Buddhists. Neo-Buddhist Serge-Christophe Kolm, for example, de-

scribes the construction of the self in terms strikingly similar to those of
Hume's nonexistent or imaginary self described earlier:

> One begins by acknowledging that a person is composed of several elements.
> The profane person would see this as a "decomposition" of the still perceptible
> person into several elements. One would then make him see that what he
> believed to be a person is only this set of elements that he stubbornly persisted in
> regarding as a whole.[112]

These comparisons often miss a critical difference, however. Buddhists'
understanding of the nature of the self does not end at the level of social
construction and mental artifices. As mentioned earlier, Buddhists believe that there is the unconditioned emptiness that is not constructed
or constituted.

This uncondition is not a concept or a thing. Emptiness is also void
of inherent condition. Emptiness cannot be grasped directly through
language because emptiness is not part of the conceptual world. Emptiness is not beyond consciousness, but it does lie beyond conceptual consciousness. Emptiness can, however, be experienced directly through the
practice of "'mindfulness,' which is the ability to sustain a calm, intense,
and steady focus when one intends to do so."[113] Mindfulness involves
accessing a state of consciousness that is beyond and ungoverned by
experience and context. Thus, much of the Buddhist practice of sitting
is directed toward gaining access to the place that is empty of concepts.
One may ask whether this place, if we can even call it a place, is essential
or unessential. The problem inherent in this question is that as soon as
we ask it we are back in the realm of conceptual duality and not in the
"unpatterned" space that is free of concepts.[114]

> It is the claim of Buddhists that through the practice of meditation, the entire
> perceptual process can be brought into awareness, including the moment of the
> first split between "self" and world. The awareness that perceives this process,
> and the ground within which it arises, is not dependent on language and is not
> oriented toward a self; therefore it is known as "nonreferential awareness."[115]

In recognizing an existence before and beyond concepts, Buddhism
asserts that the individual, as distinguished from the individual's identity
or self, "cannot be reduced to a 'site of competing discourses,' as it often
is in feminist and other postmodern descriptions."[116] I must emphasize

that my goal is not to resolve this question of essentialism and anti-essentialism.[117] My claim is a modest one: there are strong reasons to believe that the self is not unitary, transparent, and stable in the way posited by early modernists. Further, many things that we believe in, including the unconscious, strongly suggest that the self is at least fractured if not multiple. Accepting the self as fractured and/or multiple, however, does not compel a categorical adoption of the postmodern position.

Although I am not advocating an explicit acceptance of Buddhism, it is important to note that Buddhism has positive implications for personal and interpersonal interaction. Because Buddhism accepts the self as multiple and encompassing of elements that are at times conflicting or contradictory, it "departs from the urge to master, override, rein in, or otherwise manipulate the self."[118] It does not seek to construct a unitary, coherent sense of self. As Klein notes, this practice "of being nonjudgmental toward oneself has special significance in a culture where self-hatred is an issue."[119] This insight applies with equal force to minorities and to others whose self is defined as less than adequate in popular discourse.

By being nonjudgmental, Buddhism also moves beyond the psychic tension that psychoanalysis believes is the source of projecting negative traits onto the other. "When all the voices of the self are fully owned, they are less likely to be projected onto others. In this way, self-acceptance translates into acceptance of the other."[120] Thus, Buddhism requires that, in establishing relations with oneself, the mindful person "[have] models of self-engagement that do not denigrate or otherwise oppress."[121]

RECONSTITUTING THE LEGAL SUBJECT AND THE LAW

By rejecting the modern self, postmodernism strikes at the very foundation of modern jurisprudence – the legal subject. Consistent with modernism and social contract theory, the law is largely premised upon the notion of an a priori self whose "neutral" rights take precedence over societal good. This conception of the self is, however, a fallacy. In their criticism of Rawls's jurisprudential theory, Sandel and Boyle each make clear that a transparent, nonparticularized legal subject is an impossibility.

According to Sandel, Rawls premises his supposedly neutral theory of justice on the notion that there is an essence to humans that justice can serve by promulgating "principles that do not themselves presuppose any particular conception of the good."[122] Rawls, therefore, asserts that these principles should be discovered by placing oneself behind a theoretical "veil of ignorance" that blinds the individual to the "outcomes of natural chance [and] the contingency of social circumstances."[123]

Postmodernism, however, makes clear that what modernism posits as the essence of the self – that is, what aspects of identity Rawls and other modern thinkers would take behind the veil with them – is in fact based upon a specific concept of the good. The methodology, though purportedly neutral, incorporates a particular account of selfhood masquerading as a universal concept. As Boyle remarks:

> To accomplish all of this, Rawls must take a number of things away from his subjects. He says that he wants subjects that are motivated neither by altruism nor envy. . . . Self-interest, after all, is seen as rational. . . . What if the stripped-down subjects were designed by Kropotkin and Confucius, rather than by Mandeville, Smith, and Pareto?[124]

This juxtaposition of Rawls's conception of the self with those of others who have clearly contradicting conceptions makes clear that the process of determining what is essential to the universal self is far from neutral. By accepting and dismissing various aspects of the self as relevant or irrelevant, lawmakers inevitably give primacy to their own sense of self and, in so doing, divorce various other aspects of selfhood that many people perceive as vital. Grillo makes this point in the context of a woman of color:

> Under a traditional legal approach, when her situation is analyzed as a woman, it is not analyzed as a Latina. . . . Her characteristics are not connected one to the other; instead, they exist separately, suspended in time and space. This fragmenting of identity by legal analysis . . . [is] entirely at odds with the concrete life of this woman . . .[125]

Sandel exposes the non-neutrality of modern jurisprudence another way when he critiques Rawls's reliance on social contract theory. Although Rawls creates a social contract that he believes is neutral and fair, Sandel notes that the mere inquiry into fairness takes the contract out of the realm of neutrality:

> As the non-trivial coherence of the "further question" attests ("But is it fair, what they have agreed to?"), actual contracts are not self-sufficient moral instruments but presuppose a background morality in the light of which the obligations arising from them may be qualified and assessed.[126]

The question of fairness requires that we fall back upon some substantive understanding about what is just. We then necessarily rely on our own sense of self and what is good for it. "To give rights meaning," Crenshaw reminds us, "people must specify the world; they must create a picture of 'what is' that grounds their normative interpretation."[127] Although the implications of rejecting the current legal subject – declaring, as it were, the futility of searching for a universal jurisprudence – cut deep and wide, it is impossible to predict their ramifications. What is needed is a sustained project that unmasks the power and coercion of the law and removes the cloak of invisibility that is often called neutrality. This project must discover and make explicit the ways in which "the law is actually constitutive of our social existence."[128] It will require a determined community effort. I only attempt to sketch out some of the implications related to the intersectional thesis and the treatment of racism in law.

The Intersectional Thesis Reconsidered

The theory of the intersectional self presumes that identity is marked by many intersecting traits and that the implications of this cannot be understood by simply adding these traits together. As discussed earlier, an African American female's experience is not adequately captured by adding the traits of a (white) female with that of a black (male). Thus, in terms of the law, rules that prohibit racial and gender discrimination by addressing them as discrete phenomena do not adequately extend protection to a person marked by both subordinate gender and racial status. Title VII of the Civil Rights Act of 1964, for example, treats sources of discrimination as theoretically distinct by declaring: "It shall be an unlawful employment practice for an employer . . . to discriminate against any individual with respect to his compensation, terms, conditions, or privileges of employment, because of such individual's race, color, religion, sex, or national origin."[129]

The intersectionality thesis, however, can be understood to describe not just the sites of discrimination, but also the nature of the self at these intersections. That is, the intersectional self can be construed as multiple because it is defined by the intersections of oppression. One of the possible implications of this notion of intersectionality is that a self not marked by systems of oppression (white, male, heterosexual, etc.) is not necessarily multiple.

This conclusion, however, is a serious conceptual error that postmodernism and feminism have rejected, even if somewhat ambivalently. Such an understanding of the intersectional self leaves the "longing for coherence" seen in the experiences of oppressed groups uncritically situated in the dominant and dominating narrative. And if race and gender always mark the self, then the white male also is marked. He is no more a unitary, cohesive individual than is the black female, in spite of whatever lack of symmetry exists between them.

We might help expose this asymmetry by focusing on the marks of privilege as well as the marks of oppression. Marks of privilege will vary at different sites, times, and cultures, but once we develop a working list, we can consider what should be added or modified at given sites. A preliminary list might start with male, white, Christian, able-bodied, heterosexual, and middle class. If an individual possesses all the possible markings of privilege at a site, that person holds the maximum privilege available. The advantage to this method of analysis is that it marks the unmarked and helps to expose the interdependency of privilege and oppression. It also makes it clear that all selves are at least partially constituted and multiple. But a problem remains in thinking about intersectionality in this way. The approach I have just suggested implies that each of the marking categories is unitary; it implies that while gender and race may create an intersection, gender and race are unitary concepts. This is clearly wrong. Just as categories intersect to create a composite, each category itself is a composite.

As I have posited in previous chapters, when we look at whiteness, we see that it is made up in part of what it excludes, especially with respect to blackness. The excluded other does not function only externally, as in exclusion from a particular neighborhood; it also functions internally. The self is fractured by the part of the self – whiteness – that must deny the part that is equally present, yet loathed: blackness. In a non-mutual way, blackness necessarily carries whiteness with it, externally and internally.[130] It is not enough, therefore, to look at how categories intersect to create a sense of self; we also must examine how the categories are created and maintained.[131] There may be times and places where it is pragmatically important to talk about these categories as more or less unitary, because we may need the broad concepts in order to communicate. They can and should be contested, though, especially when they implicate privilege and subordination. This approach affects how we think about intersectionality in two ways: it marks the privileged individual, and it exposes the multiple and relational nature of categories without trying to do away with the categories themselves.

The Multiple Self and the Law

Acceptance of a fractured, multiple, and intersectional self would change the way we think about the law. The issue of agency and choice clearly would be altered by moving away from the unitary self. Indeed, some have tried to hold on to the unitary self by making the claim that we need agency, and that multiplicity would destroy it. Conversely, Gloria Anzaldúa and others have accepted the multiplicity of the self and used it to advocate a newfound sense of agency and self-creation:

> Don't give me your tenets and your laws. Don't give me your lukewarm gods. What I want is an accounting with all three cultures – white, Mexican, Indian. I want the freedom to carve and chisel my own face, to staunch the bleeding with ashes, to fashion my own gods out of my entrails. And if going home is denied me then I will have to stand and claim my space, making a new culture.[132]

So although we may need agency, a fractured and multiple self may entail the reformulation rather than the end of it. If we take seriously the claims of the constituted self, we cannot situate agency solely within the individual. Instead, it might be situated in the individual, the intersubjective community, and the structure of society. Claiming that agency dies with the individual assumes that if the self is fractured, it must be radically determined and arbitrary. Judith Butler makes explicit the flaw in this reasoning:

Paradoxically, the reconceptualization of identity as an *effect*, that is, as *produced* or *generated*, opens up possibilities of "agency" that are insidiously foreclosed by positions that take identity categories as foundational and fixed. For an identity to be an effect means that it is neither fatally determined nor fully artificial and arbitrary. That the *constituted* status of identity is misconstrued along these two conflicting lines suggests the ways in which the feminist discourse on cultural construction remains trapped within the unnecessary binarism of free will and determinism. Construction is not opposed to agency; it is the necessary scene of agency, the very terms in which agency is articulated and becomes culturally intelligible.[133]

The notion of the multiple self and the way we think about agency clearly challenge the validity of the intent standard in racial discrimination claims.[134] This standard is problematic in any context, but it is simply inapposite in the context of racism, because it fundamentally mischaracterizes the way that racism functions within the individual and within society. Under current jurisprudence, the claim that someone intended to discriminate on the basis of race is interpreted as an assertion that this person engaged in the conscious thought process, "I dislike or disfavor this person because of her race, and therefore I shall behave adversely toward her." Such a characterization of racism is clearly erroneous under any but the modern theory of the self. In addition to ignoring the structural and institutional roles, it is based on a unitary, transcendent view of the self. Both a psychoanalytic and a multiple view of the self reject the idea that this is possible.

Twenty-five years ago, Charles Lawrence pointed out that "requiring proof of conscious or intentional motivation . . . ignores much of what we understand about how the human mind works."[135] Contemporary research on subconscious bias confirms that unconscious thought processes play a primary role in the interaction between the self and the other, but psychoanalytical insights also clarify that the intentional/unintentional dichotomy of current discrimination jurisprudence is a false one. Lawrence explains:

> Racial matters are influenced in large part by factors that can be characterized as neither intentional – in the sense that certain outcomes are self-consciously sought – nor unintentional – in the sense that the outcomes are random, fortuitous, and uninfluenced by the decisionmaker's beliefs, desires and wishes.[136]

Yet common misconceptions of the way the self functions continue to be used to justify a demand by the courts for proof of an explicit, conscious intention to discriminate in all cases related to race and racialization. This demand has grave repercussions. It means that the courts recognize only a small subset of racist actions – those that can be proved to be the product of some specific conscious mind or minds – and leaves the vast majority of them unaddressed. In our current social context, where overtly racist theories are generally discredited, most racist actions are driven by semiconscious, subconscious, or unconscious motivations.

The postmodern critique of the self as socially constructed, constituted, and shaped by social context also undermines the rationale for the intent standard. Given the centrality of racism to the construction of both society and self (both minority and non-minority), any jurisprudential theory that assumes a static, a priori self will fail to recognize the full extent to which racist actions harm individuals and the full extent to which intersubjective discourses and structures contribute to the creation and perpetuation of these harms.

Current discrimination jurisprudence views racist actions as problematic because they remove the a priori self from its original position and treat it as if it exists at another position by virtue of certain insignificant appendages ("arbitrary contingencies") that it possesses. Specifically, the racialized self is assigned a position that causes it to be disfavored in various otherwise fair transactions (applying for jobs, seeking housing, and so on). The law remedies these transactional aberrations by returning the self to its original and rightful position, regardless of its arbitrary contingencies. Under this rubric, one understands the assertions that historical racism and race-conscious remedies such as affirmative action are equally abhorrent. Yet critiques of the modern self recognize that racism is a far more complex and entrenched phenomenon. The remedial method is necessarily inadequate because it fails to acknowledge the larger discourse that causes certain "arbitrary contingencies" to be consistently singled out. Also, it fails to acknowledge the effect of this discourse on the constitution of all subjects that exist within it.

Because the postmodern self is intersubjective, dependent upon others for definition, oppression is a relational function. As Trina Grillo put it: "You cannot get rid of subordination without eliminating the privilege as well."[137] In other words, contrary to current jurisprudential theory, there is no original position to which we can return the racialized self.[138] Furthermore, because the self is relational and context-dependent, race is an "intersubjective phenomenon"[139] whose meaning both resides in a discourse outside of the minds of particular subjects and functions to shape those subjects.

The relational and constructed nature of the self means that racial discourse can be described as both "self-making" and "world-making" in that it structures both individual identities and interpersonal relations. Toni Morrison makes this point explicit when she describes the interdependence of racial identities in the definition of the white American ethos.[140] As Mullin puts it, race relations are "not always about what happens between defined groups but also involve [the] constitution of identities and groups."[141] Thus, it is critical that we examine the way we create and utilize race in our society. For example, modern discourse views segregation as problematic because it precludes certain individuals from having access to certain resources and opportunities. But the problem goes much deeper than that. Segregation goes to the very core of the constitution of the self and the other. It deprives the racialized self of access to resources and opportunities but also plays a determinative role in the way racialized groups are constituted and controls and justifies the image the dominant self perceives of the racial other.

We must bring our focus to the way the construction of blackness and otherness is related to creating and maintaining the normal (white male) individual.[142] As Toni Morrison does from a literary perspective, it is imperative that we look at how racial structures have marked whites. For instance, David Roediger and Ruth Frankenberg suggest that it is privilege itself that creates and maintains whiteness.[143] If the law is to adequately address racism, it must acknowledge and expose the central role that racial discourse plays in the construction of self and society, as well as the process by which this discourse is created and sustained. This project requires recognizing that there will be strong, often unconscious, resistance to policies and actions that threaten the stability of the dominant self by threatening the stability of racial discourse. The power of racial discourse in the sanctity of the self can be seen in how "slaveholders from the 17th century onward created and politicized racial categories to maintain the support of non-slaveholding whites, . . . convincing whites to support a system that was opposed to their own economic interests."[144] It also requires the fundamental recognition that racism pervades and structures our society and is not merely present in the aberrant minds of a few racists.

Finally, the law must address the harm that racism causes by its stigmatic effect upon individual development. The Supreme Court recognized this effect in 1954, in *Brown v. Board of Education*, but has largely failed to use this recognition to inform its practices. The relational, constitutive self mandates that we remember the stigma identified in *Brown* and recognize both the effect on individuals and social groups of the development of racialized identities and the privilege that is buttressed by this stigmatization. What this may require in the form of jurisprudence is uncertain, but our current "tort model" analysis of racism is certainly inaccurate and inadequate.

The Use of Categories

Postmodernists have discussed the use of categories as conventions of law and social organization. Indeed, categorization plays a critical role in modernity's essentialist ordering of the self and reality. Language and discourse also have a profound effect upon the constitution of the subject. Language is not just a tool; it also shapes us. Self-awareness is largely dependent on language, and language is necessarily social. Most postmodernists seem to agree, with reservations, that categorization is a necessary tool. Some psychoanalysts would go further and assert that the tendency to categorize is a universal by-product of the human need to understand experience.[145] If we are to avoid a descent into meaningless plurality, particularly with respect to the law, we must, as Flax urges, make "claims about what we believe to be better or worse ways of being a person."[146] Harris illustrates this point in stating that "avoiding gender essentialism need not mean that the Holocaust and a corncob are the same."[147] Furthermore, even though we recognize that categories are socially constructed, they powerfully shape our experiential world and our sense of self.[148] If we are to respect each individual's sense of self, then, to the extent possible, we also must respect the intersubjective truths (categories) that shape this self. Michael Sandel makes a similar point:

> The bonds between the self and (some) others are thus relaxed on the intersubjective account, but not so completely relaxed as to give way to a radically situated subject. The bonds that remain are not given to physical bodily differences between human beings, but by the capacity of the self through reflection to participate in the constitution of its identity, and where circumstances permit, to arrive at an expansive self-understanding.[149]

When we use categories, we must do so with a functional goal in mind. Note that this effort will always be radically incomplete, however. We use and form categories behind our backs, as it were – unconsciously. We cannot be seduced by the Enlightenment goal of making all things exposed to the conscious mind, as even when we are critical of the Enlightenment dream, we are still the product of that dream. This will change. And while we cannot abandon the use of categories, we can avoid the belief that they can ever capture the world and all its emerging possibilities. Sandel would add that we also cannot "fall back on reassuring, universal standards to justify our beliefs."[150] This means, Haraway suggests, that we must abandon the quest for total explanations and instead seek "partial, real connections."[151] This requires at least two internalizations. First, a category's function must be explicit: there can be no "invisible" motive or function masked in false legitimacy. As Flax points out, we must ensure that the "benefits and limitations [of the category] are always defined and take on meaning in relation to specific purposes which we must also specify and defend as our norms."[152] Haraway argues that we also need to reconceptualize race as a "strategic essentialism" concerning "a certain set of political and moral rights and obligations that are argued to arise from a certain history."[153] Second, in order to avoid the exclusivist and imperialist functions of universal categories, a category must be, Harris reminds us, "tentative, relational, and unstable."[154] We must continually evaluate a category's viability in terms of its purpose, the manner in which it serves its function, and the degree to which it may serve other, unintended functions. The problem with the unitary self may extend beyond the problem of excluding normative logocentric, phallocentric requirements for inclusion. The problem may be that modernity's goal of unity also requires the silencing of those internal and external voices that do not fit into the narratives used to maintain unity and construct the self.

If we accept that the self is relational and multiple, it follows that our efforts to address oppression must focus on the privileged as well as the oppressed. From a pragmatic standpoint, we must acknowledge that subordination affects the position of both the dominant and the dominated. Postmodernists sometimes unwittingly accept many flawed parameters and limitations of modernism, as, for example, in the dichotomy portrayed in the essentialist/anti-essentialist debate. Given the extensive ramifications of reconstituting the self, we must critique the modern self externally as well as internally. We must not repeat the epistemological flaws of the modernist project. The discourse on the postmodern self will be ongoing, with no fixed resolution on the horizon. We can only hope that the debate is undertaken prudently and with due respect for the great personal, social, and philosophical issues it affects.

PART FOUR

Engagement

EIGHT

Lessons from Suffering

HOW SOCIAL JUSTICE INFORMS SPIRITUALITY

As people who live – in a broad sense – together, we cannot
escape the thought that the terrible occurrences that we see
around us are quintessentially our problems. They are our
responsibility – whether or not they are also anyone else's.

Amartya Sen, Development as Freedom

[The] need to face and understand our suffering, and to
change toward new values, is perhaps the basic spiritual
narrative – the common core of world spirituality.

Roger Gottlieb, Joining Hands: Politics and Religion Together for Social Change

Much of the literature on the relationship between social justice and
spirituality focuses on how spirituality has informed and inspired social
justice work. Relatively little attention is paid to how social justice might
inform the practice and development of spirituality. These spheres, however, share a deep concern with suffering, which is a central concern and
animating force of both. Social justice and spirituality are, moreover, in
a recursive relationship, on which I focus here.

SUFFERING, SPIRITUALITY, AND SOCIAL JUSTICE

It is helpful first to differentiate, broadly, between two forms of suffering.
Spiritual suffering can be thought of as ontological or existential suffering. Existential suffering reflects the sense of lack and disillusionment
inherent in material existence and in the presence of consciousness,

particularly self-consciousness. We all grow old, and we all die. Things, including the self, fall apart. The insubstantial nature of the self cut off from a more substantial source, as well as its final demise, are the heart of spiritual suffering. David Loy asserts that the sense of lack is the heart of spiritual questioning and profoundly impacts both our spiritual and secular suffering.[1] It is not simply that we will die, but that we never were the substantial being we conceived ourselves to be to begin with. We lack the substantiality that we yearn for. The very existence of a separate self or self-consciousness causes a split and suffering that is difficult to heal. All of us are subject to existential suffering.

Social suffering, unlike ontological suffering, is not inherent in self-consciousness or being but is largely the result of our social arrangements. It is visited upon different people to varying degrees. Indeed, because social practices institutionalize subjugation and suffering that need not exist, social suffering can be thought of not just as secular but also as surplus suffering. Because this suffering is the result of social arrangements and norms, it is surplus to the inherent suffering of life and can be made better or worse.

Of course there are types of suffering that lie outside of these categories and that may be implicated in how we relate to spiritual and social suffering: I may get a stomachache or suffer other pain that is not caused by social arrangements and does not implicate my sense of self. Some may indeed object that ontological or existential suffering should not be considered spiritual, given that much of philosophy addresses it without looking through a religious frame. Yet most of the philosophical rumination on existential suffering, at least historically, has been rooted in religious values and understandings. I think it is appropriate to push this even further and question a clear boundary between what is called secular and what is called spiritual.

Further, much of the cause of surplus suffering has been understood primarily in individualistic and human terms: one person beats up or kills another, or a group of people discriminates against another group. This way of looking at suffering has led some to assume that any effort to address it must also be on individualistic or human terms. These assumptions are false. As previous discussion has emphasized, much surplus suffering is caused not by individuals directly, but by structures and institutional arrangements. John Rawls makes a similar assessment in focusing on basic institutions. He notes that individual wants and desires are themselves a product of situatedness and background institutions. To put it differently, one cannot address justice by looking only at individuals.[2] What I am suggesting is that if spirituality is to engage suffering and its causes, it must also be concerned with how institutions and structures function in society. This understanding could offer a more critical and transformative dimension to spirituality and redefine the spaces between spirituality and social justice. One might also question whether other expressions of life suffer. Indeed part of the split between self and other is echoed in the split between self and other beings, as well as nature. So this is an important consideration as well, though I will not develop it here.

Rather, I ask, what is the relationship between social suffering and spiritual suffering? More pointedly for our discussion, does surplus suffering inform spiritual suffering? Many believe that it does not, or that if the two domains are related, the energy runs in only one direction; that is, spirituality is relevant for addressing social justice and the surplus suffering caused by social injustice, but social justice is not relevant for addressing spiritual suffering. Much of the social suffering that we visit on one another is, however, spiritual at its base. We are greedy and jealous; we fear and distrust one another. We deny one another's humanity because of our flawed spiritual understandings. If we correct these understandings, we could do less social harm. Spirituality requires that we engage in something larger than ourselves. Failure to do so affects the state of the social secular world, but it also limits our ability to address spiritual concerns. Many of our revered spiritual traditions are explicit about being concerned about the conditions people experience in their daily lives and not just in a transcendental realm.

On the other hand, ontological suffering is caused by the fact of being alive and self-conscious, which suggests that it cannot be avoided by changes in physical or social circumstances. From this perspective, it would seem that what we do or fail to do in the physical world has no bearing on spiritual well-being; similarly, if there is an obligation to be concerned with the spiritual suffering of others, it does not entail being concerned with their physical circumstances. Yet caring about others' suffering is not just about relieving the suffering they experience; it is also about spiritual development and relieving the suffering of the spiritual actor. If we recognize ourselves in others or the divine in others, it is inconceivable that we would be indifferent to suffering just because it is called secular. Indeed, there is possibly a greater indictment to be leveled against accepting surplus suffering, because it is unnecessary and something we inflict upon one another either directly or through our institutions. Note also that although some spiritual traditions are transcendental, many are not. The very separation of the material and mundane from the spiritual can contribute to both confusion and suffering.

I therefore wish to explore and challenge the idea of a disconnect between spiritual and social suffering. These forms of suffering are not radically separate. Spirituality should be concerned with more than ontological suffering. It has an important role to play in social justice work, defined here as work focused primarily on ameliorating social or surplus suffering. There are other ways of defining social justice work: Rawls defines it as fairness; Alasdair MacIntyre asserts that it only takes on meaning within a political-historical context. This chapter's definition, as work focused on ameliorating social suffering, is both different from and similar to the way Rawls and others write about it.[3] And even this definition is qualified with "primarily," because these concerns will naturally reach into other areas, such as physical suffering that is the result neither of social arrangements nor of existentialist suffering and spirituality. Spirituality is based on a deeper concern, but this does not and cannot mean that one is not concerned about what is thought of as the nonspiritual, whatever that might be. The relationship of social suffering to existential suffering is really about the relationship between social justice and spirituality. It is also about the relationship between the secular and the spiritual.

Some of the major spiritual traditions have a rich history of addressing social justice issues. Stories in the Bible, the Koran, and many other sacred writings focus not just on ontological suffering but also on elements of secular suffering, such as hunger, poverty, and physical illness. The effort to end slavery in the United States and the more recent civil rights movement are examples of spirituality's role within struggles for social justice. The Reverend Dr. Martin Luther King, Jr.'s articles of faith were profoundly influential in his call for civil rights, as is apparent in his "Letter from Birmingham City Jail," his "I Have a Dream" speech, and his speech about Vietnam, "A Time to Break Silence."[4] Dr. King did not believe that the racial apartheid he was challenging was unjust only in a civil or secular sense; he also correctly believed that it was in violation of broadly shared spiritual concerns. Even though he came from a rich African American Baptist tradition, he refused to limit his concern to followers of the Abrahamic religions. In "A Time to Break Silence," for example, he expresses concern for Buddhist and other traditions. Dr. King was more than a religious leader; he was a spiritual leader. Notably, he was greatly influenced by the life, work, and spiritual practices of Mohandas Karamchand Gandhi (Mahatma).

Gandhi's work and life are probably the most prominent example of a combination of social activism and spirituality. First in South Africa and later in India, Gandhi provided an enduring example of an inspired integration of these realms. He was deeply committed to nonviolence and to the achieving of just outcomes in the secular world, and his social justice work drew much of its power from his spiritual foundation. He asserted that people who thought social justice was different from spirituality did not understand either. But Gandhi was not just bringing his spirituality to the poor. He also said that he was blessed to have a chance to work with those in poverty and the downtrodden in order to lift up his own spirit, intimating that he was not just using a spiritual base to do social justice work, but that the social justice work also helped to inform and deepen his spirituality. Dr. King noted that "Gandhi was probably the first person in history to lift the love ethic of Jesus above mere interaction between individuals to a powerful and effective social force on a large scale."[5]

THE RELATIONSHIP BETWEEN
SPIRITUALITY AND RELIGION

If social justice work is a focus on or concern for addressing social suffering, what is spirituality? The word is sometimes used as coterminous with the word "religion." At other times the two are treated as completely distinct. There is clearly a relationship, but there are important differences, and the multiple ways we use both terms only add to the complexity. Integrative thinker Ken Wilber has identified several different and often conflicting ways the term "religious" is used, ranging from what he calls nonrational engagement, to religion as extremely meaningful (or integrative engagement), to religion as an immortality project, to authentic religion.[6] Wilber believes that religions can be irrational, rational, or transrational, but he believes that all involve bringing meaning to and reducing suffering in existing structures or facilitating transcendence to a higher structural form. Wilber uses two scales to validate religion. One, the *transitive* scale, helps the adherent adapt and make meaning on a horizontal level – learning to live with things as they are, within existing structures and arrangements. The other is the *transformative* scale, which helps the adherent move to a higher level and change existing arrangements.

One way to distinguish between these scales is to analyze what makes exchanges in a life system work well and have meaning within current arrangements, a process that Wilber refers to as *translation*. The exchanges can be on a physical or nonphysical level. When the needs are such that the exchanges in the current system can no longer make meaning, a change to a higher system takes place. Wilber refers to this transformative exchange as *transcendental*. But what is transcended, and why? Wilber supports the assessments of Hinduism and Buddhism that it is the fear of death and suffering that gives birth to the need for transcendence. "Wherever there is self, there is trembling; wherever there is other, there is fear."[7] Wilber also values the insight of those traditions that until separation and death are addressed, there will be pain (suffering). This is a restatement of what I have called "existentialist suffering" and what David Loy refers to as "lack." Wilber evaluates religions on how well they deal with this suffering and resolve this spiritual need. In this chapter, I will use the term "religion" to suggest an organized or institutionalized set of practices that are designed to support and effectuate a spiritual life and address spiritual suffering.

Roberto Unger uses a different typology to discuss the meaning of the terms "religion" and "spirituality." He begins by asserting that our pursuit of the meaning of our lives and our places in the world is an existential project. Unger also rejects the assumption that existential philosophical questions can be separated from religious questions. "The most significant articulation of existential projects can be found in the major religions and religiously inspired ethics of world history."[8] Unger believes that this project deals with our death and how we engage with one another, as well as with the often strange world outside of ourselves, in which people "live in mutual longing and jeopardy."[9] This longing is an expression of life that unites the secular and the spiritual. A well-lived life recognizes this.

For Unger, interpersonal engagement centers on a preoccupation with dread and on the possibility of salvation. Through engagement, we experience both mutual need and mutual fear of the other. We are exposed to power and disillusionment. We have a deep longing and need for the other that is not just for the realization of what we want, but also for who we are – an existential or ontological need. The other is thus necessary both for the constitution of our being and for the realization of self-expression and growth. Yet engagement with the other threatens the self in its constitution and its wants. "For our efforts at self assertion – at marking out a sustainable presence in the world – may be undermined both by the lack of social involvements and by these involvements themselves."[10] The tension is worked out by our relationship to the other and to our context, the world. Because we need the other and are threatened by the other, there is an interplay of love and hate.

Even our most interpersonal longings and fears are only partially worked out directly between ourselves and others; individuals' relations to others and even one's relation to oneself are mediated and partially constituted through structural and institutional arrangements. Unger refers to these structures and arrangements as context. His view is that some contexts make it more difficult to advance the existential project because of heightened vulnerability and an extraordinary threat of subjection. For Unger, then, the existential project is also about transcending and remaking our context to constantly afford and support richer engagement with the self and with other humans in the world. For him, there is no natural context: all context is made by our collective work and imagination.[11]

Some of us, Unger asserts, motivated as we are by fear and the danger of engagement with others, as well as by the constant threat of death and disappointment in life, will attempt to become invulnerable by remaining detached from human engagement and the phenomenal world in favor of a transcendental merger. Suffering animates this project of merger, as it does the projects of engagement and context transformation. Instead of engaging with the phenomenal world and with other selves who are also in a state of disillusionment, the subject in this endeavor responds to the instability of the world and others by trying to merge with the unconditional. Unger cites Hinduism and Buddhism as religions that institutionalize this form of transcendence, although he acknowledges that there are mystics within the Abrahamic religions who adopt the same approach.[12]

Unger rejects, however, a transcendental space that denies or is cut off from the immanent – a spirituality in which the secular has no impact. Such efforts at escape not only fail to address the suffering and disquiet in the phenomenal world but also create spiritual suffering by moving us toward spiritual narcissism and social conservatism that impede development in both realms. Instead of liberation, these efforts become a religion of resignation and acceptance of the status quo:

> The devotee of the impersonal absolute finds himself constantly nagged or threatened by the irrepressible demands of the real embodied person, the person who has an unlimited craving for other people's help and acceptance and even for their bodies. To be sure, he may achieve a measure of success in his attempt to find serenity through disengagement. But he can do so only by maintaining a distance from the others that deprives him of the chief means with which to experiment with his own character.[13]

While Unger's project can be seen as deeply religious and spiritual, he is critical of religious and philosophical traditions that would detach us from the world and our embodied phenomenal self. This is not just because he is concerned with the world in a secular sense; it is also because he believes that our religious existential project can only be worked out through engagement with others, by constantly remaking our context, institutions, and structures in response to the demands for engagement of embodied spiritual beings. It is not enough to remake ourselves; we must remake the world so that our selves can more appropriately think of the world as a provisional home. Unger asks: What type of institutional and social arrangements support self-assertion and love? As do most spiritual thinkers, he believes that love is the positive value that heals the breach of separation, the angst of being strangers and homeless in the world. Love, therefore, plays a central role in addressing our existential suffering, or lack.

Unger critiques major religions, such as Hinduism and Buddhism, that encourage practices that could degenerate into escapism. Hinduism, however, although it may assert that the world of phenomena is not real, is not indifferent to the world. In fact, much of Hinduism was used to justify – as divinely preordained – rigid social hierarchy in the material world, including the caste system. This is hardly otherworldly. Thus, Hinduism has been closely associated with a particular set of arrangements in the phenomenal world, such that it lacks the separation between the secular and the spiritual that modern Western cultures think so important. Hinduism then is not so much indifferent to the world as it is willing to provide some justification for its conditions. This is not a split between the secular and the spiritual; in fact, such a split did not occur until fairly recently and is largely a modern Western phenomenon.

Buddhism has been cited as the most otherworldly of the major religions, and Unger's critique is that it can be misused as simply an attempt to escape suffering by retreating to a private transcendental relationship with the divine.[14] Teacher and practitioner Ken Jones, among others, would take issue with Unger's view, but he does recognize the danger: "Of all religions Buddhism has long been associated with this quietism, this flight from the world and the institutionally embedded conservatism that commonly accompanies it. . . . At worst such a perspective can become an accessory to social injustice."[15] There is a history of social engagement in Buddhism that is not generally present in its Western reiteration, however. Buddhism in India directly challenged the caste system and rejected claims of the ordained nature of social hierarchy. Indeed, this stance is often one of the reasons cited for the substantial rejection of Buddhism in India.[16] The Buddhist tradition in India also recognized that the satisfaction of material needs is a precondition for moral development and its absence a cause of moral decay.[17] In this sense, those who are indifferent to or benefit from social suffering are a cause of spiritual decay.[18] Some may challenge Unger's description of Hinduism and Buddhism as otherworldly. A more useful way to read

Unger here may be as a critique of transcendentalism, quietism, or a sharp split between the material and spiritual worlds.

Throughout much of history – essentially until the birth of modern democracy – the social order, including the roles of kings and priests, was often based on a belief in a divine order that used a justification not dissimilar to that used by Hinduism in India. One of the great questions in much of premodern history was about the relationship between the divine and the secular. There were differences, certainly, between them, but there was little doubt that the two were intimately related. Indeed, often there was not a recognition of two realms, but instead a perceived continuum. In modern liberal society, we have assumed both that there is a sharp separation between the spiritual world and the secular world and that spirituality is a private matter concerned with a private internal world.[19] This arrangement, and the assumptions behind it, are increasingly being called into question, however. Indeed, a central part of Unger's critique of a transcendental approach is that it is cut off from the phenomenal world, which can lead to easy justifications of an unjust status quo.[20]

Criticizing the effort to find spiritual salvation in a private internal world may strike us as odd, as we often think of spiritual practices as both private and internal. Unger would urge us to consider whether this is not often a spiritual narcissism. Jim Wallis asserts that spirituality – God – is both public and political. Unger believes in the compounding effect of community: "We cannot obtain the categories that allow us to describe our situation and to reflect about ourselves unless we share in specific, historically conditioned traditions of discourse that none of us authored individually."[21]

Loy, a well-known Buddhist scholar and practitioner, offers an even more insightful challenge to the notion of a private, interiorized self, cut off from the world. He cites Max Weber in support of the proposition that the effort to retreat to the private in reaction to a rational, secularized, disenchanted world is both impossible and self-defeating.[22] The more we withdraw from the world, the more disenchanted it becomes, requiring still further withdrawal. For those who believe that the secular world is or should be radically separate from the spiritual world, this may seem heretical. But Loy reminds us that, until relatively recently, most of the world took for granted the unity of the secular and the spiritual. Adroitly citing the move to create this separation in Western society, he argues that all such efforts have failed and indeed must fail. Loy characterizes secularism as religion without God, or, in Weber's language, means without ends. The spiritual need and foundation have not disappeared; they have been driven into the unconscious.[23] At its core, spirituality is about being and meaning. Loy warns that spiritual needs pushed underground and cut off from free expression can reemerge in demonic forms. Loy would start to resolve this unhealthy split by inviting our spiritual need back into consciousness and by rejecting the duality of the spiritual and secular.

Unger's resolution of this problem is to add love to the mix – not the narcissistic love dominant in society today, but rather a love that seeks and embraces the other. This love, central to both our existentialist project and our spiritual yearning, should not be confused with altruism. Unger explains that love requires that we fully engage with the embodied self instead of with the removed and distanced space suggested by altruism. Love requires engagement with our others in their otherness and in their situated embodiedness. It is not enough to care for someone just as a spiritual being, nor can there simply be a resignation to what is. We must make our physical habitation more open to our spiritual yearning, which is self-assertion and connection, or love. Unger is particularly drawn to Christianity's commitment to addressing the need for a bridge between the transcendental spiritual and the physical world. Our disease or suffering in the world pushes us to search for the transcendental, the unconditional. Unger cautions that this search can bear fruit only if we reject the transcendental and open up to embodied, situated others. Indeed, there is no final answer or destination, but this movement is a part of what allows us to become ethical humans.

Unger reads Christianity as instructing us not to flee the conditional, material world. He encourages engagement with the world not to save it, but to save ourselves – or perhaps more accurately, to become ourselves. To seek a world with justice is to seek a world that provides for our spiritual expression. Our authentic self is both unconditional and conditional, universal and particular, corporeal and spiritual. Indeed, healing requires that these apparent binaries be expressed in each other.

We advance in self-understanding and goodness by opening ourselves up to the whole life of personal encounter, rather than by turning away to seek communion with an impersonal, nonhuman reality. We make partial peace with this world we inhabit as homeless strangers by deep engagement with our homeless fellows;[24] we engage the divine by making "our worldly habitation more open to love."[25]

For Unger, such an effort means that we must reject those institutions and structures that limit and frustrate our multiple evolving ways of embracing love, hope, and charity in our routine human relations. Accepting the falseness of what is deemed natural and necessary in our existing context is only the beginning of opening our imaginations to possibilities that can better reflect our own contingencies. Loy sees this understanding and project as central to Buddhism; Unger sees it as part of the Christian Romantic tradition. It is also part of the other great Abrahamic religions, but the heart of it does not depend on any particular religion at all. Rather, it is a spiritual journey requiring that we open ourselves up to engagement with the whole of humanity.

SPIRITUALITY AND ONTOLOGICAL SUFFERING

Spirituality is the practice of addressing ontological suffering by relating to something more authentic or larger than the egoistic self. It is informed by suffering on the one hand – particularly but not exclusively ontological suffering – and love on the other. This connection is sometimes discussed in terms of our true or deeper self, one that is not the same as the egoistic self. Indeed, the heart of Buddhism is the insight that the separate permanent self – ego, which is so important in the secular West – is a fiction, and that the false belief in such a permanent self is one of the main sources of suffering. This egoistic self is both a fiction and a source of real suffering in the secular social domain and the spiritual domain because of the way that it asserts its separateness. One only has to reflect on the damage of separation expressed in segregated speech – and dreams – to see this.

Spirituality addresses the connection with the deeper self, or no self, which is connected with something beyond the egoist self. The way we think about what this connection is has important implications for our spiritual and social practices and for the way that we imagine our structural arrangements.[26] We might conceive of it as a connection with God or the divine – something that is above and separate. Indeed, early Christians often saw sin or hell as separation from God. This could be thought of as a vertical connection. If this separate God is unconcerned with the phenomenal world, then those who adhere to such beliefs are likely to be less concerned with the world. But to adopt a position that God is unconcerned with the world is also to move to undermine our interest in God. One could instead see all beings and phenomena as manifestations of God or the divine.

Another way to think of being connected is to think of being connected to one another, to life, or to the world.[27] Joanna Macy captures the latter in *World as Lover, World as Self*.[28] While there is an apparent difference in the way religious and spiritual practices deal with connection, there seems to be agreement that the lack of connection, or more accurately, the lack of the awareness of connection, is one of the major causes of suffering in both the ontological and the secular realms.[29] Lack of connection is closely associated with suffering and not just from a spiritual perspective but also from a psychological and neurological perspective. Lack of connection with others not only scars our emotions but also restructures and distorts our brains. The need for healthy connection is required in both our secular world and our spiritual world, and our institutions and context have impacts on our connections in both. This profound need is not simply personal but is expressed at both the individual, societal, and structural levels.[30]

If spirituality is about connection, what does it mean to think of it in private terms? Some may assert that it is possible to have a private, vertical relationship with God that does not involve others, but this approach is difficult to sustain for at least two reasons. First, one must believe that God is not concerned with or reflected in others and therefore does not call on one to have engagement with them. This seems inconsistent with much of the teaching of the Abrahamic religions. Another reason that this private approach may not be successful has to do with the nature of the self. As previous discussions of contemporary understandings of this problem indicate, it is not clear that a self that is totally disconnected from other selves could have meaning or even exist.

I have described this issue from the Buddhist perspective, but the insubstantial nature of the self is also increasingly being considered within Western culture. In the language of late modernism and postmodernism, for example, we saw the self described as having a "constituted" or situated nature; as being relational and saturated with other selves.[31] A radical egoistic self that is cut off from its community is also cut off from what constitutes and sustains it. Such a self suffers and indeed may cease to exist. One of the readings of the death of Socrates is that he refused to be cut off from the political community because he understood that outside of this community he was already dead. Orlando Patterson, in his work on the meaning of slavery, demonstrates that slavery is an existence outside of the political community, and that this displacement is one that imposes a social death.[32] This socially dead self, while biologically alive, suffers constantly because of being conscious yet unable to fully constitute itself.

One may object to the notion of the constituted and relational self of late modernism, but what should take its place? The autonomous disembodied self whose privacy we wish to protect is an artifact of early modernity. The rise of the private relationship with God in the Western tradition was in part fueled by the concurrent rise of the private self. This suggests that if modernity can no longer support the existence of such a self, the private religious experience may be undermined as well.[33] Moreover, there may be a strong relationship between events in the larger social world and our self-images and spirituality.[34] In other words, our spiritual and social selves may be more strongly related than we have assumed.

In addition to opening our eyes to this relationship, we must also recognize the suffering that comes from separation from the other. This profound longing cannot be easily healed at the individual level, for the self that is constituted through relationship is constantly in the process of being co-created. Because the project is both personal and social, these realms must be interactive and porous; and because this process is mediated through language, culture, and structures, the individual and interactive selves are never just given. Embedded in social relationships that are both inter and intrarelated, in the context of a web of cultural and institutional arrangements, the self is always in process and interbeing. Indeed, much of what is necessary for the constitution of the self is subject to institutional and societal arrangements. Therefore, to address our being, to heal our suffering, we must be willing to actively engage these arrangements.

Of course the spiritual self is beyond just the political and secular community. Spirituality entails something larger and other. It moves in a different direction from mere ego satisfaction, which spends much of its energies mis-wanting. One can imagine an experience or an insight that would connect one more strongly with the divine but not necessarily with other humans or life expressions. Another approach might extend the connectedness to some select others and exclude those not in this group. At the other end of the spectrum, there might be a deep connection with other life-forms that does not invoke the divine at all. And again, this connection might be extended to a select few (but not others) or to not only all humans but also to all other life- and nonlife-forms.

Huston Smith, echoing Unger, captures the inadequacy of basing a search to end suffering on the individualistic self, noting that it is too small and too private to fully meet our needs and bring happiness.[35] The wants of this small, separate self, i.e., the ego, are both unstable and insatiable. Pursuit of them is always unsatisfying, leaving us wanting – little more than hungry ghosts. This separate self is born in sin or lack and cannot be fulfilled. Indeed, it is this effort in the phenomenal world that creates institutionalized "lack" and institutionally supported surplus suffering.[36] Smith believes that "true religion begins with the quest for meaning and value beyond self-centeredness. It renounces the ego's claim to finality."[37] It is, therefore, difficult to imagine a sense of spirituality in which the egoistic self remains largely self-contained. Spirituality suggests that wherever one draws the boundary for connectedness, one is cut off in a deep existential suffering.

Even if one accepts that the egoist separate self is too small, and indeed false and lacking in substance, there still may be good reason to remain ambivalent about the relationship between spirituality and social justice. One is the concern already addressed, that spirituality is something that can inform social justice work (or at least individual suffering) but that social practice does not inform spiritual work – the idea that caring for others' nonspiritual well-being is a service the already spiritual person provides to others. This work is not required for spirituality, the thought goes; it may be desirable, but it is not necessary. Another concern is practical and based on fear and history. It is that spiritual or, more accurately, religious concerns, when brought into the public square, may cause great harm and suffering. With a few limited exceptions, therefore, spiritual or religious values should be expressed only in private.

In spite of a strong tradition of involvement by spiritual seekers in social justice work, such work has largely been understood as having a weak relationship to spiritual development. Even when a place for concern about the poor is acknowledged, it is often presented as a permissive value rather than something that is either affirmatively required or that will affirmatively deepen spiritual practice. The assumption about Gandhi, Mother Teresa, and Dr. King is that they were deeply religious people who extended themselves to the poor. There is no recognition that their engagement with the poor informed their spiritual development. We can only hold this position, however, if we reject their own assessment of their spiritual journeys. They all strongly assert that their social justice work was essential to their spiritual practice and development, not a reflection of practice already perfected.

Unger's writing also helps us see the limitation of viewing the poor only as beneficiaries of spiritual beings by suggesting that feeding the poor is not enough; we must also open up to them. We are called upon to be vulnerable to them as embodied interbeings – not as abstract beings to be pitied, but as aspects of ourselves, the other, and the divine. As Unger suggests, if we are cut off from the poor and only related through rigid social structures, they as the needy and we as those there to help, the entire relationship is distorted.

Consider the recorded life of Buddha, father of the "otherworldly" religion discussed earlier. What motivated Siddhārtha Gautama to pursue a spiritual path was a concern for suffering. One could say that the suffering he saw in others was both his and their suffering, but his concern was not limited to how to make things good or easy for himself – they already were. And of course the motivation was love. It is not surprising, given his willingness to take on suffering out of his feeling of connection with others, that love and compassion lie at the heart of his teachings. A related observation about the importance of recognizing the unity of all existence can also be drawn from the recorded life of the Buddha: in spite of a practice of many seekers in denying the phenomenal world and the desires associated with it, it was not until Siddhārtha Gautama rejected this position and attended to his physical body that he was able to achieve enlightenment. He spoke of this approach as the middle way.

From the perspective of social justice, there is a similar set of concerns. While some welcome a spiritual foundation for social justice, others worry that such a foundation is narrow and closed. The decision is then made that in secular society it is better to base social justice on non-religious/nonspiritual concerns. But what is the foundation of values, ethics, and morals if it is not spiritual concerns about connectedness? The Enlightenment project of the West has attempted to answer the call for foundational moral concepts in contexts separate from those of spirituality and religion. It is not entirely clear that this has been successful. What would support and sustain respect for a separate individual? One approach would be to build a foundation on a separate, self-contained individual. But it is extremely doubtful that such a being exists, from either a spiritual or a psychological perspective. Another approach is to suggest that we are all the same, but this is just another form of narcissism that also fails. Instead, we must recognize both our shifting similarity and our difference. Unger anticipates this with the call to love the other. Love and connectivity is more than just an extension of vanity.[38]

All of this brings us to the widespread assumption that there is great danger in bringing spirituality into the public space. Although this concern may appear to be very different from the assumption above – that social justice efforts should be based on a nonspiritual foundation – it is not. Both positions assume that spiritual concerns can be separated, and in the latter case, should be separated, from social concerns. The concept of separation of church and state is based on an experiential history of great danger in state orthodoxy on matters of faith. This position therefore need not be, and indeed is not, anti-spiritual or anti-religious; it merely assumes that the forceful power of the state can best be used to create an environment in which religious freedom is exercised in the context of a neutral separated state.

The concern as reflected in our Constitution was not that religion would influence the state but that the state would be coercive in religious matters. The separation of church and state, at least historically, was not a mandate to keep religious values private but rather to protect space for religious values.[39] While there is undoubtedly a danger of improperly conflating the realms of church and state, there is also danger in improperly, unconsciously, separating the spiritual from the secular. Curtis White brings our attention to this danger in an examination of the rationale for the response to 9/11. Citing the work of Hegel and Derrida, White notes that the response of the United States could be understood only as religious in nature, albeit unconsciously so.[40]

Neutrality, especially in the context of our nation, is also associated with the freedom to exercise faith. It is the state that must be neutral, not the citizenry. The arrangement that is part of our history and founding documents is an effort to support religious pluralism. The concern is not with religion per se but with avoidance of a state orthodoxy that would disfavor the nonorthodox. The pluralism is implemented through respect for the rights of the individual and refusal to allow state-sponsored religion. But although state neutrality is valued, it is frequently confusing and difficult, if not impossible, to maintain.

Many of the values that some consider bedrock secular values are believed by others to be based on specific religious values. Consider the controversy over marriage and the nature of the family. Historians trace marriage from at least as long ago as the development of the concept of the self and the registering of births, deaths, and related rites. Older practices include the Incan idea that among the highest-ranking persons, only a sibling could be a worthy mate, and the practice in Mesopotamia of marriage between cousins, to help control inherited land. Eventually the rising sense of individual rights, along with the rise of institutional support, lessened the level of involvement of extended family in the choice of mates.[41] That development was solidified in the European context with the 1563 Council of Trent's proclamation that a couple's marriage was completely validated by a priest's blessing (assuming the partners were not too closely related) in spite of any objections that the families might have.[42]

In modern America, *Loving v. Virginia* expanded the rights of individuals to marry, affirming that marriage is a basic civil right, fundamental to existence and survival: "The Fourteenth Amendment requires that the freedom of choice to marry not be restricted by invidious racial discriminations. Under our Constitution, the freedom to marry, or not marry, a person of another race resides with the individual and cannot be infringed by the State."[43] But what about the freedom to marry a person of the same sex? Many would argue that, given its status as a fundamental right, marriage should be viewed in secular terms. Yet others see our culture's evolving concepts of marriage and the family not only as grounded in religion but also as originating from a particular set of religious beliefs, which they believe should continue to be honored and applied broadly across an increasingly diverse society. Does this position support using the state to prohibit others from marrying? Those who would say yes are in effect challenging the line between state and church.

Respect for the religious values of pluralistic communities and the assertion that we must all be tolerant will of course create tensions. It is simply false that all values are largely or primarily about private matters. The Mormons, for example, lost their Free Expression argument against the Morrill Act, which banned their religious doctrine of polygamy.[44] And what if one's religious values call for positions inconsistent with tolerance? If I believe that someone is about to commit a grave injustice, sin, or wrong, it is not clear that the appropriate response is that it is none of my business, and that I must necessarily respect the privacy and autonomy of that person in that act. This form of privacy may be an important liberal ideal, but it may also be in sharp contrast with religious ideas.

Life and death issues come to mind first. The intensity of the public struggles over end-of-life care, in the face of our ability to mechanically sustain physical functioning when an individual can no longer survive independently, has provoked furious debate. Questions arise as to who decides how long or under what terms such a state of being should be maintained. Also at issue are different understandings about what a given person's state and possible outcomes actually are. And what of assisted suicide, or abortion? These issues involve intimate, often painful, personal decisions. To what extent does the community have a right or obligation to intervene? We hold radically different views about the beginning and end of life. How may the state best reflect these concerns?

One of the ways we try to resolve this issue is by making these concerns private, which indeed they are, for the individuals experiencing them. As many come to realize, however, not always in pleasant ways, privacy is, in some important respects, an illusion. Even when it exists, moreover, shall we use it as a way of resolving public issues in which the public is and should be interested?[45] If not, how do we protect the rights of the individual whose beliefs are minority views, or indeed, singular? In some cases, such protection may be possible. Deep concerns about capital punishment have been addressed legislatively, for example, with the help of concurrent efforts, such as demonstrating the fallibility of human justice and the value of mercy toward those who became caught up in a life – or devastating moment – of violence.

Numerous other issues of spiritual concern remain shrouded from view. What if imprisonment involves torture? Is it all right if we hide the prisoners, or torture only non-citizens? Many view the breeding, caging, and abuse of non-human beings with great concern. Is this concern off limits because the activity is viewed as private consumption of a privately produced "commodity"? In these and other ways, the ability to draw a distinction between private and public, spiritual and governmental, has been appropriately called into question. Cardinal George, archbishop of Chicago, rejects a neat divide between spiritual and secular and public and private, maintaining that racial segregation, and the resulting inequality, is a sin.[46]

SPIRITUALITY, RELIGIOUS VALUES, AND COMMUNITY

One solution to the tension between religious values and public secular space is to have a plurality of religious doctrines but to shield issues of private concern from public debate. This effort to closet religion and wall it off from public space solves the problem by distorting religion, limiting it, even making it trivial. If religious or spiritual values are of great importance to us, it is unrealistic to suggest that they relate only to matters of personal or private concern. There are other, similar reasons to be skeptical of this arrangement. I have already explained two of these assumptions turned arrangements: The first is that we can easily distinguish between the public and private. The second is that spiritual or religious values are properly consigned to the private sphere. A third assumption is that the role of the state is to protect individual autonomy and that this is accomplished by a neutrality in public matters that allows each individual to freely choose values or religious tenets. This assumption can be thought of as a secular restatement of the Establishment Clause, extended to all values.

Such an arrangement is possible, however, only if the law can be neutral. Even the way the law conceives of and moves to protect the rights of the autonomous individual raises serious concerns about the feasibility of this stance. The nature of the individual's relationship to other individuals, as well as its nature in and of itself, is a highly contested issue with deep religious foundations. Loy offers a few examples: "Hobbes's state of nature is a secularized version of Calvin's 'natural man' without God. Socialist critiques of private property originated in allegorical interpretations of Adam's Fall and God's curse upon him. John Locke's theory of individual rights is rooted in a Protestant understanding of man's relationship with God."[47]

The nature of this Protestant individual and its relationship to the group is not only a philosophical or conceptual issue, but also an issue that implicates a number of religious tenets. It may be that there is an important recursive relationship between the notion of the individual in law and the nature of the individual in, for example, Christian Protestantism as opposed to Catholicism. It may be more than a coincidence that Protestants move toward having personal relationships with God, while Catholics are more likely to have such relationships mediated through the church. Even if one could step away from religion, there is still no clear concept of the individual. For example, the ideal of respect for the individual, which is one of the bedrock values in the secular democratic state, has been seriously called into question by many late modernists and postmodernists as well as many students of religion. They challenge the concept of the organic, essential nature of the individual and the artificial and arbitrary nature of community. But what if the self is constituted through community and relationship? This challenge to the priority of the individual would seriously disturb the claim of neutrality.

There is another reason to be skeptical of efforts to build a wall between spiritual values and public space. What if the arrangement of public space has an impact both on suffering in the phenomenal world and on our ability to pursue a spiritual life? In fact, the way we arrange our space does just that, insist Unger, Jones, and others.[48] Context matters. Social arrangements have spiritual implications in a developmental way. Oppressive arrangements or the lack of basic necessities can and do affect spiritual development. Though these conditions may not destroy such development, they can make it more difficult. Similarly, the lack of a spiritual and moral foundation can undermine well-being in the secular world. Some relationship between these two realms has been recognized, but the institutional and structural arrangements that can be important to both have not.

As Jones says, one reason for this lack is that many of the world religions came into being before the complex social structures and social theory that we have inherited. Moreover, we live in a time when the ideology of individuality blinds us to the way that structures and institutions help shape and form what we call our inner and outer lives.[49] Until we correct this ideology, we will continue to misunderstand the role of society as well as the nature of the individual that we wish to rescue from secular and existential suffering.

The story of the Garden of Eden reflects the insight that separation is the suffering-generating loss that we as spiritual beings struggle most to overcome. It portrays a separation from God that cast man and woman out into the world to suffer as aliens. Redemption is a return to God, but in this story Adam and Eve also were alienated from one another and from themselves, as indicated by their shame. So redemption must include recapture of right relationships at these other levels as well.[50] In other teachings, some of which are nontheistic, it is our lack of awareness of our interrelatedness and interbeing that causes us to believe in our separateness and to suffer because of our institutional arrangements.

Our handling of the belief that we are separate is no small matter and is fraught with difficulties. For one thing, we cannot go back, and should not go back, to some premodern time before such separation was widely perceived. Today's separation is not just a problem with tolerance; the modern self is not the same self as that of premodern times. Another issue arises from the different origins and operational modes of the different spheres. Karen Armstrong captures this difference in *The Battle for God*. Describing religious and spiritual practices as being based on myth, and modernity and public space as based on logic, Armstrong notes that the inappropriate mixing of the two can be disastrous. The solution has often been to think of the two realms as separate, rather than as different but complementary.

It is important to acknowledge the danger of conflating these two spheres, but if the solution that we have adopted is based on a misunderstanding of the problem, it is likely to be unworkable. Earlier I cited Loy for the proposition that secular society is unconsciously defined and driven by spiritual need. I have also suggested that the problem may be with orthodoxy more than with spirituality, but these issues and problems are not limited to what we formally call religion. As we think deeply about them, we are forced to think about our context and the nature of the self. Consider the public self that lives in the public space of early modernity. This self is not only not religious in public space; it is also largely devoid of passion. But how are we to reason without passion and spiritual grounding?

Much of the insight of neuroscience rejects the passion/reason split on which the private/public split is built. Hubert Dreyfus and Sean D. Kelly remind us in *All Things Shining* that the drive for meaning and awe is the human journey. Even as we have pushed God out of our public secular life, the question of meaning not only remains, but also remains deeply spiritual and philosophical. The failure to engage this question leaves our spiritual and secular life unenchanted – dull and without meaning. The move from the public toward the private for spiritual concerns is largely a Western and Christian, even Protestant, phenomenon. Martin Luther is identified with the move to communing directly with God in a private space. Indeed many have asserted this was a critical change both in the development of the public/private split and in the creation of a semi-sacred private space. That split did not occur in Islam, Confucianism, or many other world religions; nor was it a position taken by the Roman Catholic Church.[51] The Protestant position – the idea of a sharp split between the public and private and between the secular and spiritual – has been largely picked up by liberal democracies in the West, though it works inadequately.

Given the plurality of spiritual and religious approaches, there is some risk in trying to make generalizations about spirituality. The irreducible plurality of religion is the central point of Stephen Prothero's *God Is Not One*. Some religions don't have a god; some have many. Some religions focus on sin; others on harmony. One commonality Prothero does find is that religions come into being to address pressing and salient issues faced by a society. The point I have been asserting here is that if spirituality is removed from our collective questions and concerns, its absence will undermine not only spirituality but also our secular lives.

Fear of spirituality, passion, and religion causes liberal society to attempt to closet these domains and to overstate and misunderstand their differences. Human yearning and spirit can and do inform one another, however. Do we get the meaning of our lives from our reason or from our spiritual beliefs? When we look closely, it becomes clear that there is no singular entity called reason and that reason cannot be devoid of feeling or passion. That is, we see that reasoning cannot operate as early modernists had hoped it could.[52] More important in this context, reason cannot by itself address the insubstantiality that drives our secular and spiritual quest. These questions of meaning cannot be resolved in private and certainly not in the unconscious.

ORTHODOXY AND INTERBEING

I have posited that an orthodox religious perspective adopted by the state is likely to be coercive and violent; indeed, liberal modernity is partially an outgrowth of religious wars. But the problem may be lesser or greater than this statement suggests. It may be that rather than spiritual or religious values, it is orthodoxy that is the problem. Unger's writing against context that cannot be transformed, or "false necessities," is writing against orthodoxy.[53] Loy refers to orthodoxy as idolatry.[54] It is not the religious or spiritual nature of the value that is at issue, but its orthodoxy. Wilber notes that there are indeed religions that are irrational, but he points out that there are also religious and spiritual practices that are transrational.[55] Orthodoxy, with its inherent rigidity and will to control, is probably easier to maintain if one does not have to engage the other as an interbeing.

Some suffering is endemic to a self-conscious life. Ego consciousness is born out of separation and suffering, and this suffering seems unavoidable, short of redemption and/or enlightenment. But this suffering is not just individual but is reflected in our institutions and structures as part of our collective being. To try to resolve collective problems only at the individual level is a fool's errand. Moreover, surplus suffering – that which we inflict on one another – is not a necessary part of the human condition. Spousal abuse, racism, and war are not inescapable parts of human life. Spirituality, which is animated by suffering, must therefore be cognizant of both ontological and social suffering. The greater our sense of interconnectedness, the greater the scope of our empathy and compassion for those who are suffering. If we see someone or something as outside of the select group of connectedness, we are far less likely to extend the concerns regarding suffering to that being or nonbeing. Compare this view with that of those who believe not only that we are connected to the earth but also that the earth can suffer as well.

Unger suggests that the world be divided into two categories, oneself and everyone else, with the sense of self sometimes extended to family, village, race, or tribe. Care for self is different from care of others, yet this separate self is both the cause and the object of both major forms of suffering. Institutions and structures are therefore critical to an understanding of the self and of the suffering experienced by it. The Eastern tradition's insight that the issue is liberation *from* the self – not *of* the self – is of particular value here.

Indeed the divide between the self and the other in these terms also tells us more. To paraphrase Wilber: wherever there is self, there is fear; wherever there is other, there is terror. Yet escape from this fear does not automatically entail a radical separation of and from others of the type that has largely informed the early liberal modernist approach, nor does it mandate an equally disquieting forced merger of the self with others. We may need to become aware of our separateness before we become aware of our connectedness. Resolution will also be informed by the understanding that not all connectedness is the same.

THE CALL TO HEAL THE SEPARATION THROUGH LOVE

I have talked about the need to address both ontologically based and socially based suffering, but there is another important dimension to spirituality. Although we are pushed by suffering to something deeper and larger than the egoistic self, we are also pulled in that direction by love. Love gives us the hope and the reality of reconnecting. It heals the sense of loss and separation that haunts the egoistic self. The ego's self-containment limits it to a narcissistic love that can never move beyond itself and is therefore always trapped in separation. Virtually all spiritual practices therefore require a movement beyond the boundaries of the self. Love calls the ego to move beyond itself. It pushes us out of the prison of separation and the suffering of isolation. It pulls us out by the hope that it makes us feel. No wonder love plays such an important role in all major religions.

In a world that is unjust, hard, and rigid, not only is there a great deal of surplus suffering; there is also too little space for love. Existential suffering and the lack of love are, however, strongly related. Existential suffering is about being separate from the divine, the home, and atonement. It is being disconnected from what supports our authentic being. It is in our very being, our sense of self, that we experience our separateness and our sense of loss and emptiness. For Christians, this loss is the separation from God. For a child, it is separation from the birth mother. For all of us, this loss may include separation from our other mother, Earth. It is also self-consciousness. In our consciousness, the self is existential, but suffering is as well. We are haunted by the primal loss of connection and the pending loss that is death. Our very consciousness gives birth to our sense of separation.

Our project is not to return to the primal preconsciousness in which we are merged and undifferentiated; it is to move to a higher consciousness that recognizes both our relative separateness and our profound connectedness. If the suffering of an individual is not seen as a cause for concern and engagement, then there is no reason to address the role of institutions and structures in producing suffering. I have been asserting that the issue of suffering, even in the secular space, is a fundamental spiritual concern, and that, therefore, one must be cognizant of the sources of suffering. This is especially true when one is an active or passive beneficiary of such suffering.

What does holding a person in slavery do to the spiritual development of the one who asserts and enforces such a claim? Hegel and Fanon have explored this in work addressing the relationship between masters and servants, but the question needs to be enlarged.[56] To focus on the relationship between master and slave is to continue to see the relationship in individualistic terms. Slavery in the United States, however, was a peculiar institution that affected the entire society, including non-slaveholding whites and free blacks. This institutional arrangement, therefore, affects the spirit of the nation and all of its members. What does the institution of slavery do to all of those who live within its walls, within the structures of that institution – not just in physical terms, but also in spiritual terms? How does it affect the way we think of ourselves as spiritual beings? These concerns demand that we extend our focus beyond just relationships between slaves and masters to the institutional arrangements that undergird them.

Apartheid in South Africa, for example, could not be understood as or reduced to personal relationship, or adequately addressed at a merely personal level. Other examples range from the institutional and systematic subordination of females or the disabled to the hole in the ozone layer or global warming resulting from injury to the earth. These issues cannot be understood or addressed simply at the level of individuals. It is equally clear that the arrangement of our society is causing both injury to the earth and injury and suffering to various life-forms, including humans. These examples have physical implications, but they also have spiritual implications. At a very profound level, they require that our sense of self undergo a radical expansion. Verlyn Klinkenborg writes of this from the point of view of survival:

> In our everyday economic behavior, we seem determined to discover whether we can live alone on earth. E. O. Wilson has argued eloquently and persuasively that we cannot, that who we are depends as much on the richness and diversity of the biological life around us as it does on any inherent quality in our genes. Environmentalists of every stripe argue that we must somehow begin to correlate our economic behavior – by which I mean every aspect of it: production, consumption, habitation – with the welfare of other species.
>
> This is the premise of sustainability. But the very foundation of our economic interests is self-interest, and in the survival of other species we see way too little self to care.[57]

In relation to our current social arrangements, the lack of a more all-encompassing valuation of life has caused us to fail to recognize our common humanity and interbeing and has had profound impacts in both secular and spiritual domains. Many texts point to the problems in assuming that we can be close to God or the divine while being alienated from one another, and this inquiry raises the further question of what the relationship between the self and the other truly is.

From the social death of the slave as written about by Orlando Patterson,[58] to the debates about whether there is a single human species in relation to whites and non-whites, the question is who can be considered part of the human and world community. Moreover, even when someone is considered part of the community for a limited purpose, mutual respect and dignity may be withheld – with harm shared between that person and the one imposing such conditions, who denies a part of him- or herself in the process. The ambivalence many societies have demonstrated and continue to express toward women is another example. Women are certainly part of society even in such contexts, but their place too often is prescribed by men for men, and the loss is universal.

For as we deny the other or use structures to do the work of social distancing and denial, we deny ourselves, and our spiritual lives suffer. What then should our spiritual relationship be to self-denying structures already in place? One answer is captured in the observation by Cardinal George that the way we organize our metropolitan areas is spatial racism and a sin.[59] Cardinal George's statement suggests that there is a spiritual obligation to address a social problem not simply as a means of doing service to others but rather as a means of reconnecting with others and thus with ourselves. A number of the stories in the Bible and the Koran are about work related to caring for others and to rescuing the spiritually dead from failure to recognize our interconnection. There is much in religious and spiritual teaching that suggests that we approach the divine when we extend ourselves to the least among us. The engagement with the suffering of others is not just a matter of service or an expression of our spiritual grounding. It is also a way to know and claim our own spirituality.

It is not surprising, nevertheless, that efforts to reify "otherness" call on religious and spiritual values for their justification. The claims play out in our structures and in what is thought of as our public space. What is striking is the need to frame this culture of social distance, with its attendant suffering, in religious and spiritual terms. It may be equally necessary to conceive of our spiritual selves in social terms. Indeed, patterns and structures that separate us and deny our interconnectedness could be called anti-spiritual. God, the soul, salvation, redemption, and the fall are all concepts interrelated with how we imagine one another and our society. These relationships are more than personal; they are deeply embedded in our institutional and cultural arrangements. It is difficult to imagine their creation and maintenance without reference to our religious and spiritual values.

If spirituality is engagement with the deeper sense of self, the divine, or God, narrow engagement with the egoistic self is the lack of spirituality. The suffering that is caused by separation cannot be healed by this small self. Indeed it is this same self and the institutional arrangements that it collectively brings into being that cause social suffering. Most of the great atrocities have been predicated on the false belief that some group is outside our circle of concern, outside of the human family. We may reflect here on the *Dred Scott* case, in which the plaintiff was barred forever from full citizenship because of his African ancestry. In many ways, this case continues to define the central issue in our nation's political and spiritual life: Who do we as a nation consider to be part of our political community? Racism is a useful model in looking at this question, because it is a systematic denial of a mutual human relationship with the other, except for the purpose of personal exploitation or ego gratification. In giving in to its demands, we not only deny the other person's humanity and interconnectedness but also cut ourselves off from a large part of our own humanity. This problem extends to nationhood as well. Are those who are not inside the national boundaries rightfully outside of our human connection? Coming to terms with the issues of self and in-group, and other and out-group, is central to progress in social justice and spirituality. It is also increasingly and inescapably central to our survival.

One of the core messages of the religions of the world is that our ontological suffering cannot be adequately addressed through the pursuit of secular or egoistic desires. Some have responded to this message by arguing for a sharp distinction between the world of spirit and the phenomenological world. I have already discussed some of the concerns with the effort to withdraw from the phenomenal world in pursuit of a spiritual world. But most of us have not withdrawn. We live in the world, taking advantage of our cars, homes, education, health care, and other collective responses to our physical and social needs. Can we do this in a way that causes suffering to others without seeing or addressing the implications for our spiritual well-being and the spiritual well-being of others? Does the answer change if we are passively allowing suffering to be imposed on others to our benefit? It should be clear that I think there are very substantial reasons why the answer to both of these questions is no.

If one asserts that the matters of this phenomenal world are unimportant, then what is the basis for maintaining one's own advantage, especially if it entails subjecting others to surplus suffering? Ego needs are not necessarily the same as physical and emotional needs. We can agree that I need food and shelter for my physical well-being, love and engagement for my emotional well-being. But when I try to address my fear of death and lack of permanency by the house I acquire, it becomes a distortion that simply cannot be satisfied through such a project. It is an effort that reflects egoistic needs. Because the ego is inclined to elevate its needs above all others, it easily moves toward having others pay for its gratification. This allows or even calls for surplus suffering, in a project that is fundamentally anti-spiritual. In its design to maintain and enhance the ego and its needs and wants at the expense of others, it denies both our interconnectedness and the equality of other selves.

A concern for suffering animates most world religions, and teachings requiring followers to minister to those suffering in the secular world and to avoid causing unnecessary suffering are widespread if not universal. We have noted that spirituality is animated by suffering and, therefore, must respond to it. In engaging in this spiritual quest, an individual or fellowship is not only moving away from something, for the quest is a movement toward something. Given the centrality of this concern in every life, we must develop ways to engage spiritual concerns with suffering at both the personal and the institutional level with the proper degree of sensitivity to the difference between the sacred and the secular.

Compartmentalizing the world has utility, but it cannot be easily or appropriately sustained in regard to these domains. For various reasons, including what John Rawls calls our reasonable pluralism, we cannot treat them as unitary either. There is a coercive nature to the state that is ameliorated by democracy and tolerance.[60] There can be a coercive nature to spiritual beliefs as well, when they are not subject to the mediating processes of love and connection with the other. Can we respond to leaders like Jesus, Mother Teresa, Buddha, Gandhi, Muhammad, and Dr. Martin Luther King, Jr., who were bold enough to prophetically proclaim that they challenged not only secular and spiritual suffering but also the institutions that support suffering?

This is not a call to end the separation of the church and the state; nor is it a call for a continuation of the separation of the church and the state as we know it. These are different domains with differing methods and purposes, but each can support human flourishing, human spirit and body, and the amelioration of spiritual and social conditions. To call for an end to the separation of church and state at this time would be to see civil society swamped in ideological fervor. To call for simply the maintenance of the separation would be a sign of rigidity based on resignation and skepticism. The project I am suggesting is neither overly idealistic nor resigned to what is.

The concepts I propose might appear to be outside of the domain of secular society, even utopian, but the work to bridge the spiritual and the secular has to be informed by both suffering and love. Spirituality and justice call us to move beyond the egoistic self to something deeper, more intimate and authentic, but less private. This move requires recognition of our interconnectedness and our interbeing. It would be easy to assume that this call is otherworldly and idealistic, but properly understood it is neither. The call for this project to be informed by love is a call for love that is engaged in our situatedness with all its imperfections. It is not a call for an idealistic love. Instead, this is a call for what Jürgen Habermas refers to as a regulative idea – one that orients the vision and the direction of the project but is grounded in concrete reality.[61]

This idea can save us from being lost in a means with no sense of an end. But we must hold these ideas or ends open to revision. This requires that we create the structures necessary to support these ideas. It also requires that the ideas be recursively related to the reality we are co-creating. We have not created much space to recognize our interbeing. To act as if we had would prevent us from pragmatically moving in that direction based on where we are and on our current practical imagination of something better. It would also cause us to ignore the need to safeguard the world as it is. We can move toward this idea only with experimentation grounded in our current institutional arrangements, with a vision that is not limited by what is. We cannot reject where we are in hope of being someplace different: we have to lay the groundwork for common space, for sharing our common humanity, and for bulwarks against the dehumanizing tendencies of orthodoxy. This space cannot be created by goodwill alone. It will require structural and institutional support. We can be intentional, however, in reconsidering and building toward this future our larger selves can bring to life.

This is a call to enhance love, but not just private love. This is a call to enhance public love – justice. This is a call to intentionally support the creation of structures informed by and informing our sense of social justice and spirituality. This is a call to become responsible for the institutional structures we inhabit and that inhabit us. This is a call for self- and world-making and for the bridge between them, as well as recognition that the world is deeply spiritual even at its most secular. It is a call to create and live the predicate for a beloved community. As written in 1 John 4:20: "Those who say, 'I love God,' and hate their brothers and sisters are liars; for those who do not love a brother or sister they have seen, cannot love God whom they have not seen."[62]

AFTERWORD

In the course of history, there comes a time when humanity is called to
shift to a new level of consciousness, to reach a higher moral ground.
A time when we have to shed our fear and give hope to each other.
    That time is now.

Wangari Maathai, Nobel Peace Prize Lecture, 2004

Let us develop a kind of dangerous unselfishness.

Dr. Martin Luther King, Jr.

We started this discussion by questioning the idea that the United States,
in electing our first African American president, is now a post-racial
society. I have explained why I think we still have some distance ahead
of us and have offered some suggestions for how I think we can leave
the era of racialization behind us. Emerging understandings about the
interconnected and multiple nature of the self, the mutable and illusory
qualities of race, the pervasiveness of implicit bias and unconscious racial
anxiety, and the limitations of some of the more questionable tenets of
Enlightenment thinking all provide valuable keys to how our lives and
governing systems must change if we are to achieve a fully democratic
society. A greater willingness to view major elements of our lives as socially constructed opens us to more possibilities for this change, which
must begin with a recognition of the societal grounding of the justice system and indeed, of all levels of government, from local to international.

Here I wish to lift up some of the insights and conditions that should
help sharpen our understanding and better prepare us to move beyond

just awareness, to engagement and the hard work of creating change. In a number of places earlier I have mentioned the unconscious on one hand and structures and systems on the other. Our understanding of both has grown exponentially in recent years. With respect to the unconscious, we increasingly recognize that most of our cognitive and emotional response to our environment happens, as it were, behind our backs.[1] Scientists estimate that we can process eleven million bits of information per second but can only consciously process up to about forty of these.[2] Moreover, the forty or so of which we have conscious awareness will be heavily affected by prior exposures to images and metaphors that have become part of our subconscious minds. In this respect, each of us has conflicting associations or schemas that are fairly but not completely malleable. For example, our networks related to hope or fear can be salient at any given time. What is salient will be substantially influenced by cues we pick up or are offered from our environment. This process of being given cues is called priming. Because so many of our cues as well as the environment that helps structure the pathways in our brains are social, many of our unconscious associations are social as well. They are internal, but not private in the ordinary sense.

Our increasing ability to use technology to view and measure this kind of brain activity means that we no longer have to rely so heavily on self-reporting. That method of inquiry was extremely limited in terms of unconscious processes, for what we believe and feel consciously may directly contradict what we are experiencing unconsciously. Indeed, this phenomenon is most likely to occur when our unconscious feelings and judgments are inconsistent with our aspirations, as can so often happen in the context of race. Thus, applying the insights of this emerging science to social cleavages and stratifications such as race, gender, and other areas subject to often powerful socially constructed attitudes allows us to gain a better understanding of the dynamics that produce and exacerbate these cleavages. It can also help us develop ways of overcoming them.

It is important to emphasize in this context that the idea of "not noticing race," or color blindness, is a phenomenon that may or may not happen at the conscious level. There is strong evidence that most Americans are not only race-sensitive but also have racial biases that impact their feelings and decisions at unconscious levels. In other words, we cannot just decide that we will not unconsciously notice race, though we can – through interactions with one another and changes to our structural arrangements – grow beyond these biases. Some may object that only older people see race and harbor racial biases, while young people growing up today in a more tolerant and diverse world are less likely to see race. In *The Hidden Brain*, Shankar Vedantam discusses experiments that tested this very question.

Dr. Frances Aboud asked children in a Montreal preschool to look at a picture or drawing of a white and a black subject. She then read positive and negative words to the children, such as honest, nice, cruel, or ugly. There was a consistent association of positive traits with the white figure and negative traits with the black one. Dr. Aboud was interested in how these associations had developed in the children. Were they from negative stereotypes from their families or school? Dr. Aboud determined that they were not. Instead, these negative unconscious associations were coming from the larger social environment – what the children saw on television or in their day-to-day experiences. It is also interesting that older children tested this way had learned not to consciously express such negative stereotypes, though these negative associations continued to operate at an unconscious level.[3]

This is not unconscious racism or prejudice in the ways that we often think of them. It would be absurd to claim that these young children are racist. These negative racial associations are socially and culturally embedded: they are not only, or even primarily, individual thoughts. Indeed, because these biases are socially communicated and supported, groups such as women and people of color, who have been the objects of bias, will nevertheless also bear it toward members of their own and other traditionally subordinated groups. This group-based bias on the part of members of less-favored groups will not generally be as high or as strong as that of the dominant group, nor is it stable. Like other biases, it can be shifted by priming, through, for example, exposure to images that evoke empathetic (or merely non-negative) responses to people of color or women, as in the experiment described in chapter 6.

Unfortunately, we are more often primed to have negative associations with African Americans. This affects us in relatively superficial responses, but it can also diminish our ability to correctly process specific information. Dr. Aboud, in an effort to discover the impact of presenting positive images of black children to the preschoolers in her study, had a story read to them that featured a wonderful and heroic black child, "Zachariah." When questioned about the story later, the study subjects did remember his glorious deeds, but they most often misattributed them to the two white friends Zachariah had rescued, rather than to him. The associations and bias that derailed these children's memories were built up through stories and metaphors that need not be explicit. Indeed research in this field strongly calls into question the strategy of trying to avoid racial issues by not talking about them. On the contrary, the evidence indicates that efforts to adopt a color-blind approach can increase racial anxiety and negative outcomes, causing the loss of innumerable possibilities for connection, mutual support, and fairness. Dr. Susan Fiske and others have demonstrated that when a group is not liked and is not considered competent, those in the group will often not be experienced as fully human at the unconscious level. Some segments of society, including some law enforcement workers, have for example associated blacks, especially black males, with gorillas and other nonhumans.[4]

When we do not consider someone fully human or in-group – consciously or unconsciously – we will not support constructive policies that benefit or improve capacity for that group. Moreover, as formerly marginalized groups attempt to claim full participation in the public space, we may observe a withdrawal of support for and a shrinking of public space, perhaps even to the point of collapse. This is what Jeffrey Sachs worries about as the country becomes more diverse, if the growing racial and religious anxiety is not well understood or addressed.[5] To avoid such outcomes, it is important that we recognize that, in large part, which associations are salient and activated is a function of both our habitual environment and of what gets primed in a given moment. The images that we use and how we talk about things and each other matter.

We are often unskilled in talking about race. One approach has been to insist that we are all the same and that race does not matter. A second is to insist that our own racial experience is unique and must be addressed as distinct from that of all others. What I have called for – as a way to talk about issues of race and about other cleavages – is the targeted universalism discussed in chapter 1. The concept is simple, has a great deal of appeal, and avoids the problems suggested above. Targeted universalism recognizes that we have many universal goals. We all want our children to be healthy and well educated. We want to be connected to our communities and to make a contribution. We want to enjoy and share our lives. Because we are situated differently in relation to social structures and the environment, however, strategies to provide opportunities for progress toward these universal goals must be targeted for greatest effectiveness.

Our uniqueness lies within us and in our situatedness in our social and physical environment – not in our race, gender, or place of origin. Yet the nature of race can be hard for people to grasp. When we ignore our situatedness, including our relationship to power, we not only misunderstand race, we also deepen racial stratification. For example, during one talk, I was describing some of the effects our current racial arrangements can have on those outside the dominant racial group, from education to life expectancy. One of the people listening challenged me, saying that race was not what was producing these differences. He asserted that if one controls for income, wealth, place of residence, parental education, and access to other important social resources, race drops out or becomes insignificant. My response was to ask, What do you think race is? Race is not biology or phenotype. Race is social and cultural location. Moreover, its effects can be reflected not just in one lifetime, but can also be stored in the body, across generations, as we are finding in the study of epigenetic effects.

In our efforts to get beyond race, we have paid too little attention to how it is constructed and to the work that structures and the unconscious do in creating racial conditions and meaning. Race is not just an idea that we can choose to engage or not. It is structured not only into our environment but also into our brains. When we say that race is socially constructed, we mean that it is constructed in large part by our situatedness. Consider the goal of moving everyone from the first floor to the fifth floor of a building. The means of conveyance available is an escalator. For most people, this will suffice, but for those using wheelchairs, today's escalators are practically useless. The goal for a person using a wheelchair is the same as it is for everyone else, but the strategy employed will have to take situatedness into account. An escalator will not be an effective mode of transportation: the wheelchair user may need an elevator. The goal is universal, but the means to achieve it may have to be targeted. In a similar way, the saying that "a rising tide lifts all boats" can be deceptive. It assumes that we all have boats and that they are all functionally the same. But what if some people have cars but not boats, or some boats are able to rise with the tide, while others sink? The point is that different situations must be taken into account if our efforts are going to succeed.

When we look carefully, we notice that groups that seem to be similarly situated in relation to just one indicator may not be when we look at a cluster of factors, including power. Living in a neighborhood where most of the people have low incomes and a majority of the students in the schools are from low-income families has a significant impact on the residents' life chances that is not fully captured by the single indicator of individual or family income. The concentrated poverty in neighborhoods and educational environments in urban America largely defines the situatedness of poor blacks and Latinos, but not whites. Although there are more poor whites in absolute numbers, what is largely distinctive about the experience of black and brown poverty is the experience of *concentrated* poverty, because of its compounding effects, as discussed in chapter 3.

The goal, however, is not to compare levels of suffering or to simply close disparities between dominant and marginalized groups. The goal must be universal access. If, for example, 70 percent of the dominant group has adequate health insurance, but only 40 percent of the targeted group does, the goal should not be to get everyone else to 70 percent or – worse still – to, say, 60 percent. Disparities matter, but the goal is to get everyone to 100 percent. This compassionate mutual attention to situatedness, be it group-related or individual, is key to both freedom and equality.

As a way of talking more specifically about the situatedness of groups and of developing appropriate responses and implementation strategies, targeting within universal policies can and will work. But it will work only if the targeted group is within the circle of human concern, which brings us back to the work related to the unconscious. Some scholars have suggested that focusing on the unconscious will distract us from focusing on needed structural change. They assert that much inequality is reproduced by structures and by conscious racial animus or individual racial prejudice, sometimes covert. I certainly agree on the importance of structures and the work done by structures, though I would take issue with claims that racial animus is growing. More importantly though, I do not think that the effort around the unconscious should detract from engagement with structure-related issues. In fact, I view these efforts as linked at a fundamental level. The error is in viewing the unconscious in narrow individual psychological terms. As I suggested above, the unconscious is largely social. It is the environment, including our social structures and cultural meanings, that both creates the negative associations and uses them in priming. Adequately addressing unconscious bias therefore calls for an environmental shift.

Our collective unconscious bias is reflected in structures, as there is a strong mutual relationship between the constitution and function of structures and the unconscious. In addressing this structural marginalization and inequity, we should focus primarily on what the structures are in fact doing – on effects and outcomes – rather than why they were created or the motivation behind them. They exist, and we must find ways to intervene to produce better outcomes. We know, for example, that the way we fund schools produces marginalization by race and class that is not easily overcome. Regardless of how it was designed, our nation's history of funding primary education, based largely on local property taxes has become inefficient and deeply racialized. Such institutional and cultural habits are tenaciously held onto, however, even when they undermine our stated goals of inclusion and fairness. There are certainly clear examples of structures that were designed for appropriate reasons that produce racialized outcomes nonetheless. On the other hand, this school funding policy may have been designed, in part, on a racial or class basis. The purpose behind it and other failed policies is not what ultimately matters. What matters is the effectiveness of our efforts to repurpose them for a just, democratic society. This attention to outcomes and fairness is especially important today, as resources become more and more concentrated in fewer and fewer hands.

We are much more than what we own or what we can control. But today we confront the squalor of both great need and terrible excess. Corporations – entities created by judge-made law, sometimes even by sleight of hand – are wrestling with us and our governments, and they are winning. I mention this here partly because corporations have so often gained power just as citizens and workers generally, and particularly people of color, have lost it. This is more than a coincidence. In fact, race has been a favorite tool of big business for gaining both assets and power vis-à-vis workers. Today we are also rapidly losing ground in terms of our government's ability to control the corporations' inherently insatiable drive for profits. It is not just that some people are greedy. We have a serious structural imbalance.[6]

When Franklin Roosevelt was in the White House, he understood that it was economically unsustainable to have a small minority in possession of the overwhelming majority of the nation's financial resources. This was more than a question of unfairness or wasted resources. There had to be money in the pockets of the people in order for the economy to work. A large middle class with disposable income was good for the longer-term health of the country. Henry Ford also understood this. He raised the wages of the Ford Motor Company's workers so that they could own Ford automobiles. The shareholders sued in response, arguing that the purpose of the business was not to pay good wages – it was to increase the company's profits as much as possible. The shareholders reasoned that paying the workers more reduced the dividends paid out to them, and they won. To this day, corporate directors are obligated to shareholders in this way. Our laws support this system that frankly makes no sense for more than a handful of the population.

In his day, President Roosevelt went to the corporations and the public and explained that something had to be done to save the country, to preserve its economic system. People were out of work and suffering. People were in the streets, demanding change. Roosevelt pushed for decent wages not only to provide support for people at the level of basic need but also to strengthen the economy overall and – not least of all – to protect capitalism. We have to remember, this was not just a conversation, it was a fight. The New Deal now seems a given, but those were desperate times, and Roosevelt and his team were willing to pull out all the stops to make the needed changes.

Today there seems to be far less commitment and determination in Washington to address these problems, even as the corporate attitude toward the United States economy is even more problematic. Corporations may still appreciate their reliance on the middle class, but they may view the middle class in China, India, or Brazil as equal in value to the disappearing middle class of the United States. So even the imperative they saw in the 1930s is no longer there, at least not to the same extent. There's been a global shift in capitalism, to which we must respond with a global strategy. And we have to be in the streets, as we were in the 1930s.

"Free market" rhetoric, however, directly challenges the important role that governments must play in the structuring of markets. Indeed, this structuring now occurs mainly for the benefit of corporations rather than for the American people. The invocation of free markets is often used as a way to ignore situatedness and power. If American companies are indifferent or even hostile to the American people, however, in what way are they American companies? Efforts to rein in this structural inequality and greed are nevertheless met with threats by some corporations of "striking" with their capital as well as with their companies – moving to countries in which they can make and keep more profits. Earlier versions of this occurred within the United States, as companies avoided states with higher taxes and protections for workers by moving to "right to work" states with low taxes. Their strategy does not necessitate that we acquiesce; rather it requires that we develop a strategy to deal with structural inequality and the globalization of capital. Capital may be able to move, but it will continue to need some protection and support from governments. In a democracy, we have a right and an obligation to speak to these important matters.

Yet as I travel the country, I am aware of a general view that the mistake that brought us to financial crisis is that we made loans to blacks and Latinos that they couldn't repay and shouldn't have taken. The banking community, in the process of developing new regulations, has argued that the solution is to stop forcing banks to lend to black and Latino communities – to let the market do what markets do. In effect, the argument is that all these civil rights, all this concern about the environment, is distorting the market. This is based on a number of false assumptions, including the idea that there is a natural unregulated market and that this market is made of individual private actors. In formulating a response, we have to ask some basic questions: Why do we have banks? What is the reason for our public funding of private banks? If banks aren't serving democracy, then we shouldn't have them – or at least we shouldn't provide them with huge infusions of public money to do with as they please. These banks have raised considerable alarm over the repercussions if they should have to face the consequences of their greed and irresponsible behavior. They have let it be known that they are "too big to fail."

I would note two things here: First, these banks were allowed to become too big to fail not accidentally but as a result of fierce lobbying and legislative efforts that they paid for and orchestrated. Second, their rhetoric in this crisis has focused exclusively on blaming the victims of their lending scams – scams yielding enormous profits for those on the inside. How ironic it is that now, after having received staggering infusions of our tax dollars, they turn around and blame the targets and victims of their schemes, and the victims of the fallout from their schemes, for what has happened to all of us – around the world – as a result. Indeed, they frequently throw in a little lecture about the irresponsibility of their targets and victims as well.

Banks are just one example of corporate misalignment supported by government regulations with virtually no sense of responsibility or obligation to the American people. The call for deregulation is a misnomer. There will always be regulations in a market; the question is for whom are they drawn? Who benefits? Who pays? Consider the billions in national resources that were channeled to the overflowing coffers of investment bankers and their cohort under the Troubled Asset Relief Program. Those funds were also intended to purchase and modify subprime, underwater, and threatened mortgages, and provide funds for banks to restore lending. Instead, insiders in banking and government gave the money to the banks with few strings attached and *asked* them to promise to lend it for the common good. In fact, they are not lending, and the black and Latino communities are being devastated by the one-two punch of aggressively marketed predatory loans followed by the banks' complete refusal to lend. The banks are sitting on the money – our money. I describe this situation because it is such a good example of what happens when the government is in line with business rather than with the people.[7] We have to change this.

To change it, we need a new story, because in the old American story, too often the role of the villain is assigned to people of color. In today's Tea Party story, too often, the role of the villain is foisted upon immigrants. Recently the villain is becoming struggling working-class Americans of all stripes. I don't know if we really need a villain, but if we do, we have a very good one – corporate America. One only has to think of all the new rules and favorable regulations large corporations have demanded and received for the protection of capital as it moves around the world, including intellectual property. This is not about good and bad corporations but about how the misalignment of corporations in our democracy has occurred. The point is that corporations may make good servants, but they make terrible masters.

Much of the development of corporations was a racialized process, but that is not my main point in this context. The critical point is that we cannot have a sustainable, healthy, inclusive society when corporate purpose and governance are not properly aligned with the goals and requirements of democracy. Yet the metaphors used to support the current misalignment create blind spots and make a challenging problem virtually untraceable and invisible, even in addition to the threat posed by the *Citizens United* decision. For example, we talk of corporations as people. The bankruptcy of this claim is apparent to many, but the problem with the public/private metaphor may be less obvious. We think of corporations as private. Private has a special meaning in American culture. It something that Americans think of as a core value. So when we think of corporations as private, a cluster of positive associations are made. In contemporary America, public is bad, and private is good. What represents the public is both the government, especially the federal government, and people of color. Think of the response to *Brown* in the South. If blacks had the right to attend desegregated public schools, then many whites wanted to abandon the public, both with their bodies and with their tax dollars. In that respect, private also hints of fear and racial anxiety.

In private space, or in the sanctity of the market, there is a belief that government – but especially the federal government – should not regulate or intervene. Meanwhile, state governments are too weak to regulate and tax multinational corporations on behalf of (human) people. Corporations, however, are not truly private – at least not in the way that the founders conceived of the private. There was in that era certainly a mistrust of centralized governmental authority and concentration of power, but that concern was extended to corporations as well. They were largely seen as extensions of the government and also as institutions of concentrated economic power and wealth. When the courts started the long march to corporate personhood and privacy, there was an organized and strong populist response, starting with the Populist Party and extending to the Progressive Party. From early on, it was clear that the expansion of a robust public domain would constrain corporate power. It is much more than coincidental that the Gilded Age and the *Lochner* era, in which the courts were aggressively expanding and protecting corporate rights, co-occurred with Jim Crow.[8] The interaction among these spheres was rich and heavily racialized, as the courts refused to protect blacks, especially those newly freed from slavery, and simultaneously pushed a strong anti-worker agenda.[9]

So to those who argue that the "real" issue today is not race but the economy, I would suggest that this is a serious mistake. There is a profound connection between race and the economy as well as with how we have structured the institutions that we all inhabit in the United States. One only has to consider the Electoral College on one hand or opposition to taxes on the other. There has been some focus on the threat to democracy posed by the current corporate misalignment, but I would extend it, as I see the threat as much greater than is commonly realized. If we allow this misalignment to continue, we will undermine not only the public domain, including public space, but also the private. Indeed, we spend a great deal of time today in corporate space – stadiums, malls, the internet – in which we have few rights and are in fact often under surveillance.

Part of the confusion about the value of a robust public space goes back to the question of who we are and to the anxiety around having to associate with the imagined other. So the challenge we face is both economic and ontological. As I have tried to show here, there must be space for a new self that is different from the separate, fearful self that has been organized around whiteness and exclusion. For truly, who wants to be on either side of that false line? This will require a paradigm shift that may seem daunting until we realize that we are already in a major shift: the question is merely one of direction. A productive shift must use a different language that speaks to the unconscious, that makes space for all – not just the white, not just the privileged. This shift will change not only the meaning of race but also the meaning of the Western self, to bring us into a new relationship with the other and the self. We can and must expand the circle of human concern and attend to our structures and the work they are doing. This certainly includes realigning corporations with broader societal goals and reimagining and rebuilding public and private space.

In talking about framing and priming, it is clear that what we call something can be consequential, affecting the way we think and what we do in relation to our conceptualization of it. In this regard, to think of the struggle between corporations and the government or the people in terms of public and private is a serious error with confusing and negative implications. This error can be partially corrected when we notice that instead of two domains, public and private, it is more useful to think of four: public, private, non-public/non-private, and corporate. The first two we know best. The public is where there is collective action, including the government's. The second, private, is where the individual can retreat with maximum freedom, without surveillance. The third is the non-public/non-private. This is where the most socially vulnerable live, with little public voice and inadequate privacy. This is the space to which enslaved people and women were historically consigned. They could not vote or participate in the polity, nor did they have a space to which they could retreat for privacy and personal freedom. The home for man may have been a castle, but for the woman, it was often a dungeon. Today felons, undocumented immigrants, and at times, people with disabilities are in this domain. The fourth sphere is the corporate, which has been quasi public and concerned with the public good to a greater and lesser extent but is now quasi private.

These domains are dynamic, so what happens in one impacts the others. The challenge is to look at these spheres both separately and as a whole, to try to optimize their support for the best goals of our society. Yet the current discussion is more often a bullying kind of attack on government – an attack on the public sphere and public assets, with the assumption that the benefits of that attack will redound to individuals. They will not. Even if they did, moreover, under current arrangements, those benefits would flow primarily toward the increasingly small share of the 1 percent who disproportionately control our collective assets.[10] The current efforts to disable and dismantle the government are meant to enhance the power of corporations and the financial structures associated with them. Corporations – and those who serve them, profit from them – understand that civil rights, women's rights, environmental rights, and human rights limit their potentially unlimited prerogatives. They also understand that if we ever get together across these dimensions, begin to see and think about our society holistically, we will have a real democracy, which will have serious implications for how corporations are run.

Creating and exacerbating divisions that derail our awareness of common interests has therefore been a tradition in politics in the United States, which, after all, was settled and developed to a great degree by corporations. It's a tactic that may be most strongly rooted in that first division of laborers by skin color, a scheme so successful that it continues to function to this day. We often talk, for example, about working-class whites voting against their interests. I want to suggest that that's not quite right. They can be voting against their economic interests but voting for their white interests. And it's not even just interests. They're actually voting for, or fighting for, what I would call their racial identity. So part of what is needed is not just a new interest but a new identity as well.

People's identities are also threatened by the migrations of the racial other, and we need to address that in much more sophisticated ways. Otherwise, diversity will continue to cause tremendous anxiety. Jeffrey Sachs, Robert Putnam, and Tim Wise have all been saying for the last couple of years that one of the greatest threats in the United States and the world is diversity. Because as Europe and the United States become more diverse, it creates an anxiety, a racial anxiety, that is reflected in declining support for public space, public institutions, public infrastructure, and public education. As I have emphasized, our anxiety is not just a personal psychological event; it is also a collective (social) anxiety about what we have and who we are. It should go without saying that the need to consider the anxiety of whites in no way suggests that people of color should be silenced about their condition, especially given the habitual political use, veiled or overt, of communities of color as drivers of white anxiety.

This anxiety about the other is easily manipulated and exploited by elites advocating the withdrawal of support for public space – supposedly in favor of what they characterize as a superior, private space, but in fact mostly in favor of corporate space and profits. Corporate interests need announce only that the poor are not paying their fair share, and the resulting hostility is palpable. Used in this sense, "the poor" typically means the racial other, regardless of the actual color of our poor. But resulting cuts to basic needs – education, housing, employment, health care – have their greatest impact on the communities of concentrated poverty created by racial segregation. This in turn allows these communities to be used time and again not just as the emblem of unworthiness but also as the excuse for further displacements of our common concern and resources. As discussed above, these poor are at risk of being seen not only as not belonging but also as not human, not worthy. Moreover, this describes our approach to the racial other, but it also describes our attitudes toward many other stigmatized groups. To dispel the power of this move in distracting us from the greed at the top, we have to expand our notions of who we are, expand of our circle of human concern. In doing so, we must make certain that the circle includes all humans – but not corporations, which, in spite of their fully vested rights as citizens, are not people.[11]

Dr. King spoke, several decades ago, of two Americas. He also spoke of the value, indeed the necessity, of finding common ground and common purpose. Currently this endeavor in the United States must occur, institutionally at least, in an insistently color-blind context. It must occur

at a time when powerful interests promote fear and encourage anger at
the prospect that those who have enjoyed centuries of privilege will be
treated "unfairly" in favor of the poor. It must occur now, at a time when
a racial caste system of terrible origin is "invisible" in our courts but
still powerful in our psyches and social structures. And it must occur in
a time of economic inequality and corporate power not seen since the
early decades of the twentieth century, if ever.[12]

To reach our common ground, to create a sense of mutuality and
common space, we must realize that the embodiedness that spiritual
seekers know is also needed in the justice system and in efforts to end
suffering in our society. Abstract concepts and cold individualism fall
short of justice, fall short of addressing need, and allow the victory of
greed. We need to reach out to one another from a perspective that
makes group membership less determinative of opportunity and more
related to enhancement of self and community. We need to increase our
sense of abundance and improve our sense of well being, as individuals
and in relation to one another. Accomplishing this requires an identification of the white worldview along with an incorporation of the many
other visions that tell America's story. And it requires a renewed commitment by all of us to fulfill the promise of a truly democratic society.

Fortunately, as humans, we have advantages that can overcome even
the outsize power of corporations. For as humans, we are living beings,
inherently connected with one another and with the natural world. So although our brains develop partly through categorizing and organizing in
ways that can be challenging in a diverse society, our hearts orchestrate a
system hardwired to care and to respond empathically to one another's
suffering and joy. We can't allow structures – economic or political – to
block or blunt those connections, for in doing so, we harm not only the
"others" but also ourselves.

If we fail to meet this challenge, I believe we will witness the collapse of the public space and the private space. We will witness the further undermining of our civil rights, human rights, and our social and
environmental values. The stakes are high for all of us. To embrace our
commonality in an increasingly diverse public space will require new
selves, who are citizens in the true sense of the term: individual, interconnected, and inclusive in ways that reflect the highest aspirations

of our nation and our species. This is a heavy lift for all of us, and it is particularly heavy for those who continue to organize around the myth of the radically isolated individual. The alternative – a just society – requires major realignments with respect to corporations and a remaking of our institutions and ourselves. But it is a dream worth dreaming and a fight worth fighting for.

NOTES

Introduction

1. Jeremy Rifkin, "The European Dream," *Utne Reader* (Sept./Oct. 2004); available at http://www.utne.com/2004-09-01/the-european-dream.aspx (last visited 13 October 2011), 2.

1. Post-Racialism or Targeted Universalism?

1. Most Americans would be surprised to learn that the term "racism" did not come into use in the United States until the 1930s. For a good discussion of changing meanings and practices of race, see Fredrickson, *Racism*; Martinot, *The Rule of Racialization*; Roediger, *How Race Survived U.S. History*; john a. powell, "The Race Class Nexus."

2. See Omi and Winant, *Racial Formation in the United States*, 66–68.

3. See Smedley, *Race in North America*, 332.

4. Freeman, "Legitimizing Racial Discrimination through Antidiscrimination Law," 29–30.

5. 426 U.S. at 245–246 (1976).

6. King, "I Have a Dream," 217, 219.

7. 127 S. Ct. 2738, 2768 (2007) (discussing *Brown v. Board of Education*, 347 U.S. 483 [1954]).

8. See, e.g., Thernstrom and Thernstrom, *No Excuses*, 76–78.

9. *Parents Involved in Community Schools v. Seattle School District No. 1*, 127 S. Ct. 2738 at 2798 (Stevens, J., dissenting).

10. See, e.g., Michael K. Brown, et al., *Whitewashing Race*, 7–8.

11. See, e.g., *Grutter v. Bollinger*, 539 U.S. 306, 353 (2003) (Thomas, J., concurring in part and dissenting in part) ("The Constitution abhors classifications based on race, not only because those classifications can harm favored races or are based on illegitimate motives, but also because every time the government places citizens on racial registers and makes race relevant to the provision of burdens or benefits, it demeans us all.").

12. *Parents Involved*, at 2755–59.

13. See, e.g., Loury, *The Anatomy of Racial Inequality*, 142.

14. This phrase was chanted by Obama supporters made after he won the South Carolina primary, and it was not challenged by the campaign. Thompson, "Seeking Unity, Obama Feels Pull of Racial Divide."

15. Obama, *The Audacity of Hope*, 232–233.

16. See Dickerson, "Class Is the New Black"; Kotkin, "The End of Upward Mobility."

17. See Reed, "The Real Divide," 27.

18. See, e.g., Payne, *Getting beyond Race*, 78; Ifill, *The Breakthrough*.

19. As racial attitudes have improved, there has been a move from expressed racial hostility to racial resentment. Kinder and Sanders, *Divided by Color*, 92–93.

20. See Timothy D. Wilson, *Strangers to Ourselves;* and Project Implicit website.

21. For a similar discussion of formal and substantive neutrality in the First Amendment Free Exercise Clause, see Laycock, "Formal, Substantive, and Disaggregated Neutrality toward Religion," and Hanks, "Justice Souter."

22. For more on this topic, see Cavanaugh, "Towards a New Equal Protection," 384.

23. See Wechsler, "Toward Neutral Principles of Constitutional Law."

24. Charles Black, *A New Birth of Freedom,* 24.

25. Compare Herrnstein and Murray, *The Bell Curve,* 117–118, claiming that class is determined by intelligence, with Michael Brown, et al., *Whitewashing Race,* arguing that racism and organized racial advantage persist across many institutions in America.

26. See, e.g., William Julius Wilson, *The Declining Significance of Race.*

27. Even President Bush, in trying to sell his program of private savings accounts, noted that Social Security is not fair to blacks because they die earlier than whites. Kranish, "Bush Argues His Social Security Plan Aids Blacks."

28. Lieberman, *Shifting the Color Line,* 227–228. Lieberman sees Social Security as our best example of a truly universal program, but many others have challenged this claim. See, e.g., O'Connor, "The 'New Institutionalism' and the Racial Divide," 111, 117–118.

29. See Lieberman, *Shifting the Color Line,* 34.

30. See Katznelson, *When Affirmative Action Was White,* 43.

31. See Skocpol, *Social Policy in the United States,* 250–251.

32. See Obama, *The Audacity of Hope.*

33. See Skocpol, "Targeting within Universalism"; W. J. Wilson, *The Truly Disadvantaged.*

34. See M. K. Brown et al., *Whitewashing Race,* 55–56; see also Lawrence, "The Id, the Ego, and Equal Protection," 323.

35. Lipsitz, *The Possessive Investment in Whiteness.*

36. Ibid., 229–231; see also López, *White by Law* (2006), 131.

37. Roediger, *How Race Survived U.S. History.*

38. Ibid.

39. Hamilton and Hamilton, *The Dual Agenda,* 236, 241. The Hamiltons suggest that targeted universal programs were indeed pushed by civil rights groups, but that racial resentment was so high that these programs could not garner support.

40. Katznelson, *When Affirmative Action Was White,* 186.

41. Kuswa, "Suburbification, Segregation, and the Consolidation of the Highway Machine," at 47.

42. Ibid., 116.

43. Katznelson, *When Affirmative Action Was White,* 115.

44. Ibid.

45. Ibid., 114–115; see also Skocpol, "The G.I. Bill and U.S. Social Policy," 95–114.

46. Katznelson, *When Affirmative Action Was White,* 127.

47. Ibid., 107.

48. Sen, *Development as Freedom,* 136.

49. 442 U.S. 256, 284 (1979).

50. 442 U.S. at 279–281. Note that this case was decided after the establishment of the intent standard in *Washington v. Davis,* which it echoes.

51. Katznelson, *When Affirmative Action Was White,* 112.

52. See, e.g., *Parents Involved*, at 2792 (Kennedy, J., concurring); *City of Richmond v. Croson*, at 509–510.

53. Reardon, Yun, and Kurlaender report that consideration of socioeconomic status (SES) will not adequately racially integrate schools even where non-whites are overrepresented. See "Implications of Income-Based School Assignment Policies," 49, 50.

54. Myrdal, *An American Dilemma*, vol. 1, 70.

55. Ibid., 70–76.

56. See Blank, "Tracing the Economic Impact of Cumulative Discrimination," 99, 100. Blank explains that a labor economist's analysis of labor market discrimination, controlling for background characteristics and educational preparation of workers, ignores the fact that racialized outcomes are the product of cumulative effects of discrimination "over time and across domains."

57. 336 A. 2d 713, 717 (N.J. 1975).

58. Wish and Eisdorfer, "The Impact of Mount Laurel Initiatives,"1302–1305. See also Roisman, "Opening the Suburbs to Racial Integration," 70–72.

59. See N.J. Stat. Ann. § 52.27D-301–329 (West 1986); see id. § 52:27D-303 (describing the act as legislative satisfaction of "the constitutional obligation enunciated by the [New Jersey] Supreme Court"), quoted in Roisman, "Opening the Suburbs," 70–72.

60. Young, *Inclusion and Democracy*, 121–122.

61. Brooks-Gunn, et al., "Do Neighborhoods Influence Child and Adolescent Development?"; Leventhal and Brooks-Gunn, "Moving to Opportunity," 1576.

62. See, e.g., Editorial, "For Katrina Victims, Relief at Last," *New York Times*, 16 November 2010, describing the Bush administration's decision to allow Mississippi to waive requirements that at least half of $5.5 billion in federal aid must be

spent on low-and moderate-income housing. Only 20 percent of the funds were so directed. See Lawyers Committee for Civil Rights under Law, "Mississippi Housing Advocates File Suit against HUD."

63. See, e.g., Justice Scalia's opinion in *Grutter v. Bollinger*, describing the parade of horribles the justice envisions should public law schools be allowed to consider race as one of many factors in admissions. 539 U.S. 306, 347–349 (2003) (concurring in part and dissenting in part).

64. *Parents Involved*, 127 S. Ct. 2738 (2007).

65. Ibid. at 2765.

66. Ibid. at 2767–68. "Racial classifications are suspect, and that means that simple legislative assurances of good intention cannot suffice." Ibid. at 2764 (quoting *City of Richmond v. Croson*, 488 U.S. 469, 500 [1989]).

67. Ibid. at 2791–92 (2007) (Kennedy, J., concurring).

68. *Northwest Austin Municipal Utility District No. One, v. Holder*, 129 S. Ct. 2504 (2009).

69. National Voting Rights Act of 1965, 42 U.S.C.A.§1973-1973aa-6 (2009). The requirement applies to nine states – Alabama, Alaska, Arizona, Georgia, Louisiana, Mississippi, South Carolina, and Texas – along with most cities and counties in Virginia, and scores of counties and municipalities in other states in which Congress found a history of discrimination at the polls. The same reasoning that race does not matter would greatly change cases decided under the Thirteenth Amendment, such as *Jones v. Alfred H. Mayer, Co.*, 392 U.S. 409 (1968) and *Runyan v. McCrary*, 472 U.S. 160 (1976), which extend a right of private action to claims denied by the Court under the Fourteenth Amendment.

70. Brief of Appellant, *Northwest Austin Municipal Utility District No. One v. Holder*, at 1 (2009).

71. Liptak, "Supreme Court Takes Voting Rights Case."

72. 129 S. Ct. 2504, 2516.

73. U.S. Dept. of Housing and Urban Development, *Unequal Burden.*

74. Rogers et al., "Fair Credit and Fair Housing in the Wake of the Subprime Lending and Foreclosure Crisis."

75. See j. powell, "The Race Class Nexus," 355; see also Katznelson, *When Affirmative Action Was White,* 28.

76. T. L. Friedman, "Finishing Our Work."

77. See Nossiter, "For South, a Waning Hold on National Politics."

78. Westen, *The Political Brain,* 221.

79. Obama, *Audacity of Hope,* 138.

80. See Grant-Thomas and powell, "Structural Racism and Colorlines in the United States," 119; j. powell, "Structural Racism."

81. See, e.g., Project Implicit website, https://implicit.harvard.edu/implicit.

82. See also Kang, "Trojan Horses of Race."

83. Project Implicit website.

84. See, e.g., Alexander, *The New Jim Crow.*

85. See, e.g., Blasi, "Advocacy against the Stereotype."

86. Obama, *Audacity of Hope,* 139.

87. See Lawrence, "The Id, the Ego, and Equal Protection," 373–378.

88. *Parents Involved,* 127 S. Ct. at 2791–2792 (Kennedy, J., concurring).

89. Guinier and Torres, The Miner's Canary.

90. Obama, *Audacity of Hope,* 146.

91. Most of the infrastructure funds may go to routine fixes. See MacGillis and Shear, "Stimulus Package to First Pay for Routine Repairs."

92. Obama, *Audacity of Hope,* 247.

93. See, e.g., Perry, "Health Coverage in Communities of Color." This report, using 2007 data, indicates that 51 percent of African American and almost 60 percent of American Indian, Alaskan Native, and Latino workers did not have access to health insurance through their employers, compared with 34 percent of non-Latino whites.

94. U.S. Dept. of Health and Human Services. HHS *Action Plan to Reduce Racial and Ethnic Disparities: A Nation Free of Disparities in Health and Health Care.* Washington, D.C.: U.S. Department of Health and Human Services (April 2011), 1.

95. See generally, ibid.

96. The future of the Affordable Care Act, upon which this effort is largely based, is currently under review by the U.S. Supreme Court. See, e.g., *New York Times,* "Times Topics: Health Care Reform and the Supreme Court (Affordable Care Act)," 28 March 2012.

97. Jordan, *The White Man's Burden.*

98. Ibid., at 170.

99. See Patterson, *Freedom in the Making of Western Culture,* 10.

100. See especially Lopez, "Colorblind White Dominance," 18.

101. Yancey, *Who is White?* 149–164.

2. The Color-Blind Multiracial Dilemma

1. See, e.g., King, "I Have a Dream" (delivered at the March on Washington for Jobs and Freedom, 28 August 1963). For more on color blindness, see Calmore, "Critical Race Theory, Archie Shepp, and Fire Music," 2149–50; and Schlesinger, *The Disuniting of America.*

2. See Omi and Winant, *Racial Formation in the United States,* 55.

3. See Calmore, "Exploring Michael Omi's 'Messy' Real World of Race," 79.

4. See, e.g., Gotanda, "A Critique of 'Our Constitution Is Color Blind,'" 32.

5. See, e.g., *Shaw v. Reno; City of Richmond v. Croson; Arlington Heights v. Metropolitan Housing Development Corp; Brown v. Board of Education.*

6. *Parents Involved,* 127 S. Ct. 2738 (2007).

7. See Omi, "Racial Identity and the State," 14–21.

8. See Bernstein, *Beyond Objectivism and Relativism,* 18; see also powell and Menendian, "Remaking Law."

9. See j. powell, "Reflections on the Self," 1486–90. See generally Klein, *Meeting the Great Bliss Queen.*

10. This is not just a problem for late modernists and postmodernists. Hume's skepticism was based on the claim that we cannot know the world directly; that is, the world is always filtered through our senses. In his effort to construct a response, Kant accepted the basic principle that we do not have direct access to the world.

11. See Goodman, *Ways of Worldmaking,* 91–97.

12. This issue is discussed further in chapter 7. See also j. powell, "Reflections on the Self," 1486–90, and Gergen, *The Saturated Self.* Gergen argues that there are multiple selves, each of which makes its own claims and demands.

13. See j. powell, "Reflections on the Self," 1486–90. See also Klein, *Meeting the Great Bliss Queen,* discussing the Buddhist concept of no self and explaining that this position does not mean that the self does not exist, only that the permanent unconditional self posited in Western thought does not exist.

14. See Gotanda, "A Critique of 'Our Constitution Is Color Blind,'" 32; see also R. Frankenberg, *White Women, Race Matters,* 142–149.

15. See generally Bernstein, *Beyond Objectivism and Relativism.*

16. See, e.g., Wright, "Who's Black, Who's White, and Who Cares," 561–566.

17. Discussed in Hochschild and Burch, "Contingent Public Policies and Racial Hierarchy."

18. See Calmore, "Critical Race Theory, Archie Shepp, and Fire Music," 2149–50; see also R. Frankenberg, *White*

Women, 142–149; Crenshaw, "Race, Reform, and Retrenchment," 1346; j. powell, "An Agenda for the Post–Civil Rights Era," 892. See generally Omi and Winant, *Racial Formation in the United States.*

19. See generally Ansley, "Stirring the Ashes"; Calmore, "Critical Race Theory, Archie Shepp, and Fire Music," 2149–50.

20. P. Williams, *The Alchemy of Race and Rights.*

21. See Goldberg, *Racist Culture,* 2; see also Edsall and Edsall, *Chain Reaction,* 116–136.

22. Martinot, *The Rule of Racialization,* 47.

23. See Allen, *The Invention of the White Race.*

24. See, e.g., Jordan, *White over Black,* 79.

25. Wallenstein, *Tell the Court I Love My Wife,* 15.

26. *Dred Scott,* 60 U.S. 393, 408.

27. Ibid., citing Maryland law (ch. 13, s. 5).

28. Ibid.

29. Omi and Winant, *Racial Formation in the United States,* 16.

30. Hening, *Statutes,* vol. 3, 333–335. This statute was repealed in 1748, when enslaved people were deemed personal property.

31. Ibid.

32. See Tucker, "*Loving* Day Recalls a Time When the Union of a Man and a Woman Was Banned."

33. See *Loving v. Virginia,* 388 U.S. 1, 4 (1967).

34. Tucker, "*Loving* Day Recalls a Time."

35. See Passel, Wang, and Taylor, "Marrying Out"; and Taylor, Funk, and Craighill, "Guess Who's Coming to Dinner."

36. See Omi, "Racial Identity and the State," 14–21. The terms "biracial" and "multiracial" are used in this article, though they are imprecise and not free of

problems. As Omi points out, the term "mixed" implies that there is a pure race, an idea that has been called into question.

37. Saulny, "Black and White and Married in the Deep South."

38. Over 90 percent of these reported two races, most often white and black, but 8 percent chose three. U.S. Census Bureau, "Overview of Race and Hispanic Origin: 2010."

39. Office of Management and Budget, "Revisions to the Standards for the Classification of Federal Data on Race and Ethnicity."

40. See U.S. Census Bureau, "Overview of Race and Hispanic Origin: 2010." The report includes a footnote to the effect that the categories "reflect a social definition of race recognized in this country and are not an attempt to define race biologically, anthropologically, or genetically. In addition, it is recognized that the categories of the race question include race and national origin or sociocultural groups" (2).

41. See Omi, "Racial Identity and the State," 18.

42. See Graham, "The Multiracial Child."

43. See Omi, "Racial Identity and the State," 14–21. See generally Wright, "Who's Black, Who's White, and Who Cares" (suggesting that categories such as black, white, and Hispanic incorrectly imply that race is the distinguishing factor among these groups).

44. In Interracial Intimacies: Sex, Marriage, Identity and Adoption, Randall Kennedy describes and critiques the opposition to allowing white families to adopt black children. Kennedy asserts that many black professionals in the field argue that it is better for a black child to become a ward of the state than to be adopted by a white family. One may notice that this type of concern for the child enforces a racial imperative over the needs of the would-be family. Even as we have moved as a society toward acceptance of interracial relationships and marriage (an example being the widespread condemnation of George W. Bush for speaking at a college that prohibits interracial dating), it is still not uncommon to hear objections to these same couples' decisions to have children. Such comments are often along the lines that individuals can do as they please, but they should not subject children to the "confusion" or "problems" of being "interracial." This reflects the ongoing acceptance of racial boundaries and our collective discomfort at seeing them destabilized.

45. Omi, "Racial Identity and the State" at 11 (quoting Calvin Trillin, "American Chronicles: Black or White," The New Yorker, 14 April 1986, 62).

46. See U.S. Census Bureau, "Overview of Race and Hispanic Origin: 2010."

47. Ibid.

48. Omi, "Racial Identity and the State."

49. U.S. Census Bureau, "Overview of Race and Hispanic Origin: 2010," 2.

50. See ibid., 3.

51. See Omi, "Racial Identity and the State," 14–21; Wright, "Who's Black, Who's White, and Who Cares," 557.

52. See Grillo, "Anti-Essentialism and Intersectionality," 16–19.

53. See ibid.

54. See ibid. Although she was also Latina, Grillo focused on the black-white multiracial experience in part because it was the most familiar. She was careful, however, not to conflate all minority and multiracial issues under black-white dualism; nor was she prepared to assume that race and racism operate in the same manner for all racial minorities.

55. See ibid., 16–19; see also Winant, Racial Conditions, 22, 31.

56. See generally Chua, "Privatization-Nationalization Cycle"; Grillo, "Anti-

Essentialism and Intersectionality." Pigmentocracy is similar to colorism, only it extends across racial groups; the lighter the skin color, the greater the privilege. It is not that multiracial categories would necessarily lead to pigmentocracy and colorism, but without a challenge to racial hierarchy and white supremacy, the dangers increase. Grillo was especially concerned about this because of the history of colorism and pigmentocracy in the United States.

57. See Wright, "Who's Black, Who's White, and Who Cares" 562–565.

58. See j. powell, "Reflections on the Self," 1486–90. It is interesting to note for *Star Trek* fans that Spock in the original *Star Trek* and now Counselor Troi represent the mixed-race subject. Because of their mixed status they are seen as having an internal conflict based on blood or genetics that other uniracial species are not supposed to have. I have argued that we are all internally fractured. That is the nature of the self, and it is not dependent on biology. It is important to reject the assumption that there is a pure race or gene pool.

59. See generally Goldberg, *Racist Culture.*

60. See Stowe, "Uncolored People," 68, 74–75. Without relying on blood or genes, Toni Morrison asserts that all Americans are African Americans. She is suggesting that the American is a natural hybrid.

61. See Wright, "Who's Black, Who's White, and Who Cares," 513, 520–523; see also López, *White by Law,* 42–43.

62. Bradt, "'One-Drop Rule' Persists."

63. See Bradt, "'One-Drop Rule' Persists."

64. Ho et al., "Evidence for Hypodescent and Racial Hierarchy," 492–506.

65. See Wright, "Who's Black, Who's White, and Who Cares" 557–559, 563.

66. See ibid.

67. See generally Lazarre, *Beyond the Whiteness of Whiteness;* see also Baldwin,

The Price of the Ticket, 690; N. Johnson, "Race Traitor." In "Race Traitor," a white mother of black children talks about crossing over the racial divide in her multiracial family. Some have suggested that whiteness is chosen, and therefore can be unchosen. I am not clear how or if this can be done, especially on an individual level, but it does suggest that there are other ways of thinking about these issues that might affect what we think about racial categories.

68. See generally Denton, "Racial Identity and Census Categories."

69. See ibid. See generally Goldberg, *Racist Culture;* Sandel, "Political Liberalism.

70. See *Loving v. Virginia,* 388 U.S. 1, 12 (1967).

71. See generally Wright, "Who's Black, Who's White, and Who Cares."

72. See Goforth, "'What Is She?'" 9–11.

73. See ibid., 14; see also Gilanshah, "Multiracial Minorities." The 1900 census dropped the octoroon, mulatto, and quadroon categories. The 1940 census by contrast had only two racial categories: white and non-white.

74. See Gilanshah, "Multiracial Minorities," 183.

75. See *Plessy v. Ferguson,* 163 U.S. 537, 549 (1896), overruled by *Brown v. Board of Education,* 347 U.S. 483 (1954); Harris, C., "Whiteness as Property," 1758–59; see also Applebaum, "Miscegenation Statutes"; Hodgkinson, "What Should We Call People?," 174.

76. 163 U.S. 537 (1896).

77. See generally C. Black, *A New Birth of Freedom.*

78. Quoted in Thomas, Plessy v. Ferguson: *A Brief History with Documents,* 30.

79. *Plessy* at 549.

80. See j. powell, "Transformative Action." See generally Sundiata, "Late Twentieth Century Patterns of Race Relations in Brazil and the United States."

81. See powell, "Transformative Action."

82. See generally Winant, *Racial Conditions in the United States;* Hanchard, ed., *Racial Politics in Contemporary Brazil;* Reiter and Mitchell, eds., *Brazil's New Racial Politics.*

83. See j. powell, "Transformative Action."

84. See Spickard, *Mixed Blood,* 329–331.

85. See generally Lazarre, *Beyond the Whiteness of Whiteness.*

86. See generally Chua, "Privatization, Nationalization"; j. powell, "Transformative Action."

87. See generally Roediger, *Towards the Abolition of Whiteness.*

88. See Gotanda, "A Critique of 'Our Constitution Is Color Blind,'" 8. See generally Goldberg, *Racist Culture.*

89. See Omi, "Racial Identity and the State." See generally Goldberg, *Racist Culture.*

90. See, e.g., Massey, *Categorically Unequal,* and Alexander, *The New Jim Crow.*

91. In trying to develop a stance that rejects whiteness, the race traitors have contributed numerous insights that I will discuss in chapter 4. See, e.g., Ignatiev, "How to Be a Race Traitor."

92. See ibid.

93. See Lorde, "An Open Letter to Mary Daly," 94–97.

3. The Racing of American Society

1. Omi, "Racial Identity and the State," 14–21.

2. See Frankenberg, *White Women, Race Matters,* 142–149; Crenshaw, "Race, Reform, and Retrenchment," 1346; j. powell, "An Agenda for the Post–Civil Rights Era," 892.

3. *City of Richmond v. J. A. Croson,* 488 U.S. 469, 520 (1989) (Scalia, J., concurring).

4. Abram, *The Spell of the Sensuous,* 32.

5. The claim that there is no scientific basis for race can also be made for the self; yet, as Katherine Ewing notes, the concept of a unitary self remains an important fiction. Ewing, "The Illusion of Wholeness," 258; see also Ogden, describing the self as a "theoretical construct" that is "indispensable in the description of aspects of the phenomenology of subjectivity," in *The Subjects of Analysis,* 25.

6. Abram, *The Spell of the Sensuous,* 33.

7. See generally Kuhn, *The Structure of Scientific Revolutions.*

8. For a stark example of the use of race and genetics in this type of effort, see Herrnstein and Murray, *The Bell Curve.*

9. See, e.g., Lucas and Lempinen, "State GOP Pulls King Ad but Not Blitz," describing the color-blind theorists' misuse of Dr. Martin Luther King, Jr.'s "I Have a Dream" speech to assert the unfairness of racial "preferences" as just another way of overemphasizing skin color.

10. See Mahoney, "Segregation, Whiteness, and Transformation," 1661. ("Race derives much of its power from seeming to be a natural or biological phenomenon, or at the very least, a coherent social category.")

11. Abram, *The Spell of the Sensuous,* 38.

12. Omi and Winant, *Racial Formation,* 2d ed., 55.

13. Goldberg, *Racist Culture,* 2.

14. Kendall Thomas has observed that "we are 'raced' through a constellation of practices that construct and control racial subjectivities." See "The Eclipse of Reason," 1806–1807.

15. Goldberg, *Racist Culture,* 21.

16. See Allen, *The Invention of the White Race,* vol. 1, 31–38; Roediger, *Towards the Abolition of Whiteness,* 13.

17. Mahoney, *Segregation, Whiteness, and Transformation,* 1661.

18. Allen, *The Invention of the White Race,* vol. 1, 35.

19. See hooks, *Feminist Theory*, 46; McIntosh, "White Privilege and Male Privilege," 70, 81; Morrison, *Playing in the Dark*, 6–9; Stowe, "Uncolored People," 68, 74–75.

20. Omi and Winant, *Racial Formation*, 55.

21. See, e.g., McIntosh, "White Privilege and Male Privilege," 77, discussing white and male privilege.

22. Goldberg, *Racist Culture*, 197–198; see also Bell, *Race, Racism and American Law*, 806 ("If proponents of black rights point to the pressing need for more job opportunities for minority workers, the response is often that 'your people have no skills, no educational background, no experience.'"); Calmore, "Racialized Space and the Culture of Segregation,'" 1246–50; and A. M. Johnson, "How Race and Poverty Intersect to Prevent Integration," 1601–1602, 1602n19.

23. Omi and Winant, *Racial Formation*, 56 (emphasis omitted).

24. Gotanda, "A Critique of 'Our Constitution is Color-Blind,'" 32.

25. Ibid., 33.

26. Bell, *Race, Racism and American Law*, 29 (citing a quotation from Franklin's "Observations Concerning the Increase of Mankind" [1751] in Staughton Lynd, "Slavery and the Founding Fathers," in *Black History: A Reappraisal*, ed. M. Drimmer [Garden City, N.Y.: Doubleday, 1968], 130). Interestingly, Franklin is known as an ardent abolitionist and was at one time president of the Pennsylvania Abolition Society.

27. 163 U.S. 537, 549 (1896), overruled by *Brown v. Board of Education*, 347 U.S. 483 (1954).

28. *United States v. Bhagat Singh Thind*, 261 U.S. 204, 207 (1923).

29. López, *White by Law*, 42–43.

30. *U.S. v. Thind*, 261 U.S. at 215.

31. Ibid. at 209.

32. Roediger, *Towards the Abolition of Whiteness*, 182 (quoting Joan M. Jensen).

33. *U.S. v. Thind*, 261 U.S. at 213–214.

34. Roediger, *Towards the Abolition of Whiteness*, 182.

35. Ibid., 184.

36. Ibid., 185.

37. C. Harris, "Whiteness as Property," 1719 (footnote omitted).

38. Ibid.

39. Omi, "Racial Identity and the State," 7–10; Hasian and Nakayama, "The Fictions of Racialized Identities," 182, 187.

40. Hasian and Nakayama, "The Fictions of Racialized Identities," 186.

41. See C. Harris, "Whiteness as Property," 1716–21. As Harris puts it: "[A]s the system of chattel slavery came under fire, it was rationalized by an ideology of race that [by regarding Blacks as heathen and savage] further differentiated between white and Black" (1717n25).

42. Calmore, "Racialized Space," 1243–50.

43. Ibid., 1248–50.

44. For a discussion of how the working class was racialized from the beginning to mean white, see Roediger, *The Wages of Whiteness*, 19–21; see also Goldberg, *Racist Culture*, 16–20, 44, 113–114.

45. Goldberg, *Racist Culture*, 44.

46. Ibid., 16–17.

47. Conservative Charles Murray makes the deserving/undeserving dichotomy explicit:

> I am referring symptomatically to the fellow who is not just temporarily unemployed, but can't manage to hold a job for more than a few days at a time, no matter what. I'm not referring to the woman who is without a husband and trying to raise a child on her own, but to the woman who is chronically dependent on welfare and also doesn't really pay a lot of attention to her child and doesn't pay a lot of attention to the people around her as neighbours.

Keith and Cross, "Racism and the Postmodern City," 1, 12 (quoting radio broadcasts in the summer of 1990 by Charles Murray).

48. Calmore, "Racialized Space," 1247.

49. O'Reilly, *Nixon's Piano*, 360, 381–388;

50. Calmore, "Racialized Space," 1247.

51. U.S. Census Bureau, Current Population Reports, P60–238, *Income, Poverty, and Health Insurance Coverage in the United States: 2009*.

52. Mahoney, "Segregation," 1659.

53. Jargowsky, "Stunning Progress, Hidden Problems," 1, 10, 5. Twenty years earlier, the residents of the nation's poorest urban neighborhoods were 65 percent black, 22 percent Hispanic, and only 13 percent non-Hispanic white and other races. Jargowsky and Bane, "Ghetto Poverty in the United States," 235, 252.

54. Squires, *Capital and Communities in Black and White*.

55. As of 2006, the federal government alone had spent over $625 billion on highway construction. U.S. Department of Transportation, Federal Highway Administration, "Our Nation's Highways: 2008," Fig. 6.3.

56. Schill and Wachter, "The Spatial Bias of Federal Housing Law and Policy," 1308.

57. Massey and Denton, *American Apartheid*.

58. Ibid., 52.

59. By 1972, the FHA had insured 11 million home mortgage loans and 22 million home improvement loans.

60. Massey and Denton, *American Apartheid*, 30.

61. State governments have delegated their zoning power to individual municipalities. In turn, municipalities exercise this zoning power to exclude poor minorities from their suburbs by zoning in ways that preclude the development of low-and moderate-income housing. See, e.g., Rothwell and Massey, "The Effect of Density

Zoning on Racial Segregation"; and Roisman and Tegeler, "Improving and Expanding Housing Opportunities," 343.

62. In the Boston area in 2006, 30.8 percent of blacks and 26.5 percent of Latinos were rejected for a mortgage to purchase a house, compared with 13.1 percent of whites. Blanton, *More Minorities Denied Mortgages*.

63. See generally powell and Reece, "The Future of Fair Housing and Fair Credit."

64. McArdle, *Beyond Poverty*, 10.

65. See powell and Reece, "The Future of Fair Housing and Fair Credit."

66. See Bocian, Ernst, and Li, "Unfair Lending."

67. Ibid., discussing *Curbing Predatory Home Mortgage Lending*, U.S. Department of Housing and Urban Development and U.S. Department of the Treasury.

68. Bocian, Ernst, and Li, "Unfair Lending" at 5.

69. Frankenberg, *White Women, Race Matters*, 52.

70. Frankenberg, "Whiteness and Americanness," 62, 63.

71. See ibid. (articulating a relationship between power and the social construction of race).

72. Neil Gotanda, for example, has identified four distinct uses of race in color-blind jurisprudence. See Gotanda, "A Critique of 'Our Constitution Is Color Blind,'" 3–5.

73. This insight was conveyed to me by a former jurisprudence student, Jonathan Levy, who spoke of the tensions he experienced as an avowed anti-racist permeated by the racism of our society.

74. See also Ewing, "The Illusion of Wholeness," 258–259.

75. Hurston, "How It Feels to Be Colored Me," 152.

76. Genevieve Lloyd addresses the analogous problem of trying to imagine a

world without sexism. See Lloyd, *The Man of Reason,* 102–110.

77. Goldberg, *Racist Culture,* 10.

78. Gotanda, "A Critique," 4.

79. Jennifer Gratz, plaintiff in a challenge to the University of Michigan's undergraduate admissions program, began the campaign for Prop. 2 along with Ward Connerly, a former regent of the University of California and activist in opposition to affirmative action. See Lewin, "Michigan Rejects Affirmative Action, and Backers Sue"; see also Lempinen, "Confusion on Affirmative Action Ban."

80. See *Operation King's Dream et al v. Connerly et al,* U.S. District Court, Eastern District of Michigan, Southern Division, 06-12773, Arthur J. Tarnow, Opinion and Order, 29 August 2006.

81. Initiative 200 was a ballot initiative creating a law to ban race and gender "preferences" (Washington, 1998); Prop. 54, the failed "Racial Privacy Initiative," would have amended the California constitution to prohibit the use of racial classifications by the state (2003); Initiative 424 amended the Nebraska constitution in 2008 to ban affirmative action programs for women and minorities.

82. See Page, "Anti-Gay Law Flies in the Face of the 14th Amendment" (describing the statements of the executive director for the group sponsoring Amendment 2, which expressed general support for "equal rights" but characterized equal rights for gays and lesbians as "special rights"); see also Greenberg, "Court to Review Gay Rights Laws." The amendment was framed as "prohibiting new laws giving preferences on the basis of sexual orientation." It read as follows:

> Neither the State of Colorado, through any of its branches or departments, nor any of its agencies, political subdivisions, municipalities or school districts, shall enact, adopt or enforce any statute, regulation, ordinance or policy whereby homosexual, lesbian or bisexual orientation, conduct, practices or relationships shall constitute or otherwise be the basis of, or entitle any person or class of persons to have or claim any minority status, quota preferences, protected status or claim of discrimination.

The Supreme Court invalidated the amendment as a violation of the Equal Protection Clause in *Romer v. Evans,* 116 S. Ct. 1620, 1623 (1996).

83. See, e.g., *Adarand Constructors v. Pena,* 115 S. Ct. 2097, 2117 (1995), discussed in chapter 5.

84. See, e.g., *Gratz v. Bollinger,* 539 U.S. 244 (2003) and *Hopwood v. Texas,* 78 F.3d 932, 944–948 (5th Cir. 1996), *cert. denied,* 116 S. Ct. 2581 (1996) (striking down affirmative action admissions programs at two large state universities).

85. For example, John Rawls has asserted that the concept of justice and the organization of society are developed through the interactions of "individuals" and "persons." See Rawls, *A Theory of Justice,* 3–6.

86. See Goldberg, *Racist Culture,* 187–188; Omi and Winant, *Racial Formation,* 55.

87. See Abram, *The Spell of the Sensuous,* 33 ("Even the most detached scientist must begin and end her study in this indeterminate field of experience, where shifts of climate or mood may alter his experiment or her interpretation of 'the data.'"); and Unger, *Knowledge and Politics,* 31–32.

88. Gotanda presents this view when he asserts that, from a jurisprudential standpoint, "[o]nly by treating culture-race as analytically distinct from other usages of race can one begin to address the link between the cultural practices of Blacks and the subordination of Blacks, elements that are, in fact, inseparable in the lived experience of race." Gotanda, "A Critique," 56.

89. See Omi and Winant, *Racial Formation*, 67.

90. In 2003 the Census Bureau reported that average wealth of blacks was 11 percent of that held by whites. U.S. Census Bureau, "Net Worth and Asset Ownership 1998–2000."

91. A 2010 Census report listed the 2004 median assets of all kinds by household race and ethnicity, with non-Hispanic white households averaging three times the assets of Hispanics and four times those of blacks. A further breakdown showed that 45 percent of black households held less than $5,000 in assets, while only 21 percent of white households did, and that 50 percent of white households held over $100,000. "Mean Value of Assets for Households by Type of Asset Owned and Selected Characteristics" and "Percent Distribution of Household Net Worth, by Amount of Net Worth and Selected Characteristics" at U.S. Census Bureau, "Wealth and Asset Ownership: Detailed Tables: 2004." The 2000 census had found that 71.3 percent of white households owned their homes as opposed to 46.3 percent of black households. U.S. Census Bureau, "Historical Census of Housing Tables: Homeownership by Race and Hispanic Origin."

92. In 2010, the median income for black households was $32,068, compared with $51,846 for white. U.S. Census Bureau, "Income, Poverty, and Health Insurance Coverage in the United States: 2010" at 6; available at http://www.census.gov/hhes/www/income/income.html. Poverty levels in 2009 were more than twice as high for black families as for white: 24.7 percent compared to 9.4 percent. U.S. Census Bureau, Current Population Reports, P60–238, *Income, Poverty, and Health Insurance Coverage in the United States: 2009*.

93. See j. powell, "How Government Tax and Housing Policies Have Racially Segregated America," 80; see also Rothwell and Massey, "The Effect of Density Zoning and Segregation in U.S. Urban Areas."

94. Mahoney, "Segregation, Whiteness, and Transformation," 1663.

95. See C. Harris, "Whiteness as Property," 1714–15. See also Roediger, *Towards the Abolition of Whiteness*, 181–194.

96. Harris, "Whiteness as Property," 1730–31.

97. See ibid., 1734.

98. But see ibid., 1735–36 (discussing the manifestations of "[p]rivate identity based on racial hierarchy").

99. Allen, *The Invention of the White Race*, vol. 1, 185.

100. See C. Harris, "Whiteness as Property."

101. Ibid., 1736. Cheryl Harris tells the story of her light-skinned grandmother who "passed" as white, and in doing so gained employment at a department store that excluded blacks. Ibid., 1710–12. This story demonstrates one way in which designating a black person white was more a conveyance of a property interest than a removal of one.

102. Gotanda, "A Critique," 56.

103. A frequent occurrence of this characterization of racism as minority exclusion rather than majority inclusion in the use of the phrase "blacks are less likely than whites" to receive a particular social or economic benefit, rather than "whites are more likely than blacks." See, e.g., Associated Press, "Blacks Found Less Likely Than Whites to Be Promoted in the Military."

104. See Omi and Winant, *Racial Formation in the United States*, 66; and Mahoney, "Segregation, Whiteness, and Transformation," 1661.

105. J. Berger, et al., *Ways of Seeing*, 10.

106. Minh-ha, *Woman, Native, Other*, 27.

107. Fanon, *The Wretched of the Earth*, 250 (1963).

108. Yancy, *Who is White?*

109. See generally, Martinot, *The Rule of Racialization.*

4. Interrogating Privilege, Transforming Whiteness

1. Wildman, *Privilege Revealed,* 29.

2. See, e.g., Saussure, "Course in General Linguistics," 718–726.

3. See M. Armstrong, "Privilege in Residential Housing," 52.

4. See, e.g., Derrida, "Structure, Sign, and Play in the Discourse of the Human Sciences," 1117–1126.

5. See R. Williams, *Keywords,* 324.

6. Wildman, *Privilege Revealed,* 14.

7. See ibid., 27.

8. See ibid., 31–32.

9. M. Armstrong, "Privilege in Residential Housing," 59.

10. Wildman, *Privilege Revealed,* 13.

11. Ross, "Innocence and Affirmative Action," 311, 313.

12. See generally Lipsitz, *The Possessive Investment in Whiteness.*

13. See Ross, "Innocence and Affirmative Action," 315.

14. See McIntosh, "White Privilege and Male Privilege," 75–76.

15. See ibid.

16. Ibid., 79.

17. See generally T. Morrison, *Playing in the Dark.*

18. See especially Roediger, *The Wages of Whiteness.*

19. See, e.g., Du Bois, "The Souls of White Folk."

20. See, e.g., Shear, "Obama Campaign Grapples With New Voter ID Laws."

21. Minow, "Making All the Difference," 93.

22. See, e.g., Lloyd, *The Man of Reason,* 101.

23. See Minow, "Making All the Difference," 93.

24. Minow, "Partial Justice and Minorities," 17.

25. Aanerud, "Fictions of Whiteness," 42, 43.

26. Frankenberg, "Introduction: Local Whitenesses, Localizing Whiteness," 15–16.

27. Wildman, *Privilege Revealed,* 24.

28. See generally Allen, *The Invention of the White Race,* vol. 1; Young, *Justice and the Politics of Difference.*

29. For a good critique of this position, see generally Frye, "Oppression."

30. See, e.g., Farber and Sherry, *Beyond All Reason* ; and Calmore, "Random Notes of an Integration Warrior – Part 2."

31. See Jordan, *White over Black;* see also Karst, *Belonging to America.*

32. See, e.g., Young, *Justice and the Politics of Difference;* MacKinnon, *Feminism Unmodified;* Minow, *Not Only for Myself;* Frye, "Oppression."

33. See Young, *Justice and the Politics of Difference;* see also Minow, "Partial Justice and Minorities."

34. See j. powell, "Is Racial Integration Essential to Achieving Quality Education for Low-Income Minority Students?" 7.

35. See generally Jencks, *Rethinking Social Policy.*

36. See Allen, *The Invention of the White Race,* vol. 1, 35.

37. See West, "Jurisprudence and Gender."

38. See Peller, "Race Consciousness," 761–762.

39. See Fordham and Ogbu, "Black Students' School Success," 177.

40. See, for example, Buck, *Acting White.*

41. Tyson, Darity, and Castellino, "It's Not 'A Black Thing,'" 582, 600; see also Tough, "The Acting White Myth"; and Mickelson and Velasco, "Bring It On!"

42. Mickelson, "The Incomplete Desegregation of the Charlotte-Mecklenburg Schools."

43. See, e.g., Burris and Welner, "Classroom Integration and Accelerated Learning through Detracking."

44. See, e.g., Duggan, "Making It Perfectly Queer."

45. See Omi, "Racial Identity and the State."

46. Marshall continued for some time to call himself and other blacks "Negro," challenging the appropriateness of the terms "Black" and "African American." See Linzer, "White Liberal Looks at Racist Speech," 214n121.

47. See, for example, j. powell, "A New Theory of Integrated Education."

48. See Crenshaw, "Race, Reform, and Retrenchment."

49. See Jencks, *Rethinking Social Policy*; Katz, *White Awareness*.

50. McIntosh, "White Privilege and Male Privilege," 71.

51. Young, *Justice and the Politics of Difference*.

52. Ibid., 165.

53. See ibid., 166.

54. Ibid., 169 (quoting Boxill, *Blacks and Social Justice*).

55. Ibid., 170.

56. Ortiz, "Categorical Community, 771, 803.

57. Ibid. at 804.

58. Ibid. at 803.

59. See, ibid., 804.

60. Young, *Justice and the Politics of Difference*, 171.

61. Ibid.

62. Young, *Justice and the Politics of Difference*, 171; see also, Reed, W. C., "A New and Accurate Way to Identify Elite Athletes."

63. See Young, *Justice and the Politics of Difference*.

64. See Goldberg, *Racist Culture* .

65. See Lloyd, *The Man of Reason*.

66. See ibid.

67. See ibid., 100–101.

68. See Lloyd, *The Man of Reason*, 102–104.

69. Ibid., 104–105.

70. Ibid., 106.

71. See, e.g., Omi, "Racial Identity and the State"; Goldberg, *Racist Culture*; Allen, *The Invention of the White Race*, vol. 1.

72. Lloyd, *The Man of Reason*, 109.

73. See Young, *Justice and the Politics of Difference*.

74. See j. powell, "Worlds Apart" (citing Unger, *Knowledge and Politics*).

75. See ibid.

76. Young, *Justice and the Politics of Difference* .

77. Martinot, *The Rule of Racialization*, 201.

78. Ignatiev, *How the Irish Became White*.

79. Warren, "Performing Whiteness Differently."

80. Wiegman, "Whiteness Studies and the Paradox of Particularity," 115, 141.

81. See, e.g., Kahneman, *Thinking, Fast and Slow*.

5. White Innocence and the Courts

1. See Massey, *Categorically Unequal*.

2. 426 U.S. 229, 242 (1976).

3. As Peggy McIntosh describes it, "My schooling gave me no training in seeing myself as an oppressor, as an unfairly advantaged person, or as a participant in a damaged culture. I was taught to see myself as an individual whose moral state depended on her individual moral will." McIntosh, "White Privilege and Male Privilege," 72.

4. *Ricci v DeStefano*, 557 U.S., 608–609 (2009).

5. See C. Powell, "Blinded by Color," 200.

6. *Regents of the University of California v. Bakke*, 438 U.S. 265, 272–277.

7. 438 U.S. 265, 298.

8. Freeman, "Legitimizing Racial Discrimination through Antidiscrimination Law," 29.

9. J. Morrison, "Colorblindness, Individuality, and Merit," 338, 324.

10. Voting Rights Act of 1965, § 5.

11. *United Jewish Organizations of Williamsburgh, Inc. v. Carey,* 177–178 (Brennan, J., concurring) (footnote omitted).

12. 430 U.S. 144, 174 (1977) (Brennan, J., concurring).

13. *Fullilove v. Klutznick,* 448 U.S. 448, 484 (1980).

14. Ibid. at 488.

15. Ibid. at 471.

16. Ibid., 484.

17. Ibid., 477–478 (Burger, C.J.)

18. Ross, "Innocence and Affirmative Action," 300–301, 306.

19. Wildman and Davis, "Making Systems of Privilege Visible," 7, 8.

20. *City of Richmond v. J. A. Croson Co.,* 488 U.S. 469, at 479–480 (1989).

21. Ibid.

22. Ibid. at 492 (O'Connor, J., quoting *Wygant,* 476 U.S. at 274).

23. Ibid. at 505–506 (O'Connor, J.).

24. Ibid. at 516 (Stevens, J., concurring).

25. Ibid. at 526–528 (Scalia, J., concurring).

26. Ibid. at 527.

27. Ibid. at 490 (O'Connor, J.)

28. *Adarand Constructors, Inc. v. Pena,* 515 U.S. 200, 205 (1995).

29. Ibid. at 229–230.

30. See ibid. at 235–237.

31. Ibid. at 243 (Stevens, J., dissenting) (citation omitted).

32. Ibid. at 270 (Souter, J. dissenting).

33. Rosenfeld, "Decoding Richmond," 1790.

34. Byrnes, "Unmasking White Privilege," 558.

35. *McCleskey v. Kemp,* 481 U.S. 279, 286 (1987).

36. See 481 U.S. at 283.

37. See ibid. at 2876.

38. See ibid. at 287.

39. See ibid. at 297 (Powell, J.) 426 U.S. 229, 239 (1976).

40. *McCleskey* at 298 n20.

41. See ibid. at 292–293 (citing *Whitus v. Georgia,* 385 U.S. 545, 550 [1967] and *Wayte v. United States,* 470 U.S. 598, 608 [1985]).

42. Ibid. at 344 (Brennan, J., dissenting).

43. 481 U.S. at 290.

44. See ibid. at 287. The Court's Title VII jurisprudence did not require multiple regression analysis to account for every conceivable variable, as long as it accounted for the major factors that are likely to influence decisions, as Justice Brennan noted in dissent. See ibid. at 327–328.

45. Ibid. at 328 (Brennan, J., dissenting).

46. *Plessy v. Ferguson,* 163 U.S. 537, 544 (1896).

47. Ibid. at 550.

48. 347 U.S. 483, 495 (1954).

49. *Brown v. Board of Educ.,* 349 U.S. 294, 300 (1955) [*Brown II*].

50. *Washington v. Davis,* 426 U.S. 229, 248 (1976).

51. Ibid. at 248, n14 (citations omitted).

52. Ibid. (citations omitted).

53. *McCleskey v. Kemp,* 481 U.S. at 315–317.

54. Ibid. at 339 (Brennan, J., dissenting).

55. Ibid. at 320 (quoting *Gregg v. Georgia*).

56. Kentucky's Racial Justice Act prohibits the imposition of a sentence of death sought on the basis of race, as shown by statistical or other evidence that death was sought more often for defendants of one race or as punishment for crimes against victims of one race. Kentucky Revised Statutes Annotated §

532.300–309 (West 1998); North Carolina Racial Justice Act, N.C. Gen. Stat. Ann. §§ 15A-2010–2012 (West 2009).

57. See Robertson, Campbell, "Bias Law Used to Move a Man off Death Row," *New York Times,* 20 April 2012.

58. See O'Brien, Barbara and Catherine M. Grosso, "Report on Jury Selection Study" (2011) available at http://digital commons.law.msu.edu/facpubs/331/.

59. Editorial, "Justice under North Carolina's Racial Bias Law," *New York Times,* 20 April 2012.

60. See "North Carolina Racial Justice Research Project" available at http:// www.law.msu.edu/racial-justice/index .html.

61. See N.C. House Bill 615, "No Discriminatory Purpose in Death Penalty" (N.C.G.A. Session 2011).

62. See, e.g., Rosenthal, Andrew, "North Carolina Regresses on Race and Gender Bias," *New York Times,* 5 July 2012. Available at http://takingnote.blogs .nytimes.com/2012/07/05/north-carolina -regresses-on-race-and-gender-bias/.

63. See ibid.; see also Blythe, "Racial Justice Act before Judge."

64. *Swann v. Charlotte-Mecklenburg Board of Education,* 402 U.S. 1, 20–21.

65. *Freeman v. Pitts,* 503 U.S. 467–480.

66. Ibid. at 495.

67. *Grutter v. Bollinger,* 539 U.S. 306, 332 (2003).

68. *Parents Involved,* 551 U.S. 701, 788 (2007) (Kennedy, J., concurring).

69. Ibid. at 789.

70. *Local 28 of the Sheet Metal Workers' International Ass'n v.* EEOC, 478 U.S. 421, 474 (1986).

71. *Johnson v. Transportation Agency, Santa Clara County, California,* 480 U.S. 616, 647 (1987) (Stevens, J. concurring) (quoting Kathleen M. Sullivan, "The Supreme Court: 1985 Term: Comment, Sins of Discrimination: Last Term's Affirmative Action Cases" 100 *Harvard Law Review* 78 (1986)).

72. *Adarand,* 515 U.S. at 272 (Ginsburg, J. dissenting) (citing *Loving v. Virginia,* 388 U.S. 1, 11 [1967]).

73. NAACP v. *Claiborne Hardware, Co.,* 458 U.S. 886, 898–900, n26 (1982).

74. Ibid. at 933, 934 (1982) (Stevens, J.).

75. See, e.g., Confirmation Hearing on the Nomination of John G. Roberts, Jr., to be Chief Justice of the United States: Hearing before the Senate Committee on the Judiciary, 109th Congress 55 (2005).

76. *Dred Scott v. Sanford,* 60 U.S. 393, 409 (Taney, C.J.). The chief justice was explaining the reasons that African Americans were ineligible for citizenship.

77. 42 U.S.C. 2000d (2000).

78. D. Black, "Picking Up the Pieces after *Alexander v. Sandoval,* " 356.

79. 532 U.S. 275 (2001). For an excellent discussion of the challenges posed by this case and possible solutions, see D. Black, "Picking Up the Pieces after *Alexander v. Sandoval.*"

80. See D. Black, "Picking Up the Pieces after *Alexander v. Sandoval,* " 382–383.

81. See generally ibid.

82. See D. Black, "The Contradiction between Equal Protection's Meaning and Its Legal Substance."

83. See ibid.

84. For more on this see powell and Menendian, "Remaking Law," 1105–11.

85. Sterba, *Affirmative Action for the Future.*

86. Ibid.

87. Ibid.

88. Pager, "The Mark of a Criminal Record."

89. Ibid.; see also Pager, *Marked.*

90. D. Hall, "Black and Busted in Dane County."

91. For more on this, see Alexander, *The New Jim Crow,* 220–221.

92. Stevenson, "We Need to Talk about an Injustice."

93. Ibid.

94. Kim, Losen, and Hewitt, *The School to Prison Pipeline*, 128.

95. Ibid.

96. New York City Civil Liberties Union, "Report: NYPD Stop-and-Frisk Activity in 2011" (2012). Available at http://www.nyclu.org/publications /report-nypd-stop-and-frisk-activity -2011–2012.

97. See Kennedy, *Race, Crime, and the Law* at 339, discussing Justice Scalia's "Memorandum to the Conference" in *McCleskey v. Kemp* File, THURGOOD MARSHALL PAPERS box 425, The Library of Congress.

98. See Armour, "Stereotypes and Prejudice," 11–32.

99. See, e.g., *Jackson v. Chicago Transit Authority*, 273 N.E. 2d 748 (Ill. App. Ct. 1971).

100. *Metro Broadcasting, Inc. v. FCC*, 497 U.S. 547 (1990).

101. 497 U.S. 547, 604 (O'Connor, J., dissenting).

102. Poindexter, "African-American Images in the News."

103. See generally Gilens, *Why Americans Hate Welfare*.

104. *Santa Clara County v. Southern Pacific Railroad Company*, 118 U.S. 394, 397 (1886); *Citizens United v. Federal Election Commission*, 130 S. Ct. 876 (2010).

105. *Grutter v. Bollinger*, 539 U.S. 306, 333 (2003).

106. Ibid. at 332.

6. Dreaming of a Self beyond Whiteness and Isolation

1. Hacker, *Two Nations*, 31–32.

2. López, "White by Law," 542–550.

3. Bell, "White Superiority in America," 138.

4. Frye, *The Politics of Reality*, 10–12.

5. Ford, "The Boundaries of Race," 1843–59.

6. See generally Laguerre, *Minoritized Space*; Marx, *Making Race and Nation*.

7. Laguerre, *Minoritized Space*, 17–18.

8. See generally Berry and Henderson, *Geographical Identities of Ethnic America*; Cashin, *The Failures of Integration*; Jackson, *Crabgrass Frontier*; Massey and Denton, *American Apartheid*.

9. Martinot, *The Rule of Racialization* 180–181; j. powell, "The Needs of Members in a Legitimate Democratic State," 986–997.

10. See generally Aspen/Pitkin County Housing Authority, Aspen/Pitkin County Housing Guidelines.

11. Tilly, *Durable Inequality*, 6–8.

12. *Dred Scott v. Sandford*, 60 U.S. 393 (1856).

13. Ibid. at 454.

14. Ibid.

15. See generally Foner, *The Story of American Freedom*; Patterson, *Freedom*, vol. 1: *Freedom in the Making of Western Culture*.

16. For more on this issue and this case, see powell and Menendian, "Little Rock and the Legacy of *Dred Scott*."

17. Although it is true that some abolitionists who opposed slavery saw blacks as potential equals, many more of those who wanted free states surely would not have described an emancipated black as "free." Freedom was whiteness. Their opposition to the introduction of slavery into free states was more an opposition to blacks than to slavery as an unjust institution.

18. Foner, *The Story of American Freedom*, 20.

19. Ibid.; see also Roediger, *The Wages of Whiteness*.

20. As mentioned above, membership may be the most important benefit in a truly democratic state, as it in turn distributes all other privileges. See Marx, *Mak-

ing Race and Nation, 5–6; j. powell, "The Needs of Members," 969–970, 987–988.

21. *Slaughter-House Cases*, 83 U.S. 36 (1873). It is also worth noting that early civil rights laws were explicit regarding the privilege associated with whiteness, so that sections 1981 and 1982 of the Civil Rights Act of 1871 gave all citizens the same rights as whites. These statutes were both acknowledging the boundaries of whiteness and attempting to open them up.

22. For a good analysis of this under the modern civil rights laws, see generally Lipsitz, *The Possessive Investment in Whiteness*.

23. The notion that black progress equates with white loss was exacerbated by such moves, not only during Reconstruction, when rights were taken away from southern whites just as they were extended to blacks, but also in desegregation cases a century later, when non-elite whites would be forced to give up their control of white space (at least temporarily) for the perceived benefit of blacks, while the elites continued to protect their space. This is not to say that non-elite whites were simply the pawns of the elite, or that they would have easily accepted the demise of white boundaries if they hadn't been drawn in such a zero-sum way. But it is important to note that the choice of redrawing these boundaries shifted change, cost, and adaptation to less powerful whites.

24. Marx, *Making Race and Nation*, 134–135.

25. Wallenstein, *Tell the Court I Love My Wife*, 54–55.

26. Mills, *The Racial Contract*, 52.

27. Omi and Winant, *Racial Formation*, 3.

28. Omi and Winant, *Racial Formation*.

29. See generally Allen, *The Invention of the White Race*.

30. See generally the work of Roediger, especially *The Wages of Whiteness*. See also Ignatiev, *How the Irish Became White*; Allen, *The Invention of the White Race*.

31. *Plessy*, 163 U.S. at 544 (1896).

32. Ibid. The Court cites *Roberts v. The City of Boston* – a Massachusetts case that upheld racially segregated schools – without mentioning that in 1855, the Massachusetts legislature had banned racial discrimination with regard to applicants to public schools. See, e.g., Brown Foundation, "Prelude to *Brown* – 1849: *Roberts v. City of Boston*."

33. *Plessy*, at 559.

34. Marx, *Making Race and Nation*.

35. The Republican Party rose to power as the party of Lincoln and of freedom – "free labor, free land, free men" – while the Democratic Party was the party of the so-called Redeemers and their reign of terror during Reconstruction. Having lost power in the wake of the Great Depression, however, the Republican Party eventually reinvented itself in a racial realignment that made it the party of southern whites. (See, e.g., Omi and Winant, *Racial Formation*, 118–122.) The Democrats have yet to develop an effective counterstrategy. The closest they have come was probably with Bill Clinton's efforts to appear to be tough on blacks with his welfare policies, law and order rhetoric, and expansion of the criminal justice system.

36. See, e.g., Soja, *Seeking Spatial Justice*.

37. See generally Jackson, *Crabgrass Frontier*; Massey and Denton, *American Apartheid*.

38. In 1942, there were 24,500 municipalities and special districts in the U.S. By 2002, that number had more than doubled to 54,481. U.S. Dept. of Commerce, 2002 Census of Governments, xiii (2002).

39. See generally Cashin, *The Failures of Integration;* Massey and Denton, *American Apartheid.*

40. Ford, "The Boundaries of Race," 1859.

41. Cashin, *The Failures of Integration,* 104–107.

42. Winant, *The World Is a Ghetto,* 167–168.

43. See, e.g., Halberstam, *The Children,* 517.

44. See, e.g., *New York Times,* "President Map."

45. Van Osdol, "Lawyer Analyzes Landmark Case Progress."

46. Thorsen, dir., *James Baldwin: The Price of the Ticket.*

47. Allen, *The Invention of the White Race,* vol. 1, 16–17.

48. Martinot, *The Rule of Racialization,* 64.

49. Malcolmson, *One Drop of Blood,* 299.

50. See generally Institute on Race & Poverty, University of Minnesota, Minnesota Statewide Racial Profiling Reports.

51. *Plessy* at 541.

52. Unger, *Passion,* 20.

53. See generally Goldberg, *Racist Culture.*

54. Winnubst, "Vampires, Anxieties and Dreams," 4.

55. See Roediger, *Towards the Abolition of Whiteness;* Ignatiev, "The Point Is Not to Interpret Whiteness but to Abolish It."

56. *Dred Scott v. Sandford,* 60 U.S. 393 (1856) at 403–406.

57. *Brown v. Board of Education,* 347 U.S. 483 (1954).

58. j. powell, "The Needs of Members," 994–997.

59. Bennett, "Jack Johnson and the Great White Hope," 88.

60. Foucault, *Discipline and Punish,* 202–203.

61. Patterson, *Slavery and Social Death,* 100.

62. Guinier and Torres, *The Miner's Canary,* 225.

63. Baldwin, "East River, Downtown," 180.

64. See, e.g., Davis, *The Wayfinders.*

65. Klein, *Meeting the Great Bliss Queen,* 25–37; see also "The Racing of American Society," chapter 3 of this volume.

66. Unger, *Democracy Realized.*

67. Jones, "The Zen of Social Action."

68. Ibid.

69. Todd et al., "Perspective Taking Combats Automatic Expressions of Racial Bias," 3; see also B. Berger, "Walking in Another's Shoes."

70. See Todd, et al., "Perspective Taking," 8–9.

71. Ibid., 7–11.

72. Ibid., 13.

7. The Multiple Self

1. Kenneth Gergen articulated a relational view of the self as well as the insight that there are indeed multiple selves, which he attributes primarily to environmental and technological changes. See Gergen, *The Saturated Self.* Implicit in this argument is the notion that the unitary self has been fractured. While there are some postmodernists who argue for the decentering of the self, others have suggested abandoning it. Most, however, call for a rethinking and resituating of the self.

2. Theories of language assert that one of the powers of language is its ability to determine that which is considered normal and that which is considered abnormal. See, e.g., Foucault, *The Order of Things.*

3. Young, *Justice and the Politics of Difference,* 112.

4. As a linguistic convenience, I will use the overly general terms "feminism" and "postmodernism." In doing so, my intent is not to assert that there is a single

voice or vantage point for either of these categories, or that these categories are in any way mutually exclusive. I wish only to avoid being paralyzed by the task of articulating the infinite nuances and wrinkles that exist within and among them.

5. See, e.g., Grillo, "Anti-Essentialism and Intersectionality," 17–19.

6. See, e.g., Ewing, "The Illusion of Wholeness," 251; A. Harris, "Foreword: The Unbearable Lightness of Identity," 211. Jennifer Wicke notes the postmodern recognition of the self's "fissuring by the myriad social discourses which construct it." See Wicke, "Postmodern Identity and the Legal Subject," 463.

7. See Damasio, Descartes' Error, and Nørretranders, The User Illusion.

8. See, e.g., powell and Menendian, "Remaking Law"; Brooks, The Social Animal.

9. S. Hall, "The Question of Cultural Identity," 595, 602.

10. Ibid.

11. Ibid., 602–603. Although this notion of the sovereign and essential self had important implications for the liberation of those oppressed by premodern society, many of the principal proponents of this self felt that it inhered only in white Europeans. David Theo Goldberg points out that, for example, David Hume asserted that "negroes" were akin to parrots in their intellectual capacities, only capable of mimicry; Immanuel Kant felt that blacks were intellectually inferior; and John Stuart Mill believed that blacks lacked the capacity for self-government. See, e.g., Goldberg, Racist Culture, 6.

12. Dunning, "Post-Modernism and the Construct of the Divisible Self," 135.

13. Kant, Critique of Pure Reason, Smith trans., 58 (St. Martin's Press, 1968).

14. Ibid., 45.

15. Ibid., 154.

16. Ibid., 60.

17. Descartes, A Discourse on Method and Selected Writings, trans. Veitch.

18. Ibid., 1.

19. Ibid., 2.

20. Descartes, Discourse on the Method, ed. Weissman, 21.

21. Locke, An Essay Concerning Human Understanding, ed. Pringle-Pattison, 9.

22. Locke, Treatise of Civil Government, ed. Sherman, 90.

23. See Rawls, A Theory of Justice.

24. Ibid., 18–19. Critics claim that Rawls, like Kant before him, fails in this effort. See Sandel, Liberalism and the Limits of Justice, 11; see also Benhabib, Situating the Self, 161–169.

25. Rawls, A Theory of Justice, 141. The assumption Rawls makes is that "if a knowledge of particulars is allowed, then the outcome is biased by arbitrary contingencies." Ibid.

26. Ibid.

27. In A Theory of Justice, Rawls argues that in a just society "each person possesses an inviolability founded on justice that even the welfare of society as a whole cannot override," 3–4; Sandel, in Liberalism and the Limits of Justice, asserts that the concepts of self as independent of its object and of the right as prior to the good are essential to the deontological vision (2–7).

28. Hume, A Treatise of Human Nature, 251.

29. Ibid., 260

30. Ibid., 261.

31. Hegel, Reason in History, 31–34.

32. Hinchman, Hegel's Critique of the Enlightenment, 33.

33. Goldberg, Racist Culture, 44; see also chapter 3, this volume.

34. In the epistemologies of modern philosophers, Christian conceptions of God played a central role. See, e.g., Descartes, "Meditations," 197–199.

35. Goldberg, Racist Culture, 16.

36. See, e.g., Hofstadter, *Social Darwinism in American Thought.*

37. Ibid., 33–34; see also Goldberg, *Racist Culture.*

38. For more on this move, see, e.g., Calmore, "Racialized Space and the Culture of Segregation"; Crenshaw, "Race, Reform, and Retrenchment."

39. Du Bois, *The Souls of Black Folk,* 8–9.

40. As James Boyle notes, there is a tension in writings on the self between the role of structure (or context) in defining the self and the agency or ability of the individual to self-define. Boyle, "Is Subjectivity Possible?" 492. My belief is that both of these forces tell part of the story and are not mutually exclusive, though they are mutually limiting.

41. Hurston, "How It Feels to Be Colored Me," 152–53.

42. Ibid., 154.

43. Ibid.

44. This is provided, of course, that they do not transgress other constructed borders such as those of gender and sexuality.

45. What this invisibility masks is the myriad ways that whiteness has been defined and redefined in order to maintain the privileged status of whites. In fact, given the scientific unreality of race, one can argue that to be white mostly means to be privileged.

46. Fanon, *Black Skin, White Masks,* 116. Elsewhere Fanon writes, "As long as the black man is among his own, he will have no occasion, except in minor internal conflicts, to experience his being through others." Ibid., 109.

47. See generally French, *Beyond Power,* 482–483; Gilligan, *In a Different Voice,* 6–8; West, "Jurisprudence and Gender," 1–3.

48. See, e.g., A. Harris, "Race and Essentialism in Feminist Legal Theory," 590–605 (critiquing Catharine MacKinnon's dominance theory and Robin West's "essential woman" theory).

49. Haraway, "A Manifesto for Cyborgs," 190, 202.

50. See, e.g., MacKinnon, *Feminism Unmodified,* 16.

51. A. Harris, "Race and Essentialism," 588.

52. An anthology on black women's studies makes this phenomenon explicit in its title: *All the Women Are White, All the Blacks Are Men, but Some of Us Are Brave,* ed. Hull et al.

53. Grillo, "Anti-Essentialism and Intersectionality," 18; and Crenshaw, "Mapping the Margins."

54. A. Harris, "Foreword: The Unbearable Lightness of Identity," 210.

55. A. Harris, "Race and Essentialism," 584.

56. Grillo, "Anti-Essentialism and Intersectionality," 17.

57. Ewing, "The Illusion of Wholeness," 251.

58. Ibid., 255.

59. Ibid., 251.

60. Ibid., 253.

61. Ibid., 270–271.

62. A. Harris, "Foreword: The Unbearable Lightness of Identity," 211.

63. Haraway, "A Manifesto for Cyborgs," 192 and 196–197.

64. S. Friedman, "Beyond White and Other," 1, 7.

65. Ibid.

66. Ibid., 17.

67. Dunning, "Post-Modernism and the Construct of the Divisible Self," 133.

68. This concept applies equally to gender, sexual orientation, and other matrices of oppression. Haraway recognizes this when she refers to the "noninnocence of the category woman." Haraway, "A Manifesto for Cyborgs," 199. Amy Mullin describes a similar insight: "Given that ours is still a racist, sexist, and homophobic society, it is easy to predict that self-mastery will become associated with mastery over people who are not white, as well as

other women and homosexuals." Mullin, "Selves, Diverse and Divided," 7–8.

69. Crenshaw, "Race, Reform, and Retrenchment," 1373.

70. A. Harris, "Race and Essentialism," 608.

71. Baldwin, *The Price of the Ticket,* 690.

72. Frankenberg, "Whiteness and Americanness," 62, 63.

73. T. Morrison, *Playing in the Dark,* 34–35.

74. Ibid., 38.

75. Ibid., 6.

76. See generally Dallymayr, *Twilight of Subjectivity;* Foucault, *The Order of Things.*

77. Haraway, "A Manifesto for Cyborgs," 206.

78. Boyle, "Is Subjectivity Possible?," 500.

79. Ewing, "The Illusion of Wholeness," 259 (citations omitted).

80. Ibid., 268.

81. See A. Harris, "Race and Essentialism."

82. Mullin, "Selves, Diverse and Divided," 1–2.

83. Mullin describes the multiple self as the theory that the self is "composed of relatively fixed or agent-like aspects or parts." Ibid., 2.

84. Ibid., 8.

85. Ibid., 20.

86. Ibid., 17.

87. Ewing, "The Illusion of Wholeness," 257.

88. Ibid., 274.

89. Flax, "Multiple," 38. Flax goes on to assert that "naturalizing and universalizing this developmental history obscures its fictive qualities and prescriptive purposes." Ibid.

90. Hillman, *Healing Fiction,* 53–70.

91. Ogden, *The Subjects of Analysis,* 14.

92. Hillman, *Healing Fiction,* 53–70.

93. Lawrence, "The Id, The Ego, and Equal Protection," 331.

94. Ogden, *The Subjects of Analysis,* 18. ("The subject for Freud is to be sought in the phenomenology corresponding to that which lies in the relations between the consciousness and unconsciousness.")

95. Ibid., 7.

96. Ibid., 20.

97. Ibid., 21.

98. Lawrence, "The Id, the Ego, and Equal Protection," 331–332.

99. See Ogden, *The Subjects of Analysis,* 63. Ogden uses the examples of infant and mother, and analyst and analysand, asserting that in these dialectical pairs, the existence of one is dependent upon the existence of the other. Ibid.

100. Ibid., 47.

101. Ibid., 44.

102. Some have situated Freud between the romantic and the rationalist, or between the modern and the postmodern. Lifton, *The Protean Self,* 24.

103. Lawrence, "The Id, the Ego, and Equal Protection," 322–323.

104. Lawrence illustrates this point by referring to the controversy created when sportscaster Howard Cosell referred to a black football player as a "monkey." See ibid., 339–340. Accepting that Cosell was not racist in any willful respect and that he could only be harmed by engaging in deliberately racist behavior, Lawrence notes the unmistakably racist undertones in Cosell's choice of metaphor. Lawrence argues that Cosell's "inadvertent slip of the tongue was not random... , [but] evidence of the continuing presence of a derogatory racial stereotype that he [had] repressed from consciousness and that [had] momentarily slipped past his Ego's censors." See ibid., 340.

105. Lawrence, "The Id, the Ego, and Equal Protection," 333–34. This framework of analysis also provides insight into Toni Morrison's account of the role of blacks in American literature and her assertion that slavery was a possibly in-

dispensable corollary to the freedom of white Americans. See T. Morrison, *Playing in the Dark*, 38.

106. See, e.g., Lawrence, "The Id, the Ego, and Equal Protection," 333–334.

107. See generally Benhabib, *Situating the Self*, 2 (addressing "what is living and what is dead in universalist moral and political theories of the present, after their criticism in the hands of communitarians, feminists, and postmodernists"); Bernstein, *Beyond Objectivism and Relativism*, 18–20.

108. Klein, *Meeting the Great Bliss Queen*, 140.

109. Ibid., 127.

110. Ibid., 136.

111. While Buddhists agree that self-consciousness is largely constructed by language, they also believe that the process of self-consciousness starts at a pre-language level. Ibid., 11.

112. Kolm, "The Buddhist Theory of 'No-self,'" 233, 255.

113. Klein, *Meeting the Great Bliss Queen*, 11.

114. It may be that the essentialism debate is analogous to the scientific debate over whether light is a wave or a particle. The possibilities that something is constructed either of particles or of waves were considered mutually exclusive. So if the experiment designed to answer the question was set up to measure waves, light was found to be a wave. Conversely, if it was designed to measure particles, light was found to be particles. See Hayward, *Shifting Worlds, Changing Minds*, 18. Thus, the parameters of the question "What is light?" are found to be inconsistent with the true nature of light, because light is composed of both waves and particles.

Similarly, Buddhism asserts that the parameters of the essentialist/nonessentialist debate are flawed in that both "anti-

nomes" are in part correct. Moreover, how we ask and verify the question does not affect just the conclusion we reach, but also our very reality. Our questions and methods of observing the world are participants in the world we are observing. Thus, the answer to the question "Is there anything in the world essential, or is everything unessential?" may be "It depends."

115. Ibid., 132.

116. Klein, *Meeting the Great Bliss Queen*, 81.

117. Such questions and the apparent answers are often products of a limited cultural discourse, even when the aim is to critique the limits of that discourse. Thus postmodernism may be an internal criticism of modernism, because it adopts certain fundamental premises of the modernist paradigm.

118. Klein, *Meeting the Great Bliss Queen*, 80.

119. Ibid.

120. Ibid., 81.

121. Ibid., 80.

122. Sandel, *Liberalism and the Limits of Justice*, 1.

123. Rawls, *A Theory of Justice*, 12.

124. Boyle, "Is Subjectivity Possible?," 507. Flax also posits that "this metanarrative requires a certain form of subject – an undetermined one, who can be the discoverer of truth. It requires a particular view of reality – rational, orderly and accessible to and through our thought." Flax, "Multiple," 35.

125. Grillo, "Anti-Essentialism and Intersectionality," 17.

126. Sandel, *Liberalism and the Limits of Justice*, 109.

127. Crenshaw, "Race, Reform, and Retrenchment," 1353.

128. Gabel, "The Phenomenology of Rights-Consciousness and the Pact of the Withdrawn Selves," 1564.

129. 42 U.S.C. 2000e-2(a)(1) (1994).

130. See generally Baldwin, *The Price of the Ticket*.

131. See "The Racing of American Society," chapter 3 of this volume; and Butler, "Gender Trouble," 147–149.

132. Anzaldúa, *Borderlands/La Frontera*, 22.

133. Butler, "Gender Trouble," 147.

134. As discussed in chapter 1, "Post-Racialism or Targeted Universalism?," this requirement was promulgated in *Washington v. Davis*, 426 U.S. 229, 239 (1976).

135. Lawrence, "The Id, the Ego, and Equal Protection," 323.

136. Ibid., 322. For a more recent look at these issues, see Lawrence, "Unconscious Racism Revisited."

137. Grillo, "Anti-Essentialism and Intersectionality," 18–19.

138. At least one court, however, has softened its stance on the notion of a single original position. *Robinson v. Jacksonville Shipyards, Inc.*, 760 F. Supp. 1486, 1524 (M.D. Fla. 1991), applies a "reasonable woman" standard to a claim of employment discrimination.

139. See Abram, *The Spell of the Sensuous*, 38.

140. See T. Morrison, *Playing in the Dark*.

141. Mullin, *Selves, Diverse and Divided*, 22.

142. See generally Allen, *The Invention of the White Race*, vol. 1; T. Morrison, *Playing in the Dark*.

143. See generally Roediger, *Towards the Abolition of Whiteness*; Frankenberg, "Whiteness and Americanness."

144. Crenshaw, "Race, Reform, and Retrenchment," 1374.

145. See discussion in Lawrence, "The Id, the Ego, and Equal Protection," 337.

146. Flax, "Multiple," 40.

147. A. Harris, "Race and Essentialism," 586.

148. David Abram in *The Spell of the Sensuous* provides a cogent discussion of the difference between scientific and experiential truth, and the power that particularly the latter holds, in spite of its subjective nature.

149. Sandel, *Liberalism and the Limits of Justice*, 144.

150. Ibid.

151. Haraway, "A Manifesto for Cyborgs," 202–203.

152. Flax, "Multiple," 41.

153. Haraway, "A Manifesto for Cyborgs," 211.

154. A. Harris, "Race and Essentialism," 586.

8. Lessons from Suffering

1. For an excellent discussion of lack and suffering, see Loy, *A Buddhist History of the West*.

2. See Rawls, *A Theory of Justice*.

3. See ibid.; and MacIntyre, *Whose Justice? Which Rationality?*

4. These works can be found in Washington, ed., *I Have a Dream*.

5. King, "My Pilgrimage to Nonviolence."

6. Wilber, *A Sociable God*, 98–104.

7. Ibid., 94.

8. Unger, *Passion*, 47.

9. Ibid., 95.

10. Ibid., 21.

11. Ibid., 5–18; see also Unger, *False Necessity*.

12. Unger, *Passion*.

13. Ibid., 61.

14. Some challenge the claim that Buddhism is a religion. Many Buddhists assert that it is not. See, e.g. Kung, *Buddhism Is an Education, Not a Religion*.

15. Jones, *The New Social Face of Buddhism*, 12.

16. See Macy, *Mutual Causality in Buddhism and General Systems Theory*.

17. Ibid., 19.

18. There is a substantial body of literature that suggests that the failure to deal with our existential angst in a constructive way, a spiritual way, is one of the reasons that we produce so much social suffering in the secular world. See N. O. Brown, *Life against Death;* Jones, *The New Social Face of Buddhism;* Unger, *Passion;* and Wilber, *A Sociable God.*

19. For a good discussion of this assumption and the problem with it, see Jones, *The New Social Face of Buddhism.*

20. See K. Armstrong, *The Battle for God;* and Carter, *The Culture of Disbelief;* see also, Unger, *Passion.*

21. Unger, *Passion,* 20–21.

22. See Loy, *A Buddhist History.*

23. Ibid.

24. Some would not limit this engagement to humans but would extend it to all beings, and some would include the planet. See Jones, *The New Social Face of Buddhism;* also, generally, Unger, *Passion.*

25. See Unger, *Passion,* 47.

26. Robin West has said that it is our fear of others and engagement that informs the law's obsession with relationship and its need to protect a fictitious autonomous individual. See West, "Jurisprudence and Gender."

27. Those with whom we share a connection are also in the sphere of our concern. Those outside the connection are in danger of being less and of being subject to the infliction of suffering and indifference.

28. See Macy, *World as Lover, World as Self.*

29. When I asked my father, a deeply religious man who was an elder in a Christian church for many decades, what hell is, he replied, "It is the separation from God."

30. See, e.g., Dreyfus and Kelly, *All Things Shining;* and Maté, *In the Realm of Hungry Ghosts.*

31. This is discussed in more depth in chapter 7, this volume.

32. See Patterson, *Slavery and Social Death.*

33. See K. Armstrong, *The Battle for God.*

34. See ibid.

35. Houston Smith, *The Illustrated World's Religions,* 19.

36. Ibid.

37. Ibid.

38. Hegel also addresses this issue in the problem of the infinite other.

39. See, e.g., Carter, *The Culture of Disbelief,* 105–123.

40. See White, *The Middle Mind,* 172–177.

41. See, e.g., Quale, *A History of Marriage Systems.*

42. Ibid., 128.

43. *Loving v. Virginia,* 388 US 1 (1967).

44. *Reynolds v. United States,* 98 U.S. 145 (1879).

45. See, e.g., Young, *Justice and the Politics of Difference.*

46. George, *Dwell in My Love.*

47. Loy, *A Buddhist History,* 127.

48. There are those who argue for bringing spiritual concerns out of the closet, but it is usually because the person with the concern has a conviction that has social implications. See, e.g., Carter, *The Culture of Disbelief.*

49. Jones, *The New Social Face of Buddhism.*

50. Wilber asserts that the original fall was the creation itself, because it marked the illusionary separation of all things from Spirit. Wilber, *Up from Eden,* 326.

51. See Loy, *A Buddhist History.*

52. Hegel was one of the first modern thinkers to articulate a theory of reason as contextual and not historic. Weber distinguished between instrumental reasoning and substantive reasoning. Hegel, *Reason in History,* 31–34.

272   NOTES TO PAGES 220–244

53. See generally Unger, *False Necessity*.

54. Loy, *A Buddhist History,* 121–124.

55. Wilber, *Up from Eden.*

56. See Hegel, *The Phenomenology of Spirit;* and Fanon, *Black Skin, White Masks.*

57. Klinkenborg, "Millions of Missing Birds, Vanishing in Plain Sight"; see also, e.g., E. O. Wilson, *The Diversity of Life.*

58. See Patterson, *Slavery and Social Death.*

59. See George, *Dwell in My Love.*

60. Although there is a need for tolerance, we should not overvalue the concept. Much of the tolerance that is in public space is built on the thinness of values. We may be more and more tolerant of less and less. This is the point made by both Carter and Loy. Loy observes that religious tolerance became acceptable because religion became private. See Loy, *A Buddhist History,* 142. Of course tolerance may be better than intolerance, but it is thin compared with understanding.

61. Habermas, *Between Facts and Norms,* 296–300.

62. 1 John 4:20 (New Revised Standard Version 1989).

Afterword

1. Brooks, *The Social Animal;* see also, Vedantam, *The Hidden Brain.*

2. Nørretranders, *The User Illusion.*

3. Vedantam, *The Hidden Brain,* 66–86.

4. Evidence of such views appeared in the 1991 trial of officers charged with the beating of black motorist Rodney G. King. Having responded to a domestic dispute involving African Americans on the day of King's arrest, a Los Angeles police officer reported over squad car computers that the scene had reminded him of the documentary film "Gorillas in the Mist." See, e.g., Associated Press, "Judge Says Remarks on 'Gorillas' May Be Cited in Trial on Beating."

5. See, e.g., Sachs, *The Price of Civilization.*

6. This argument and a more detailed analysis of the challenges we face with respect to corporate misalignment is developed in an article I wrote with Stephen Menendian, "Beyond Public/Private: Understanding Excessive Corporate Prerogative," *Kentucky Law Journal,* 100 Ky. L.J. (2011/2012).

7. Ibid.

8. *Lochner v. New York,* 198 U.S. 45 (1905).

9. David R. Roediger and Elizabeth D. Esch have written about this recently in *The Production of Difference.*

10. See, e.g., Galbraith, *Inequality and Instability;* Noah, *The Great Divide.*

11. For a different view, see Rucker, "Mitt Romney says 'corporations are people' at Iowa State Fair."

12. Galbraith, *Inequality and Instability;* Noah, *The Great Divide.*

REFERENCES

Aanerud, Rebecca. "Fictions of Whiteness: Speaking the Names of Whiteness in U.S. Literature." In *Displacing Whiteness: Essays in Social and Cultural Criticism,* ed. Ruth Frankenberg. Durham, N.C.: Duke University Press, 1997.

Abram, David. *The Spell of the Sensuous: Perception and Language in a More-than-Human World.* New York: Pantheon, 1996.

Alesina, Alberto, and Edward L. Glaeser. *Fighting Poverty in the US and Europe: A World of Difference.* Oxford: Oxford University Press, 2004.

Alexander, Michelle. *The New Jim Crow: Mass Incarceration in the Age of Colorblindness.* New York: The New Press, 2010.

Allen, Theodore W. *The Invention of the White Race.* Vol. 1, *Racial Oppression and Social Control.* New York: Verso, 1994.

———. *The Invention of the White Race.* Vol. 2, *The Origin of Racial Oppression in Anglo-America.* New York: Verso, 1994.

Ansley, Frances Lee. "Stirring the Ashes: Race, Class and the Future of Civil Rights Scholarship." *Cornell Law Review* 74 (1989): 993.

Anzaldúa, Gloria. *Borderlands/La Frontera: The New Mestiza.* San Francisco: Spinsters/Aunt Lute, 1987.

Applebaum, Harvey M. "Miscegenation Statutes: A Constitutional and Social Problem." *Georgetown Law Journal* 53, no. 1 (Fall 1964).

Armour, Jody. "Stereotypes and Prejudice: Helping Legal Decisionmakers Break the Prejudice Habit." In *Critical Race Realism: Intersections of Psychology, Race, and Law,* ed. Gregory S. Parks, Shyne Jones, and Jonathan Cardi. New York: The New Press, 2008.

Armstrong, Karen. *The Battle for God: A History of Fundamentalism.* New York: Alfred A. Knopf, 2000.

Armstrong, Margalynne. "Privilege in Residential Housing." In *Privilege Revealed: How Invisible Preference Undermines America,* ed. Stephanie M. Wildman and Adrienne D. Davis. New York: New York University Press, 1996.

Aspen Institute. Roundtable on Community Change: Structural Racism and Community Building (2004). Washington, D.C. The Aspen Institute. Available at www.aspeninstitute.org /policy-work/community-change /racial-equity/publications.

Aspen/Pitkin County Housing Authority. Aspen/Pitkin County Housing Guidelines (2003). Available at http:// www.aspenhousingoffice.com/images /other/guide.pdf.

Associated Press, "Blacks Found Less Likely than Whites to Be Promoted in the Military." *NewYork Times*, 22 November 1995, A20.

———. "Judge Says Remarks on 'Gorillas' May Be Cited in Trial on Beating." *NewYork Times*, 12 June 1991. Available at http://www.nytimes.com/articles.html.

Baldwin, James. "East River, Downtown: Postscript to a Letter from Harlem." In *Collected Essays*, ed. Toni Morrison. New York: Library of America, 1998.

———. *The Price of the Ticket*. New York: St. Martin's/Marek, 1985.

Bell, Derrick. *Race, Racism and American Law*. Boston: Little, Brown, 1992.

———. "White Superiority in America." In *Black on White*, ed. D. R. Roediger. New York: Schocken Books, 1998.

Bender, Leslie, and Daan Braveman. *Power, Privilege, and Law*. St. Paul, Minn.: West Publishing, 1995.

Benhabib, Seyla. *Situating the Self: Gender, Community, and Postmodernism*. New York: Routledge, 1992.

Bennett, Lerone, Jr. "Jack Johnson and the Great White Hope." *Ebony*, April 1994.

Berger, Betsy. "Walking in Another's Shoes." Website of the Kellogg School of Management, Northwestern University, 6 April 2011; available at http://www.kellogg.northwestern.edu/News_Articles/2011/walking-in-shoes.aspx.

Berger, John, et al. *Ways of Seeing* 10. BBC Television; Penguin Books, 1972.

Bernstein, Richard J. *Beyond Objectivism and Relativism: Science, Hermeneutics, and Praxis*. Philadelphia: University of Pennsylvania Press, 1983.

Berry, Kate A., and Martha L. Henderson. *Geographical Identities of Ethnic America: Race Space and Place*. Reno: University of Nevada Press, 2002.

Black, Charles L., Jr. *A New Birth of Freedom: Human Rights, Named and Unnamed*. New York: Grosset/Putnam, 1997.

Black, Derek W. "The Contradiction between Equal Protection's Meaning and Its Legal Substance: How Deliberate Indifference Can Cure It." *William and Mary Bill of Rights Journal* 15 (2006): 533.

———. "Picking Up the Pieces after *Alexander v. Sandoval*: Resurrecting a Private Cause of Action for Disparate Impact." *North Carolina Law Review* 81 (2002): 356.

Blank, Rebecca M. "Tracing the Economic Impact of Cumulative Discrimination." *American Economic Review* 95, no 2 (May 2005): 99–103.

Blanton, Kimberly. "More Minorities Denied Mortgages." *Boston Globe*, 13 September 2007. Available at http://www.boston.com/business/articles/2007/09/13/more_minorities_denied_mortgages/.

Blasi, Gary. "Advocacy against the Stereotype." In *Critical Race Realism: Intersections of Psychology, Race, and Law*, ed. Gregory S. Parks, Shayne Jones, and W. Jonathan Cardi. New York: The New Press, 2008.

Blythe, Anne. "Racial Justice Act before Judge." Newsobserver.com, 8 February 2011. Available at http://www.newsobserver.com/2011/02/08/974941/racial-justice-act-before-judge.html.

Bocian, Debbie Gruenstein, Keith S. Ernst, and Wei Li. "Unfair Lending: The Effect of Race and Ethnicity on the Price of Subprime Mortgages." Center for Responsible Lending, 2006. Available at http://www.responsiblelending.org/mortgage-lending/research-analysis/unfair-lending-the-effect-of-race-and-ethnicity-on-the-price-of-subprime-mortgages.html.

Boxill, Bernard R., *Blacks and Social Justice*, Totowa, N.J.: Rowman & Allanheld, 1984.

Boyle, James. "Is Subjectivity Possible? The Postmodern Subject in Legal Theory." *University of Colorado Law Review* 62 (1991): 489.

Bradt, Steve. "'One-Drop Rule' Persists: Biracials Viewed as Members of Their Lower-Status Parent Group." *Harvard Gazette,* 9 December 2010. Available at http://news.harvard.edu/gazette/story/2010/12/%E2%80%98one-drop-rule%E2%80%99-persists/.

Brooks, David. *The Social Animal: The Hidden Sources of Love, Character, and Achievement.* New York: Random House, 2012.

Brooks-Gunn, Jeanne, et al. "Do Neighborhoods Influence Child and Adolescent Development?" *American Journal of Sociology* 99, no. 2 (1993): 353.

Brown Foundation. "Prelude to *Brown*–1849: *Roberts v. City of Boston.*" Available at http://brownvboard.org/content/prelude-brown-1849-roberts-v-city-boston; last visited 28 September 2011.

Brown, Michael K., et al. *Whitewashing Race: The Myth of a Color-Blind Society.* Berkeley: University of California Press, 2003.

Brown, Norman Oliver. *Life against Death: The Psychoanalytical Meaning of History.* 2d ed.; Middletown, Conn.: Wesleyan University Press, 1985.

Buck, Stuart H. *Acting White: The Ironic Legacy of Desegregation.* New Haven, Conn.: Yale University Press, 2010.

Burris, Carol Corbett, and Kevin G. Welner. "Classroom Integration and Accelerated Learning through Detracking." In *Lessons in Integration: Realizing the Promise of Racial Diversity in American Schools,* ed. Erica Frankenberg and Gary Orfield. Charlottesville: University of Virginia Press, 2007.

Butler, Judith. "Critically Queer." In *Bodies That Matter: On the Discursive Limits of "Sex."* New York: Routledge, 1993.

———. *Gender Trouble: Feminism and the Subversion of Identity.* New York: Routledge, 1990.

Byrnes, Erin E. Note, "Unmasking White Privilege to Expose the Fallacy of White Innocence: Using a Theory of Moral Correlativity to Make the Case for Affirmative Action Programs in Education." *Arizona Law Review* 41 (1999): 535.

Calmore, John O. "Critical Race Theory, Archie Shepp, and Fire Music: Securing an Authentic Intellectual Life in a Multicultural World." *Southern California Law Review* 65 (1992): 2129.

———. "Exploring Michael Omi's 'Messy' Real World of Race: An Essay for 'Naked People Longing to Swim Free.'" *Law & Inequality Journal* 15 (1997): 25.

———. "Racialized Space and the Culture of Segregation: 'Hewing a Stone of Hope from a Mountain of Despair.'" *University of Pennsylvania Law Review* 143 (1995): 1233.

———. "Random Notes of an Integration Warrior – Part 2: A Critical Response to the Hegemonic 'Truth' of Daniel Farber and Suzanna Sherry." *Minnesota Law Review* 83 (1999): 1589.

Carter, Steven L. *The Culture of Disbelief: How American Law and Politics Trivialize Religious Devotion.* New York: Basic-Books, 1993.

Cashin, Sheryll. *The Failures of Integration: How Race and Class Are Undermining the American Dream.* New York: Public Affairs, 2004.

Cavanaugh, Maureen B. "Towards a New Equal Protection: Two Kinds of Equality." *Law & Inequality* 12 (1994): 381.

Chua, Amy L. "Privatization-Nationalization Cycle: The Link between Markets and Ethnicity in Developing Countries." *Columbia Law Review* 95 (1995): 223.

Crenshaw, Kimberlé Williams. "Mapping the Margins: Intersectionality, Identity Politics, and Violence against Women of Color." *Stanford Law Review* 43 (1993): 1241.

———. "Race, Reform, and Retrenchment: Transformation and Legitimation in Antidiscrimination Law." *Harvard Law Review* 101 (1988): 1331.

Dallymayr, Winfried Reinhard. *Twilight of Subjectivity: Contributions to a Post-Individualist Theory Politics.* Amherst: University of Massachusetts Press, 1981.

Damasio, Antonio. *Descartes' Error: Emotion, Reason and the Human Brain.* London: Vintage, 2006.

Davis, Wade. *The Wayfinders: Why Ancient Wisdom Matters in the Modern World.* Toronto: House of Anansi Press, 2009.

Denton, Nancy A. "Racial Identity and Census Categories: Can Incorrect Categories Yield Correct Information?" *Law & Inequality Journal* 15 (1997): 83.

Derrida, Jacques. "Structure, Sign, and Play in the Discourse of the Human Sciences." In *Critical Theory since Plato.* New York: Harcourt Brace Jovanovich, 1971.

Descartes, René. *A Discourse on Method and Selected Writings.* Trans. John Veitch. New York: E. P. Dutton, 1951.

———. *Discourse on the Method of Rightly Conducting the Reason and Seeking for Truth in the Sciences.* Ed. David Weissman. New Haven, Conn.: Yale University Press, 1996.

———. "Meditations." in I *Philosophical Works of Descartes.* Trans. E. S. Haldane and G. R. T. Ross. London: Cambridge University Press, 1967.

Dickerson, Debra. "Class Is the New Black." *Mother Jones,* Jan./Feb. 2009; http://www.motherjones.com/news/feature/2009/01/class-is-the-new-black.html.

Dreyfus, Hubert, and Sean Dorrance Kelly. *All Things Shining: Reading the Western Classics to Find Meaning in a Secular Age.* New York: Free Press, 2011.

Du Bois, W. E. B. *The Souls of Black Folk.* New York: Signet Classic, 1995.

———. "The Souls of White Folk," in *Darkwater: Voiced from within the Veil.* Mineola: Dover Publ., 1999.

Duggan, Lisa. "Making It Perfectly Queer." *Socialist Review* 22 (1992): 11; reprinted in *Sex Wars: Essays on Sexual Dissent and American Politics,* ed. Lisa Duggan and Nan D. Hunter. New York: Routledge, 1995.

Dunning, William V. "Post-Modernism and the Construct of the Divisible Self." British Journal of Aesthetics 33, no. 2 (1993): 132–141.

Edsall, Thomas B., and Mary D. Edsall. *Chain Reaction: The Impact of Race, Rights, and Taxes on American Politics.* New York: Norton, 1991.

Ewing, Katherine P. "The Illusion of Wholeness: Culture, Self, and the Experience of Inconsistency." *Ethos* 18 (1990): 251.

Fanon, Frantz. *Black Skin, White Masks.* Trans. Charles Lam Marchkmann. New York: Grove Press, 1967.

———. *The Wretched of the Earth.* Trans. Constance Farrington. 1963; New York: Grove Weidenfeld, 1991.

Farber, Daniel A., and Suzanna Sherry, *Beyond All Reason: The Radical Assault on Truth in American Law.* New York: Oxford University Press, 1997.

Flax, Jane. "Multiple: On the Contemporary Politics of Subjectivity." *Human Studies* 16 (1993): 33.

Foner, Eric. *The Story of American Freedom.* New York: W. W. Norton, 1999.

Ford, Richard Thompson. "The Boundaries of Race: Political Geography in Legal Analysis." *Harvard Law Review* 107 (1994): 1843.

Fordham, Signithia, and John U. Ogbu. "Black Students' School Success:

Coping with the 'Burden of "Acting White."'" *Urban Review* 18 (1986): 176.

Foucault, Michel. *Discipline and Punish: The Birth of the Prison.* New York: Vintage Books, 1979.

———. *The Order of Things: An Archaeology of the Human Sciences.* London: Tavistock Publications, 1970.

Frankenberg, Ruth. "Introduction: Local Whitenesses, Localizing Whiteness." In *Displacing Whiteness: Essays in Social and Cultural Criticism.* Durham, N.C.: Duke University Press, 1997.

———. "Whiteness and Americanness: Examining Constructions of Race, Culture, and Nation in White Women's Life Narratives." In *Race,* ed. Steven Gregory and Roger Sanjek. New Brunswick, N.J.: Rutgers University Press, 1994.

———. *White Women, Race Matters: The Social Construction of Whiteness.* Minneapolis: University of Minnesota Press, 1993.

Fredrickson, George M. *Racism: A Short History.* Princeton, N.J.: Princeton University Press, 2002.

Freeman, Alan David. "Legitimizing Racial Discrimination through Antidiscrimination Law: A Critical Review of Supreme Court Doctrine." In *Critical Race Theory: The Key Writings That Formed the Movement,* ed. Kimberlé Crenshaw et al. New York: New Press, 1995.

French, Marilyn. *Beyond Power: On Women, Men, and Morals.* New York: Summit Books, 1985.

Friedman, Susan Stanford. "Beyond White and Other: Relationality and Narratives of Race in Feminist Discourse." *Signs: Journal of Women in Culture and Society* 21, no. 1 (1995): 1–49.

Friedman, Thomas L. "Finishing Our Work." *New York Times,* 5 November 2008, A35. Available at http://www.nytimes.com/2008/11/05/opinion/05friedman.html?ref=opinion.

Frye, Marilyn. "Oppression." In *Power, Privilege, and Law: a Civil Rights Reader,* ed. Leslie Bender. St. Paul, Minn.: West Publishing, 1995.

———. *The Politics of Reality: Essays in Feminist Theory.* Trumansburg, N.Y.: Crossing Press, 1983.

Gabel, Peter. "The Phenomenology of Rights-Consciousness and the Pact of the Withdrawn Selves." *Texas Law Review* 62 (1984): 1563.

Galbraith, James. *Inequality and Instability: A Study of the World Economy Just Before the Great Crisis.* New York: Oxford, 2012.

George, Cardinal Frances, OMI, Archbishop of Chicago. *Dwell in My Love: A Pastoral Letter on Racism,* 4 April 2001. Available at http://www.archdiocese-chgo.org/cardinal/dwellinmylove/dwellinmylove.shtm; last visited 4 April 2011.

Gergen, Kenneth J. *The Saturated Self: Dilemmas of Identity in Contemporary Life.* New York: Basic Books, 1991.

Gilanshah, Bijan. "Multiracial Minorities: Erasing the Color Line." *Law & Inequality Journal* 12 (1993): 183.

Gilens, Martin. *Why Americans Hate Welfare: Race, Media, and the Politics of Antipoverty Policy.* Chicago: University of Chicago Press, 1999.

Gilligan, Carol. *In a Different Voice: Psychological Theory and Women's Development.* Cambridge, Mass.: Harvard University Press, 1982.

Goforth, Carol R. "'What Is She?': How Race Matters and Why It Shouldn't." *DePaul Law Review* 46 (1996): 1.

Goldberg, David Theo. *Racist Culture: Philosophy and the Politics of Meaning.* Oxford, UK: Blackwell, 1993.

Goodman, Nelson. *Ways of Worldmaking.* Hassocks, Sussex: Harvester Press, 1978.

Gotanda, Neil. "A Critique of 'Our Constitution Is Color Blind." *Stanford Law Review* 44 (1991): 1.

Gottlieb, Roger. *Joining Hands: Politics and Religion Together for Social Change.* Boulder, Colo.: Westview Press, 2002.

Graham, Susan. "The Multiracial Child." *Merced Sun-Star,* 18 March 2011. Available at http://www.mercedsunstar.com/2011/03/18/v-print/1816173/susan-graham-the-multiracial-child.html.

Grant-Thomas, Andrew, and john a. powell, "Structural Racism and Colorlines in the United States." In *Twenty-First Century Color Lines: Multiracial Change in Contemporary America,* ed. Andrew Grant-Thomas and Gary Orfield. Philadelphia: Temple University Press, 2009.

Greenberg, Jan Crawford. "Court to Review Gay Rights Laws: Justices to Decide If Ballot Initiatives Deny Civil Liberties." *Chicago Tribune,* 22 February 1995, 3.

Grillo, Trina. "Anti-Essentialism and Intersectionality: Tools to Dismantle the Master's House." *Berkeley Women's Law Journal* 10 (1995): 16.

Guinier, Lani, and Gerald Torres, *The Miner's Canary: Enlisting Race, Resisting Power, Transforming Democracy.* Cambridge, Mass.: Harvard University Press, 2002.

Habermas, Jürgen. *Between Facts and Norms: Contributing to a Discourse Theory of Law and Democracy.* Trans. William Rehg. Cambridge, Mass.: MIT Press, 1996.

Hacker, Andrew. *Two Nations: Black and White, Separate, Hostile, Unequal.* New York: Scribner's, 1992.

Halberstam, David. *The Children.* New York: Random House, 1998.

Hall, Dee J. "Black and Busted in Dane County: Reasons for Racial Disparity in Dane County Penal System

Are Complex." Available at http://host.madison.com/wsj/news/local/crime_and_courts/article_fea23fac-b625-11e0-b588-001cc4c002e0.html. Posted 25 July 2011.

Hall, Stuart. "The Question of Cultural Identity." In *Modernity and Its Futures: Understanding Modern Societies, Book 4,* eds. Stuart Hall, Tony McGrew, and David Held. Cambridge, UK: Polity Press and Blackwell Publishers, 1992.

Hamilton, Dona Cooper, and Charles V. Hamilton. *The Dual Agenda: Race and Social Welfare Policies of Civil Rights Organizations.* New York: Columbia University Press, 1997.

Hanchard, Michael, ed., *Racial Politics in Contemporary Brazil*: Durham, N.C.: Duke University Press, 1999.

Hanks, Liza Weiman. Note, "Justice Souter: Defining 'Substantive Neutrality' in an Age of Religious Politics." *Stanford Law Review* 48 (1996): 903.

Haraway, Donna. "A Manifesto for Cyborgs: Science, Technology, and Socialist Feminism in the 1980s." In *Feminism/Postmodernism,* ed. Linda J. Nicholson. Originally published in *Socialist Review* 15, no. 2 (1985).

Harris, Angela P. "Foreword: The Unbearable Lightness of Identity." *Berkeley Women's Law Journal* 11 (1996): 207.

———. "Race and Essentialism in Feminist Legal Theory." *Stanford Law Review* 42 (1990): 581.

Harris, Cheryl I. "Whiteness as Property." *Harvard Law Review* 106 (1993): 1709.

Hasian, Marouf A., Jr., and Thomas K. Nakayama. "The Fictions of Racialized Identities." In *Judgment Calls: Rhetoric, Politics, and Indeterminacy,* ed. James P. McDaniel and John M. Sloop. Boulder, Colo.: Westview Press, 1998.

Hayward, Jeremy M. *Shifting Worlds, Changing Minds: Where the Sciences and Buddhism Meet.* Boston: Shambhala Publications, 1987.

Hegel, Georg W. F. "Independence and Dependence of Self-Consciousness: Relations of Master and Servant." In *The Phenomenology of Spirit.* Trans. A. V. Miller. Oxford: Clarendon Press, 1977.

———. *Reason in History: A General Introduction to the Philosophy of History.* Trans. Robert S. Hartman. New York: Liberal Arts Press, 1953.

Hernandez-Truyol, Berta Esperanza. "Borders (En)gendered: Normativities, Latinas, and a LatCrit Paradigm." 72 *New York University Law Review* 882 (1997).

Herrnstein, Richard J. & Charles Murray, *The Bell Curve: Intelligence and Class Structure in American Life.* New York: Free Press, 1994.

Higginbotham, A. Leon, Jr. *In the Matter of Color: Race and the American Legal Process; The Colonial Period.* New York: Oxford University Press, 1978.

Hillman, James, *Healing Fiction.* Woodstock, Conn.: Spring Publications, 1983.

Hinchman, Lewis P. *Hegel's Critique of the Enlightenment.* Gainesville: University Presses of Florida, 1984.

Ho, Arnold K., Jim Sidanius, Daniel T. Levin, and Mahzarin R. Banaji. "Evidence for Hypodescent and Racial Hierarchy in the Categorization and Perception of Biracial Individuals." *Journal of Personality and Social Psychology* 100, no. 3 (March 2011): 492–506.

Hochschild, Jennifer, and Traci Burch. "Contingent Public Policies and Racial Hierarchy: Lessons from Immigration and Census Policies." In *Political Contingency: Studying the Unexpected, the Accidental, and the Unforeseen,* ed. Ian Shapiro and Sonu Bedi. New York: New York University Press, 2007.

Hodgkinson, Harold L. "What Should We Call People? Race, Class, and the Census for 2000." *Phi Delta Kappan* 77 (1995): 173.

Hofstadter, Richard. *Social Darwinism in American Thought.* Boston: Beacon Press, 1992.

hooks, bell. *Feminist Theory: From Margin to Center.* Boston: South End Press, 1984.

Hull, Gloria, et al., eds. *All the Women Are White, All the Blacks Are Men, but Some of Us Are Brave.* Old Westbury, N.Y.: Feminist Press, 1982.

Hume, David. *A Treatise of Human Nature.* Ed. L.A. Selby-Bigge. Oxford: Clarendon Press; 1978.

Humes, Karen R., Nicholas A. Jones, and Roberto R. Ramirez. "Overview of Race and Hispanic Origin: 2010," March 2011. Available at http://2010. census.gov/news/releases/operations/ cb11-cn125.html.

Hurston, Zora Neale. "How It Feels to Be Colored Me." In *I Love Myself When I Am Laughing . . . and Then Again When I Am Looking Mean and Impressive: A Zora Neale Hurston Reader,* ed. Alice Walker. Old Westbury, N.Y.: Feminist Press, 1979.

———. *Their Eyes Were Watching God: A Novel.* Philadelphia: J. B. Lippincott, 1937.

Ifill, Gwen. *The Breakthrough: Politics and Race in the Age of Obama.* New York: Doubleday, 2009.

Ignatiev, Noel. *How the Irish Became White.* New York: Routledge, 1995.

———. "How to Be a Race Traitor: Six Ways to Fight Being White." *Utne Reader,* November-December 1994.

———. "The Point Is Not to Interpret Whiteness but to Abolish It." Remarks at the University of California, Berkeley, 11–13 April 1997; available at http:// racetraitor.org/abolishthepoint.pdf.

Institute on Race and Poverty, University of Minnesota, Minnesota Statewide Racial Profiling Reports. Available at http://umn.edu/irp/mnrpreport.html.

Jackson, Kenneth T. *Crabgrass Frontier: The Suburbanization of the United States*. New York: Oxford University Press, 1985.

Jargowsky, Paul." Stunning Progress, Hidden Problems: The Dramatic Decline of Concentrated Poverty in the 1990s." Brookings Institute, May 2003. Available at http://www.brookings .edu/reports/2003/05demographics _jargowsky.aspx.

Jargowsky, Paul A., and Mary Jo Bane, "Ghetto Poverty in the United States, 1970–1980." In *The Urban Underclass*, ed. Christopher Jencks and Paul E. Peterson . Washington, D.C.: Brookings Institution, 1991.

Jencks, Christopher. *Rethinking Social Policy: Race, Poverty, and the Underclass*. Cambridge, Mass.: Harvard University Press, 1992.

Jencks, Christopher, and Paul E. Peterson, eds. *The Urban Underclass*. Washington, D.C.: Brookings Institution, 1991.

Johnson, Alex M., Jr. "How Race and Poverty Intersect to Prevent Integration: Destabilizing Race as a Vehicle to Integrate Neighborhoods." *University of Pennsylvania Law Review* 143 (1995): 1595.

Johnson, Noelle. "Race Traitor: The New Abolitionism." *New York Beacon*, 29 January 1997.

Jones, Ken. *The New Social Face of Buddhism: A Call to Action*. Boston: Wisdom Publications, 2003.

———. "The Zen of Social Action" (1995), *Western Chan Fellowship* website; available at http://westernchanfellowship. org/reading/ncf11_TheZenOfSocial-Action.html.

Jordan, Winthrop D. *The White Man's Burden: Historical Origins of Racism in the United States*. New York: Oxford University Press, 1974.

———. *White over Black: American Attitudes toward the Negro 1550–1812*. Cha-

pel Hill: Published for the Institute of Early American History and Culture at Williamsburg, Va., by the University of North Carolina Press, 1968.

Kahneman, Daniel. *Thinking, Fast and Slow*. New York: Farrar, Straus and Giroux, 2011.

Kang, Jerry. "Trojan Horses of Race." *Harvard Law Review* 118 (2005): 1489.

Kant, Immanuel. *Critique of Pure Reason*. Trans. Norman Kemp Smith. New York: St. Martin's Press, 1968.

Karst, Kenneth L. *Belonging to America: Equal Citizenship and the Constitution*. New Haven, Conn.: Yale University Press, 1989.

Katz, Judy H. *White Awareness: Handbook for Anti-Racism Training*. Norman: University of Oklahoma Press, 1978.

Katznelson, Ira. *When Affirmative Action Was White: An Untold History of Racial Inequality in Twentieth-Century America*. New York: W. W. Norton, 2005.

Keith, Michael, and Malcolm Cross. "Racism and the Postmodern City." In *Racism, the City and the State*, ed. Malcolm Cross and Michael Keith. London: Routledge, 1993.

Kennedy, Randall. *Interracial Intimacies: Sex, Marriage, Identity and Adoption*. New York: Vintage, 2004.

———. *Race, Crime, and the Law*. New York: Vintage, 1997.

Kim, Catherine Y., Daniel J. Losen, and Damon T. Hewitt. *The School to Prison Pipeline: Structuring Legal Reform*. New York: New York University Press, 2010.

Kinder, Donald R., and Lynn M. Sanders. *Divided by Color: Racial Politics and Democratic Ideals*. Chicago: University of Chicago Press, 1996.

King, Dr. Martin Luther, Jr. "I Have a Dream" (1963). In *A Testament of Hope: The Essential Writings and Speeches of Martin Luther King, Jr.*, ed. James M. Washington. San Francisco: Harper & Row, 1986.

———. "My Pilgrimage to Nonviolence" (1 September 1958, New York). The Martin Luther King, Jr., Research and Education Institute, Stanford University. Available at http://mlk-kpp01 .stanford.edu/index.php/encyclopedia /documentsentry/my_pilgrimage _to_nonviolence1.

Klein, Anne Carolyn. *Meeting the Great Bliss Queen: Buddhists, Feminists and the Art of the Self.* Boston: Beacon Press, 1995.

Klinkenborg, Verlyn. "Millions of Missing Birds, Vanishing in Plain Sight." *New York Times,* 19 June 2007.

Kolm, Serge-Christophe. "The Buddhist Theory of 'No-self.'" In *The Multiple Self,* ed. Jon Elster. Cambridge: Cambridge University Press, 1986.

Kotkin, Joel. "The End of Upward Mobility." *Newsweek,* 26 January 2009; http://www.newsweek.com/id/ 180041.

Kranish, Michael. "Bush Argues His Social Security Plan Aids Blacks." *Boston Globe,* 30 January 2005, A1.

Kuhn, Thomas. *The Structure of Scientific Revolutions.* Chicago: University of Chicago Press, 1996.

Kung, Chin. *Buddhism Is an Education, Not a Religion.* Available at www.amtb .org.tw/e-bud/releases/educati.htm.

Kuswa, Kevin Douglas. "Suburbification, Segregation, and the Consolidation of the Highway Machine." *Journal of Law and Society* 3 (2002): 31.

Laguerre, Michel S. *Minoritized Space: An Inquiry into the Spatial Order of Things.* Berkeley: Institute of Governmental Studies Press, Institute of Urban and Regional Development, University of California, 1999.

Lawrence, Charles R., III. "The Id, the Ego, and Equal Protection: Reckoning with Unconscious Racism." *Stanford Law Review* 39 (1987): 317.

———. "Unconscious Racism Revisited: Reflections on the Impact and Origins of 'The Id, the Ego, and Equal Protection.'" *Connecticut Law Review* 40 (2008): 931.

Lawyers Committee for Civil Rights under Law and Mississippi Center for Justice. "Mississippi Housing Advocates File Suit against HUD over Diversion of Hurricane Recovery Funds." Available at http://www.lawyerscommittee .org/newsroom/press_releases?id= 0011.

Laycock, Douglas. "Formal, Substantive, and Disaggregated Neutrality toward Religion." *DePaul Law Review* 39 (1990): 993.

Lazarre, Jane. *Beyond the Whiteness of Whiteness: Memoir of a White Mother of Black Sons.* Durham, N.C.: Duke University Press, 1996.

Lempinen, Edward W. "Confusion on Affirmative Action Ban: Voters Seem Ambivalent toward Ballot Initiative." *San Francisco Chronicle,* 22 April 1996, A17.

Leventhal, Tama, and Jeanne Brooks-Gunn. "Moving to Opportunity: An Experimental Study of the Neighborhood Effects on Mental Health." *American Journal of Public Health* 93, no. 9 (2003): 1576.

Lewin, Tamar. "Colleges Regroup after Voters Ban Race Preferences." *New York Times,* 26 January 2007.

———. "Michigan Rejects Affirmative Action, and Backers Sue." *New York Times,* 9 November 2006.

Lieberman, Robert C. *Shifting the Color Line: Race and the American Welfare State.* Cambridge, Mass.: Harvard University Press, 1998.

Lifton, Robert Jay. *The Protean Self: Human Resilience in an Age of Fragmentation.* New York: Basic Books, 1993.

Linzer, Peter. "White Liberal Looks at Racist Speech." *St. John's Law Review* 65 (1991): 187.

Lipsitz, George. *The Possessive Investment in Whiteness: How White People Profit from Identity Politics.* Philadelphia: Temple University Press, 1998.

Liptak, Adam. "Supreme Court Takes Voting Rights Case." *New York Times,* 10 January 2009, A13.

Lloyd, Genevieve. *The Man of Reason: "Male" and "Female" in Western Philosophy.* Minneapolis: University of Minnesota Press, 1984.

Locke, John. *An Essay Concerning Human Understanding.* ed. A. S. Pringle-Pattison. Atlantic Highlands, N.J.: Humanities Press, 1978.

———. *Treatise of Civil Government and A Letter Concerning Toleration.* ed. Charles L. Sherman. New York: Appelton-Century-Crofts, 1937.

López, Ian Haney. "Colorblind White Dominance" (2006) (unpublished ms., on file with author).

———. "White by Law." In *Critical Race Theory,* ed. Richard Delgado. Philadelphia: Temple University Press, 1995.

———. *White by Law: The Legal Construction of Race.* New York: New York University Press, 1996.

———. *White by Law: The Legal Construction of Race.* Rev. ed., New York: New York University Press, 2006.

Lorde, Audre. "An Open Letter to Mary Daly." In *This Bridge Called My Back: Writings by Radical Women of Color,* ed. Cherríe Moraga and Gloria Anzaldúa. Watertown, Mass.: Persephone Press, 1981.

Loury, Glenn C. *The Anatomy of Racial Inequality.* Cambridge, Mass.: Harvard University Press, 2002.

Loy, David R. *A Buddhist History of the West: Studies in Lack.* Albany: State University of New York Press, 2002.

———. *The World Is Made of Stories.* Boston: Wisdom Publications, 2010.

Lucas, Greg, and Edward W. Lempinen. "State GOP Pulls King Ad but Not Blitz: Party Still Will Spend Millions to Push Prop. 209." *San Francisco Chronicle,* 25 October 1996, A21.

MacGillis, Alec, and Michael Shear. "Stimulus Package to First Pay for Routine Repairs." *Washington Post,* 14 December 2008, A01; available at http://www.washingtonpost.com/wp-dyn/content/article/2008/12/13/AR2008121301819_pf.html.

MacIntyre, Alasdair. *Whose Justice? Which Rationality?* Notre Dame, Ind.: University of Notre Dame Press, 1988.

MacKinnon, Catharine A. *Feminism Unmodified: Discourses on Life and Law.* Cambridge, Mass.: Harvard University Press, 1987.

Macy, Joanna R. *Mutual Causality in Buddhism and General Systems Theory: The Dharma of Natural Systems.* Albany: State University of New York Press, 1991.

———. *World as Lover, World as Self.* Berkeley, Calif.: Parallax Press, 1991.

Mahoney, Martha R. "Segregation, Whiteness, and Transformation." *University of Pennsylvania Law Review* 143 (1995): 1659.

Malcolm X. *Malcolm X Speaks: Selected Speeches and Statements.* Ed. George Breitman. New York: Grove Weidenfeld, 1990.

Malcolmson, Scott. *One Drop of Blood: The American Misadventure of Race.* New York: Farrar, Straus and Giroux, 2000.

Manuel, Michael L. "*Adarand Constructors, Inc. v. Pena*: Is Strict Scrutiny Fatal in Fact for Governmental Affirmative Action Programs?" *New England Law Review* 31 (1997): 975.

Martinot, Steve. *The Rule of Racialization: Class, Identity, Governance.* Philadelphia: Temple University Press, 2003.

Marx, Anthony. *Making Race and Nation: A Comparison of the United States, South Africa, and Brazil.* Cambridge: Cambridge University Press, 1998.

Massey, Douglas S. *Categorically Unequal: The American Stratification System.* New York: Russell Sage Foundation, 2007.

Massey, Douglas S., and Nancy A. Denton. *American Apartheid: Segregation and the Making of the Underclass.* Cambridge, Mass.: Harvard University Press, 1993.

Maté, Gabor. *In the Realm of Hungry Ghosts: Close Encounters with Addiction.* Toronto: Knopf Canada, 2008.

McArdle, Nancy. *Beyond Poverty: Race and Concentrated-Poverty Neighborhoods in Metro Boston.* The Civil Rights Project (2003). Available at http://civilrightsproject.ucla.edu.

McIntosh, Peggy. "White Privilege and Male Privilege: A Personal Account of Coming to See Correspondences through Work in Women's Studies." In *Race, Class, and Gender: An Anthology,* ed. Margaret L. Andersen and Patricia Hill Collins. Belmont, Calif.: Wadsworth, 1992.

Mickelson, Roslyn A. "The Incomplete Desegregation of the Charlotte-Mecklenburg Schools and Its Consequences, 1971–2004." In *School Resegregation: Must the South Turn Back?* ed. John C. Boger and Gary Orfield. Chapel Hill: University of North Carolina Press, 2005.

Mickelson, Roslyn Arlin, and Anne E. Velasco. "Bring It On! Diverse Responses to 'Acting White' Among Academically Able Black Adolescents." In *Beyond Acting White: Reframing the Debate on Black Student Achievement,* ed. Erin McNamara Horvat and Carla

O'Connor. Lanham, Md.: Rowman & Littlefield, 2006.

Mills, Charles W. *The Racial Contract.* Ithaca, N.Y.: Cornell University Press, 1997.

Minh-ha, Trinh T. *Woman, Native, Other: Writing, Postcoloniality and Feminism.* Bloomington: Indiana University Press, 1989.

Minow, Martha. "Making All the Difference." In *Power, Privilege, and Law,* ed. Leslie Bender and Daan Braveman. St. Paul, Minn.: West Publishing, 1995.

———. *Not Only for Myself: Identity, Politics, and the Law.* New York: New Press, 1997.

———. "Partial Justice and Minorities." In *Power, Privilege, and Law,* ed. Leslie Bender and Daan Braveman. St. Paul, Minn.: West Publishing, 1995.

Morrison, John E. "Colorblindness, Individuality, and Merit: An Analysis of the Rhetoric against Affirmative Action." *Iowa Law Review* 79 (1994): 313.

Morrison, Toni. *Playing in the Dark: Whiteness and the Literary Imagination.* Cambridge, Mass.: Harvard University Press, 1992.

Mullin, Amy. "Selves, Diverse and Divided: Can Feminists Have Diversity without Multiplicity?" *Hypatia* 10 (1995): 1.

Myrdal, Gunnar. *An American Dilemma: The Negro Problem and Modern Democracy,* vol. 1. New York: Harper & Brothers Publishers, 1944.

New York Civil Liberties Union, "Report: NYPD Stop-and-Frisk Activity in 2011 (2012)." Available at http://www.nyclu.org/publications/report-nypd-stop-and-frisk-activity-2011-2012.

New York Times, Editorial, "For Katrina Victims, Relief at Last." 16 November 2010.

———. "President Map." 9 December 2008. Available at http://elections

.nytimes.com/2008/results/president
/map.html.

———. "Times Topics: Health Care Reform and the Supreme Court (Affordable Health Care Act)," 28 March, 2012.

Nicholson Linda J., ed., Feminism/Post-
modernism. New York: Routledge,
1990.

Noah, Timothy. The Great Divide:
America's Growing Inequality Cris and
What We Can Do about It. New York:
Bloomsbury, 2012.

Nørretranders, Tor. The User Illusion: Cut-
ting Consciousness Down to Size. New
York: Viking Penguin, 1998.

North Carolina House Bill 615, "An Act to
Reform the Racial Justice Act of 2009
to Be Consistent with the United States
Supreme Court's Ruling in McCleskey
v. Kemp, /03/09." Available at http://
www.scribd.com/doc/52392458/HB-
615-Filed-North-Carolina-General-
Assembly-via-MyGov365-com.

Nossiter, Adam. "For South, a Waning
Hold on National Politics." New York
Times, 11 November 2008, A1; available
at: http://www.nytimes.com/2008/11/
11/us/politics/11south.html.

Obama, Barack. The Audacity of Hope.
New York: Crown Publishers, 2006.

O'Connor, Alice. "The 'New Institutionalism' and the Racial Divide." Reviews
in American History 29 (2001): 111–118.

Office of Management and Budget. "Revisions to the Standards for the Classification of Federal Data on Race and
Ethnicity." 30 October 1997. Available
at http://www.whitehouse.gov/omb/
fedrg-1997standards.

Ogden, Thomas H. The Subjects of Analysis. Lanham, Md.: Jason Aronson, 1977.

Omi, Michael. "Racial Identity and the
State: The Dilemmas of Classification."
Law & Inequality Journal 15 (1997): 7.

Omi, Michael, and Howard Winant.
Racial Formation in the United States:

From the 1960s to the 1990s. 2d ed. New
York: Routledge, 1994.

O'Reilly, Kenneth. Nixon's Piano: Presidents and Racial Politics from Washington to Clinton. New York: Free Press,
1995.

Ortiz, Daniel R. "Categorical Community." Stanford Law Review 51 (1999): 769.

Page, Clarence. "Anti-Gay Law Flies in
the Face of the 14th Amendment." Chicago Tribune, 11 October 1995, 19.

Pager, Devah. Marked: Race, Crime, and
Finding Work in an Era of Mass Incarcer-
ation, Chicago: University of Chicago
Press, 2007.

———. "The Mark of a Criminal Record."
American Journal of Sociology 108, no. 5
(March 2003): 937–975.

Parks, Gregory S., Shayne Jones, and W.
Jonathan Cardi, eds. Critical Race Real-
ism: Intersections of Psychology, Race, and
Law. New York: The New Press, 2008.

Passel, Jeffrey S., Wendy Wang, and Paul
Taylor. "Marrying Out: One-in-Seven
New U.S. Marriages is Interracial or
Interethnic." Pew Research Center, 4
June 2010; available at http://
pewresearch.org/pubs/1616/american-
marriage-interracial-interethnic.

Patterson, Orlando. Freedom. Vol. 1, Freedom in the Making of Western Culture.
New York: Basic Books, 1991.

———. Slavery and Social Death. Cambridge, Mass.: Harvard University
Press, 1982.

Payne, Richard J. Getting beyond Race.
Boulder, Colo.: Westview Press, 1998.

Peller, Gary. "Race Consciousness." Duke
Law Journal 1990, no. 4 (September
1990): 758.

Perry, Sherice. "Health Coverage in
Communities of Color: Talking about
the New Census Numbers." Minority
Health Initiatives, Families USA. September 2008.

Poindexter, Paula. "African-American Images in the News: Understanding the

Past to Improve Future Portrayals." In *Images That Injure: Pictorial Stereotypes in the Media*, ed. Susan D. Ross and Paul M. Lester. Santa Barbara, Calif.: Praeger, 2011.

Powell, Cedric Merlin. "Blinded by Color: The New Equal Protection, the Second Deconstruction, and Affirmative Inaction." *University of Miami Law Review* 51 (1997): 191.

powell, john a. "An Agenda for the Post–Civil Rights Era." *University of San Francisco Law Review* 29 (1995): 889.

———. "A New Theory of Integrated Education: *True* Integration." In *School Resegregation: Must the South Turn Back?* ed. John Charles Boger and Gary Orfield. Chapel Hill: University of North Carolina Press, 2005.

———. "How Government Tax and Housing Policies Have Racially Segregated America." In *Taxing America*, ed. Karen B. Brown and Mary Louise Fellows. New York: New York University Press, 1996.

———. "Is Racial Integration Essential to Achieving Quality Education for Low-Income Minority Students, in the Short Term? In the Long Term?" *Poverty & Race* 5 (September/October 1996): 7.

———. "Reflections on the Self: Exploring Between and Beyond Modernity and Postmodernity." *Minnesota Law Review* 81 (1997): 1481.

———. "Structural Racism: Building upon the Insights of John Calmore." *North Carolina Law Review* 86 (2008): 791.

———. "Talking Race." *Hungry Mind Review* 31 (1994): 15.

———. "The Needs of Members in a Legitimate Democratic State." *Santa Clara Law Review* 44 (2004): 969.

———. "The Race Class Nexus: An Intersectional Perspective." *Law & Inequality* 25 (2007): 355.

———. "Transformative Action: A Strategy for Ending Racial Hierarchy and Achieving True Democracy." In *Beyond Racism: Race and Inequality in Brazil, South Africa, and the United States*, ed. Charles V. Hamilton et al. Boulder, Colo.: Lynne Rienner Publishers, 2001.

———. "Worlds Apart: Reconciling Freedom of Speech and Equality." *Kentucky Law Journal* 85 (1996–1997): 9.

powell, john a., and Stephen Menendian. "Little Rock and the Legacy of *Dred Scott*." The Childress Lecture. *Saint Louis University Law Journal* 52 (Summer 2008): 1153.

———. "Remaking Law: Moving beyond Enlightenment Jurisprudence." *Saint Louis University Law Journal* 54 (2010): 1035–40.

powell, john a., and Jason Reece. "The Future of Fair Housing and Fair Credit: From Crisis to Opportunity." Kirwan Institute for the Study of Race and Ethnicity (2009).

Project Implicit. https://implicit.harvard.edu/implicit.

Prothero, Stephen R. *God Is Not One: The Eight Rival Religions That Run the World – and Why Their Differences Matter*. New York: HarperOne, 2010.

Quale, G. Robina. *A History of Marriage Systems*. New York: Greenwood Press, 1988.

Rawls, John. *A Theory of Justice*. Cambridge, Mass.: Belknap Press of Harvard University Press, 1971.

Reardon, Sean F., John T. Yun, and Michael Kurlaender. "Implications of Income-Based School Assignment Policies for Racial School Segregation." *Educational Evaluation & Policy Analysis* 28, no. 1 (2006): 49–75.

Reed, Adolph L., Jr. "The Real Divide." *The Progressive*, November 2005; available at http://progressive.org/mag_reed1105.

Reed, Warren C. "A New and Accurate Way to Identify Elite Athletes." *Journal of Medical Ethics*. Published Online First: 9 August 2011.

Reiter, Bernd, and Gladys L. Mitchell, eds. *Brazil's New Racial Politics*. Boulder, Colo.: Lynne Rienner Publishers, 2010.

Rifkin, Jeremy. "The European Dream." *Utne Reader* (Sept./Oct. 2004). Available at http://www.utne.com/2004-09-01/the-european-dream.aspx.

Roediger, David R. *How Race Survived U.S. History: From Settlement and Slavery to the Obama Phenomenon*. London: Verso, 2008.

———. *The Wages of Whiteness: Race and the Making of the American Working Class*. London: Verso, 1991.

———. *Towards the Abolition of Whiteness: Essays on Race, Politics, and Working Class History*. London: Verso, 1994.

Roediger, David R. and Elizabeth D. Esch. *The Production of Difference: Race and the Management of Labor in U.S. History*. New York: Oxford University Press, 2012.

Rogers, Christy, et al. "Fair Credit and Fair Housing in the Wake of the Subprime Lending and Foreclosure Crisis: Findings from the Kirwan Institute Initiative." In *The Future of Fair Housing*. Kirwan Institute for the Study of Race and Ethnicity, the Ohio State University, February 2010.

Roisman, Florence W. "Opening the Suburbs to Racial Integration: Lessons for the 21st Century." *Western New England Law Review* 23 (2001): 65.

Roisman, Florence W., and Philip Tegeler. "Improving and Expanding Housing Opportunities for Poor People of Color: Recent Developments in Federal and State Courts." *Clearinghouse Review* 24 (1990): 312.

Rosenfeld, Michel. "Decoding *Richmond*: Affirmative Action and the Elusive Meaning of Constitutional Equality." *Michigan Law Review* 87 (1989): 1729.

Ross, Thomas. "Innocence and Affirmative Action." *Vanderbilt Law Review* 43 (March 1990): 297.

Rothwell, Jonathan T., and Douglas S. Massey. "The Effect of Density Zoning on Racial Segregation in U.S. Urban Areas." Woodrow Wilson School of Public and International Affairs, Princeton University (December 16, 2008). Available at Social Science Research Network (SSRN): http://ssrn.com/abstract=1260802.

Rucker, Phillip. "Mitt Romney says 'corporations are people' at Iowa State Fair," *Washington Post*, 11 August 2011.

Sachs, Jeffrey. *The Price of Civilization: Reawakening American Virtue and Prosperity*. New York: Random House, 2011.

Sandel, Michael J. *Liberalism and the Limits of Justice*. Cambridge: Cambridge University Press, 1982.

———. "Political Liberalism." *Harvard Law Review* 107 (1994): 1765.

Saulny, Susan. "Black and White and Married in the Deep South: A Shifting Image." *New York Times*, 19 March 2011.

Saussure, Ferdinand de. "Course in General Linguistics." In *Critical Theory since Plato*, ed. Hazard Adams. Fort Worth, Texas: Harcourt Brace Jovanovich College Publishers, 1992.

Schill, Michael H., and Susan M. Wachter. "The Spatial Bias of Federal Housing Law and Policy: Concentrated Poverty in Urban America." *University of Pennsylvania Law Review* 143 (1995): 1285.

Schlesinger, Arthur M., Jr., *The Disuniting of America*. New York: W. W. Norton, 1992.

Sen, Amartya. *Development as Freedom*. New York: Knopf, 1999.

Sentencing Project, "Death Row Inmates File Racial Justice Act Claims." 18 August 2010; available at http://www

.sentencingproject.org/detail/news
.cfm?news_id=974.

Shear, Michael. "Obama Campaign Grapples with New Voter ID Laws," *New York Times*, 29 April 2012.

Skocpol, Theda. *Social Policy in the United States: Future Possibilities in Historical Perspective.* Princeton, N.J.: Princeton University Press, 1995.

———. "Targeting within Universalism: Politically Viable Policies to Combat Poverty in the United States." In *The Urban Underclass*, ed. Christopher Jencks and Paul E Peterson. Washington, D.C.: Brookings Institution, 1991.

———. "The G.I. Bill and U.S. Social Policy, Past and Future." *Social Philosophy & Policy* 14 (June 2007): 95.

Smedley, Audrey. *Race in North America: Origin and Evolution of a Worldview.* 3d ed. Boulder, Colo.: Westview Press, 2007.

Smith, Huston, *The Illustrated World's Religions: A Guide to Our Wisdom Traditions.* San Francisco: HarperCollins.

Soja, Edward. *Seeking Spatial Justice.* Minneapolis: University of Minnesota Press, 2010.

Spickard, Paul R. *Mixed Blood: Intermarriage and Ethnic Identity in Twentieth-Century America.* Madison: University of Wisconsin Press, 1989.

Squires, Gregory D. *Capital and Communities in Black and White: The Intersection of Race, Class, and Uneven Development.* Albany: State University of New York, 1994.

Sterba, James P. *Affirmative Action for the Future.* Ithaca, N.Y.: Cornell University Press, 2009.

Stevenson, Bryan. "We Need to Talk about an Injustice." TED: Ideas Worth Spreading: "*McCleskey v. Kemp* 25 Years Later," 31 March 2012.

Stowe, David W. "Uncolored People." *Lingua Franca*, Sept.-Oct. 1996.

Sundiata, I. K. "Late Twentieth Century Patterns of Race Relations in Brazil and the United States." *Phylon* 48 (1987): 65.

Taylor, Paul, Cary Funk, and Peyton Craighill. "Guess Who's Coming to Dinner: 22% of Americans Have a Relative in a Mixed-Race Marriage." Pew Research Center, 14 March 2006. Available at http://pewresearch.org/pubs/304/guess-whos-coming-to-dinner.

Thernstrom, Abigail, and Stephan Thernstrom. *No Excuses: Closing the Racial Gap in Learning.* New York: Simon & Schuster, 2003.

Thomas, Brook. *Plessy v. Ferguson: A Brief History with Documents.* Boston: Bedford/St. Martin's, 1997.

Thomas, Kendall. "The Eclipse of Reason: A Rhetorical Reading of *Bowers v. Hardwick*." *Virginia Law Review* 79 (1993): 1805.

Thompson, Ginger. "Seeking Unity, Obama Feels Pull of Racial Divide." *New York Times*, 12 February 2008, A1; available at http://www.nytimes.com/2008/02/12/us/politics/12obama.html?emc=eta1.

Thorsen, Karen, director. *James Baldwin: The Price of the Ticket.* Produced by Thorsen in association with Maysles Films, Inc.; WNET, New York; & William Miles; written by Thorsen and Douglas K. Dempsey. Imprint [S.l.]: Nobody Knows Productions, 1989.

Tilly, Charles. *Durable Inequality.* Berkeley: University of California Press, 1998.

Todd, A. R., G. V. Bodenhausen, J. A. Richeson, and A. D. Galinsky. "Perspective Taking Combats Automatic Expressions of Racial Bias." *Journal of Personality and Social Psychology* 3 (March 2011): 7.

Tough, Paul. "The Acting White Myth." *New York Times Magazine*, 12 December 2004; available at http://

www.nytimes.com/2004/12/12/ magazine/12ACTING.html.

Trillin, Calvin. "American Chronicles: Black or White." *The New Yorker*, 14 April 1986.

Tucker, Neely. "*Loving* Day Recalls a Time When the Union of a Man and a Woman Was Banned." , *Washington Post*, 13 June 2006.

Tyson, Karolyn, William Darity, Jr., and Domini R. Castellino. "It's Not 'a Black Thing': Understanding the Burden of Acting White and Other Dilemmas of High Achievement." *American Sociological Review* 70, no. 4 (August 2005). Available at http://links.jstor.org/sici?sici=0003-1224%28200508%2970%3A4%3C582%3AIN%22BTU%3E2.0.CO%3B2-3.

Unger, Roberto M. *Democracy Realized: The Progressive Alternative*. London: Verso, 1998.

———. *False Necessity: Anti-Necessitarian Social Theory in the Service of Radical Democracy*. Cambridge: Cambridge University Press, 1987.

———. *Knowledge and Politics*. New York: Free Press, 1976.

———. *Passion: An Essay on Personality*. New York: Free Press/Macmillan, 1984.

U.S. Census Bureau. Current Population Reports, P60–238: *Income, Poverty, and Health Insurance Coverage in the United States: 2009*. Washington, D.C.: U.S. Government Printing Office, 2010.

———. "Historical Census of Housing Tables: Homeownership by Race and Hispanic Origin" (2004). Available at http://www.census.gov/hhes/www/housing/census/historic/ownershipbyrace.html.

———. "Net Worth and Asset Ownership 1998–2000." Household Economic Studies, 2003.

———. "Overview of Race and Hispanic Origin: 2010." March 2011. Available at http://2010.census.gov/news/releases/operations/cb11-cn125.html.

———. "Wealth and Asset Ownership: Detailed Tables: 2004." Available at http://www.census.gov/hhes/www/wealth/2004_tables.html.

———. Census of Governments, 2002, Vol. 1, no. 1, Government Organization, GC02(1)-U.S. Government Printing Office. Washington, DC.

U.S. Department of Health and Human Services. "HHS Announces Plan to Reduce Health Disparities: National Partnership for Action Launches Strategy to Strengthen and Expand Community-Led Efforts to Achieve Health Equity." 8 April 2011. Available at www.minorityhealth.hhs.gov/npa.

U.S. Department of Housing and Urban Development. *Unequal Burden: Income and Racial Disparities in Subprime Lending in America* (2000).

U.S. Department of Transportation. Federal Highway Administration. "Our Nation's Highways: 2008." Fig. 6.3 (2008): http://www.fhwa.dot.gov/policyinformation/pubs/pl08021/fig6_3.cfm.

U.S. Office of Management and Budget. "Revisions to the Standards for the Classification of Federal Data on Race and Ethnicity." 30 October 1997. Available at http://www.whitehouse.gov/omb/fedreg_1997standards.

Van Osdol, Adam. "Lawyer Analyzes Landmark Case Progress." *Indiana Daily Student*, IDSNews.com, 17 Nov. 2004. Available at http://www.idsnews.com/news/story.aspx?id=38205.

Wallenstein, Peter. *Tell the Court I Love My Wife: Race, Marriage and Law – an American History*. New York: Palgrave Macmillan, 2002.

Warren, John. "Performing Whiteness Differently: Rethinking the Abolitionist Project." *Educational Theory* 51 (2001): 454.

Wechsler, Herbert. "Toward Neutral Principles of Constitutional Law." *Harvard Law Review* 73 (1959): 1.

West, Robin. "Jurisprudence and Gender." *University of Chicago Law Review* 55 (1988): 1.

Westen, Drew. *The Political Brain: The Role of Emotion in Deciding the Fate of the Nation*. New York: Public Affairs, 2007.

White, Curtis. *The Middle Mind: Why Americans Don't Think for Themselves*. San Francisco: HarperSanFrancisco, 2003.

Wicke, Jennifer. "Postmodern Identity and the Legal Subject." *University of Colorado Law Review* 62 (1991): 455.

Wiegman, Robyn. "Whiteness Studies and the Paradox of Particularity." *Boundary* 26 (1999): 2.

Wilber, Ken. *A Sociable God*. Boulder, Colo.: New Science Library, 2005.

———. *Up from Eden: A Transpersonal View of Human Evolution*. Rev. ed. Wheaton, Ill.: Theosophical Publishing House, 1996.

Wildman, Stephanie. *Privilege Revealed: How Invisible Preference Undermines America*. New York: New York University Press, 1996.

Wildman, Stephanie M., and Adrienne D. Davis. "Making Systems of Privilege Visible." In *Privilege Revealed: How Invisible Preference Undermines America*, New York: New York University Press, 1996.

Williams, Patricia J. *The Alchemy of Race and Rights*. Cambridge, Mass.: Harvard University Press, 1991.

Williams, Raymond. *Keywords: A Vocabulary of Culture and Society*. Rev. ed. London: Fontana, 1983.

Wilson, E. O. *The Diversity of Life*. Cambridge, Mass.: Harvard University Press, 1992.

Wilson, Timothy D. *Strangers to Ourselves: Discovering the Adaptive Unconscious*. Cambridge, Mass.: Belknap Press of Harvard University Press, 2002.

Wilson, William Julius. *The Declining Significance of Race*. 2d ed. Chicago: University of Chicago Press, 1980.

———. *The Truly Disadvantaged*. Chicago: University of Chicago Press, 1990.

Winant, Howard. *Racial Conditions: Politics, Theory, Comparisons*. Minneapolis: University of Minnesota Press, 1994.

———. *The World Is a Ghetto: Race and Democracy since World War II*. New York: Basic Books, 2001.

Winnubst, Shannon. "Vampires, Anxieties and Dreams: Race and Sex in the Contemporary United States." *Hypatia* 18 (2003): 3.

Wish, Naomi Bailin, and Stephen Eisdorfer. "The Impact of Mount Laurel Initiatives: An Analysis of the Characteristics of Applicants and Occupants." *Seton Hall Law Review* 27 (1997): 1268.

Wright, Luther, Jr. "Who's Black, Who's White, and Who Cares: Reconceptualizing the United States's Definition of Race and Racial Classifications." *Vanderbilt Law Review* 48 (1995): 513.

Yancey, George. *Who Is White? Latinos, Asians, and the New Black/Nonblack Divide*. Boulder, Colo.: Lynne Rienner, 2003.

Young, Iris Marion. *Inclusion and Democracy*. Oxford: Oxford University Press, 2000.

———. *Justice and the Politics of Difference*. Princeton, N.J.: Princeton University Press, 1990.

INDEX

religious freedom, 213
religious traditions, xix
Renaissance, 165
Republicans, 115
resistance, white, xi
Revolutionary War, 147
Ricci v. DeStefano, 104
Richmond, Va., 108
Rifkin, Jeremy, xviii, xix, xx
Roberts, Justice John R.: equating race
    conscious integration with discrimina-
    tion, 6; in Stevens, J. dissent in *Parents
    Involved,* 7
Roediger, David R., xi–xiv; on slavery and
    freedom, xxiv; white emptiness, 154;
    white fear, 80; white privilege, 97, 191
Rogin, Michael, xiii
Romanticists, 154
Roosevelt, President Franklin D., 236, 237
Rosenfeld, Michel, 110
Ross, Thomas, 78, 107

Sachs, Jeffrey, 232
Said, Edward, xi, xii
Salience, 232
salvation, 225
sameness/difference debate, 84–89
sanctity of markets, 240
Sandel, Michael, 185, 193
*Santa Clara County v. Southern Pacific Rail-
    road Company,* 130
Scalia, Justice Antonin, 109; unconscious
    bias ineradicable, 128
school discipline, 126
school funding, 235
scientific revolution, 165
Seattle school district: in *Parents Involved*
    case, 5–7
Sebelius, Kathleen, Secretary of HHS, 26
Section 5 preclearance, 106
secularism, xviii, xix, 207, 219
secular suffering, 198
segregation, xvii, 149; spatial, 59, 68, 149
self, xvii, xviii; contextual, xx, 158; fear
    and the other, 157–158; multiple, 158;
    racialized, xx, 159; separate modern, xx,
    161–162

Sen, Amartya, 14, 197
separate but equal: regime made law under
    Plessy v. Ferguson, 43
Separate Car Act of 1890 (Louisiana), 42
separation of church and state, 213
sexuality, xiv
shareholders suit, 236
simultaneity, xi
situatedness: in policy design, 9, 233
Slaughter-House Cases, 144
Slavery, xxi; affecting whole society, 223;
    children, 41, 57; after Civil War, 144,
    145; in colonies, 34, 55, 191–192; *Dred
    Scott,* 142; in Greece, 157; peoples affect-
    ed, 35; property interest, 35; rape, 41, 57;
    and self, 169, 175; and social death, 210
slippery slope, 103, 111, 112, 113, 117
Smith, Huston, 211
social change, xii
social construction of race, xvii, 30, 62,
    66, 142
social contract theory, 185
social death, 54, 86, 224
social justice: as informing institutional
    structures, 228; as a source of spiritual
    pursuits, xxiv, 197, 200
social needs, xx
Social Security Act: limitations by age,
    gender, employment, 11
social space: new, for reconceptualization
    of selfhood, xxiii
social suffering: and institutions, xxv; and
    spiritual suffering, xxiv
societal cohesiveness, xxi
Socrates, 210
Souter, Justice David, 110
South: and explicit racism, 8
Southern Democrats, 144
Southern Strategy, 21, 23, 149
spatial segregation: and racial hierarchy,
    47, 147
spiritual development, 200, 218
spirituality, xix; and public life, xix, 213
spiritual need, xx, 161; and secularism, 207
spiritual suffering, 199
spiritual traditions: and common values,
    xxiv

JOHN A. POWELL is Director of the Haas Diversity Research
Center at the University of California, Berkeley, where he holds the
Robert D. Haas Chancellor's Chair in Equity and Inclusion. He
is the founder and former executive director of both the Kirwan
Institute for the Study of Race and Ethnicity at the Ohio State
University and the Institute on Race and Poverty at the University
of Minnesota School of Law. Editor of *In Pursuit of a Dream Deferred*
(with Gavin Kearney and Vina Kay) he is the author of *Structural
Racism in a Diverse Society* (with M. Omi, forthcoming); *The Rights
of Racial Minorities: The Basic ACLU Guide to Racial Minority Rights*
(with L. McDonald); and many essays on race, equality, and law.